UNDERSTANDING
SOCIAL MEDIA

UNDERSTANDING SOCIAL MEDIA

SECOND EDITION

LARISSA HJORTH
AND SAM HINTON

Los Angeles | London | New Delhi
Singapore | Washington DC | Melbourne

Los Angeles | London | New Delhi
Singapore | Washington DC | Melbourne

SAGE Publications Ltd
1 Oliver's Yard
55 City Road
London EC1Y 1SP

SAGE Publications Inc.
2455 Teller Road
Thousand Oaks, California 91320

SAGE Publications India Pvt Ltd
B 1/I 1 Mohan Cooperative Industrial Area
Mathura Road
New Delhi 110 044

SAGE Publications Asia-Pacific Pte Ltd
3 Church Street
#10-04 Samsung Hub
Singapore 049483

Editor: Michael Ainsley
Assistant editor: John Nightingale
Production editor: Imogen Roome
Copyeditor: Sarah Bury
Proofreader: Neil Dowden
Indexer: Adam Pozner
Marketing manager: Lucia Sweet
Cover design: Lisa Harper-Wells
Typeset by: C&M Digitals (P) Ltd, Chennai, India
Printed in the UK

Library of Congress Control Number: 2018963590

British Library Cataloguing in Publication data

A catalogue record for this book is available from
the British Library

ISBN 978-1-5264-2595-9
ISBN 978-1-5264-2596-6 (pbk)

At SAGE we take sustainability seriously. Most of our products are printed in the UK using responsibly sourced
papers and boards. When we print overseas we ensure sustainable papers are used as measured by the PREPS
grading system. We undertake an annual audit to monitor our sustainability.

Contents

Figures

Acknowledgements

The authors would like to thank series editor Michael Ainsley for his guidance and support in the development of this second edition of *Understanding Social Media*.

Larissa would like to thank her collaborators on the two Australian Research Council (ARC) projects of which some of the findings are discussed in this book. First, the collaborators on the ARC Linkage Project *Locating the Mobile* with Intel, Keio University and Fudan University. These collaborators include Professor Heather Horst, Distinguished Professor Sarah Pink, Professor Genevieve Bell, Professor Fumitoshi Kato, Professor Baohua Zhou, Dr Kana Ohashi and Dr Jolynna Sinanan. Second, the collaborators on the ARC Discovery Project *Games of Being Mobile* Associate Professor Ingrid Richardson. In addition, we acknowledge the important work by research assistants Dr William Balmford, Dr Brendan Keogh, Gina Krone and Olivia Efthimiou. We thank all our participants in Australia, Japan and China for their time and insights. We also acknowledge the great editorial work by Klare Lanson.

And, of course, the authors wish to thank friends, family and colleagues – their support cannot be underestimated. Larissa would like to acknowledge the importance of both her mother Noela Hjorth and son Jesper Hjorth, and David Keir in shaping ethnographic inquiry into digital media practices. Sam would especially like to thank his biggest supporters: his wife Nicole and daughters Catherine and Sarah, who have been patient and understanding while he stressed and agonized over the manuscript.

1

Introduction

Writing a book about social media is about as hard as it can get. Once the platform practices have been documented and analysed, they have already passed their hashtagged used-by date. #solastyear. Doing a second edition of the *Understanding Social Media* book isn't just a process of providing an updated preface. Rather, it requires a complete rewriting in which we attend to all the diversities of complex social media practices, cultures and industries that have rapidly emerged. Like the previous edition, this book seeks to provide an overview of some of the key issues relating to studying social media through key paradoxes – concepts such as invisibility/visibility, empowerment/exploitation, autonomy/algorithmic platforma-tivity, user-generated/platform corporate personalization, power and powerlessness, tactics and strategies.

Since the first edition, a key phenomenon has emerged – the role of the mobile as synonymous with social media and also, interrelatedly, the rise of the visual. Core to these practices are the integral role sharing and datafication has played in recalibrating what is social media today. As noted by scholars such as Mark Deuze (2012) and José van Dijck (2007) while media has always been *social*, what it means to conceptualize and practise the *social* in contemporary automated and datafied culture is changing. The social is a contested and dynamic space – epitomized by social media.

The rise of mobile media, visuality and sharing has a long history in the inception of camera phones, in which the role of sharing forms part of its logic (Frohlich et al., 2002; Kindberg et al., 2005; Van House et al., 2005; Koskinen, 2007). As mentioned above, the logic of sharing is the default function for much of social media (van Dijck, 2007). For van Dijck in *The Culture of Connectivity* (2013), sharing has become the 'social verb'. A doing word. An embodied practice of contemporary digital media lives. Expanding on this idea further, Nicholas A. John argues in *Age of Sharing* (2016) that sharing is central to how we live our lives today – it is not only what we do online but also a model of economy and therapy.

And yet the rise of the social dimensions of sharing social media – in the form of memes, Instagrams, hashtags, to name but a few – has a core paradox in that it partakes in the rhythms and logic of platforms and corporate algorithms and datafication. Here, at the core of this 'datafication' paradox, users willingly hand over their data and other forms of social, creative and emotional labour to platforms (corporations) which then monetize their preferences in order to sell back to the users (van Dijck, 2017).

According to van Djick and Poell (2013), social media logic has four grounding principles: programmability, popularity, connectivity and datafication. These principles and strategies are pervasive across all areas of public life. Or what Zizi Papacharissi (2014) calls 'affective publics' – the digital storytelling processes of public engagement that create affect and emotions in ways that fully erode boundaries between political, public and intimate lives. For Papailias (2016), contemporary mobile social media elicits certain types of affect that blur boundaries between witness and mourner. Social media is now often framed as digital intimate publics (Hjorth & Arnold, 2013; Dobson et al., 2018), as a way to make sense of the paradoxes that see old divisions challenged – between self and society, public and private, digital and offline. This phenomenon is a consequence of the role mobile media plays in providing a particular embodied and intimate context for social media (Hinton & Hjorth, 2013; Hjorth & Arnold, 2013; Goggin, 2014; Carr & Hayes, 2015; Fuchs, 2017).

Figure 1.1 #catsoninstagram continues to dominate as an extension of Ethan Zuckerman's activist theory of cute cats

In this Introduction we will outline some of the key paradoxes explored in this book. We will begin with contextualizing the paradoxes around social media, and then outline some of the multiple and contested definitions. We will then outline the role of each chapter in the logic of this book. From the outset, we should make it clear that this book does not intend to be an exhaustive guide, but rather an examination of key arguments. For a more holistic guide, please refer to *The Sage Social Media Handbook* (Burgess et al., 2018).

Instead, we wish to provide critical analyses and insight into the various contested histories, methods, economies, cultures and practices to give readers a conceptual overview. We draw on fieldwork studies in various locations, such as China and Japan, to provide English speakers with a broader context for the ways in which global social media is playing out in various ways at the level of the local.

Key debates

At the beginning of 2018, two events represented one of the core paradoxes of social media in terms of sharing and disclosure, visibility and invisibility, empowerment and exploitation. The first was the fact that the top new entry in the *Macquarie Dictionary* for 2017 was 'milkshake duck,' the term used to describe the volatile rhythms of social media publics whereby someone can become famous on social media only to then have their reputation ruined by those same social media publics.

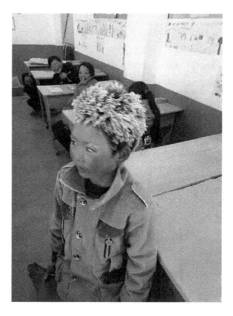

Figure 1.2 'Snowflake Boy' or 'Ice Boy'

At the same time in January 2018, a story in rural China went viral, the story of an eight-year-old boy (Wang Fuman) who walked four kilometres to school in freezing snow and arrived with head, eyebrows and eyelashes full of icicles. Wang was dubbed 'Snowflake Boy' or 'Ice Boy'. The primary school teacher took a picture of Wang and shared it on WeChat, China's most popular social media platform. The image and story took on political dimensions, with some arguing that Wang represented the tenacity of the rural people, while others argued that the rural poor people like Wang were being forgotten in the narratives of Chinese modernity and its focus on urban megacities. During an interview with Wang on national TV he announced that he wasn't sure his fame was a good thing, despite receiving reports of US$200 million in donations globally.

What these two social media phenomena highlight is the paradoxical nature of social media to create what Papacharissi (2014) calls 'affective publics' – that is, an entanglement between visibility/invisibility and agency/disempowerment that are subject to global storytelling, contestations and whimsy. As social media becomes indivisible from mobile media, we see the acceleration of users' ability to take and share images and stories. Events and activities become measured through their *Instagrammable* quality as part of broader tensions around user creativity and datafication, in terms of what Thomas LaMarre calls 'platformativity' (2017: 24). As LaMarre further explains: 'In platformativity, the platforms and infrastructures play an active role, or more precisely, an intra-active role, as they iterate, over and again' (2017: 25). What becomes apparent in the accelerated cycles of social media discourses is the amplification of inequality within digital intimate publics.

For example, take the successful augmented reality (AR) game *Pokémon GO*, which created a phenomenon across much of the world in 2016. It was so successful, it even surpassed porn in terms of downloads. And in its collective social orchestration of playful performativity around urban cartography, *Pokémon GO* harnessed core debates around datafied (or gamified) worlds, from a variety of perspectives including wellbeing (the fact that games make people exercise to achieve goals which in turn can impact positively upon mental wellbeing issues) and the social dimensions of games, to the more dark debates around safely, surveillance and risk (Hjorth & Richardson, 2017).

As platforms such as Facebook throw resources and capabilities around the mainstreaming of AR and virtual reality (VR), we see paradoxes persist around agency and disempowerment, especially as digital literacies continue to remain unequal across generational, socio-economic and cultural divides. The rise of social VR, spearheaded by companies such as Facebook's Oculus, presents some challenges and opportunities in this space. Moreover, as bots and artificial intelligence (AI) start to inhabit social media to the point that 'followers' are now viewed as fake news, the debates around user agency and datafication become magnified. In these Big Data narratives, alternative human-centred (and 'more-than-human') social digital methods emerge around ethnography and critical making.[1]

As a social medium, understanding social media requires attending to some core fundamental issues to being human. While much of social media has focused on life (Deuze, 2012), and especially birth – or even before birth, as can be seen in Tama Leaver's intimate surveillance work (2013) – the significance of death becomes increasingly pertinent. For example, estimates have Facebook having more dead users than live ones in five years' time. What does it mean to have death and the afterlife constantly streaming in our lives? And what is the politics of Facebook owning our loved one's accounts? Emerging fields of compassion studies (Brubaker et al., 2014) are attempting to attend to this growing area of complex ethical issues that in turn impact upon how we practise and experience social media now and in the future (as we discuss in Chapter 12).

Figure 1.3 Dr John Troyer, director for the Centre for Death & Society (UK), on the rise of dead users

To understand the life and death of, and in, social media we need to survey the diversity of contesting and dynamic definitions. Scholars such as van Djick and Graeme Meikle identify the role of sharing and visibility as central to the logic of social media. For Meikle (2016), the tension between sharing, visibility and privacy constantly plays out through social media as today's dominant form of mass communication. Indeed, tensions and paradoxes around visibility and agency, surveillance alongside privacy, invisibility and intimacy have attracted much attention from a variety of social media scholars (Fuchs, 2014, 2017; Meikle, 2016; van Dijck, 2017; Marwick & boyd, 2018).

While it is uncontested that we live in the 'age of social media' (Lamberton & Stephen, 2016), and social media services such as Facebook, WhatsApp, WeChat, LINE and YouTube have amassed billions of users, definitions remain multiple and disputed. Beyond definitions understood broadly as 'digital technologies emphasizing user-generated content or interaction' (Carr & Hayes, 2015: 47; see also Kaplan & Haenlein, 2010), social media definitions are as varied as the platforms themselves. Many of the more encompassing definitions of social media are criticized for their lack of delineation between social media and 'traditional' new media (email, text-messaging, etc.) and/or for 'obscuring the ways the [social media] technology may influence behaviors' (Treem & Leonardi, 2013: 145) and 'missing the unique technological and social affordances that distinguish social media' from non-social media (Carr & Hayes, 2015: 48).

Narrower classifications of social media are equally problematic, often referencing specific social media services (i.e. Facebook, Twitter) in their definition or conflating them with social media subcategories – social networking sites in particular – resulting in definitions of social media with limited scope and poor interdisciplinary utility (Treem & Leonardi, 2013; Carr & Hayes, 2015).

However, one definition of social media that traverses the broad and narrow perspectives is given by Caleb Carr and Rebecca Hayes (2015) in their article 'Social Media: Defining, Developing, and Divining'. Building on a review of a decade of social media definitions across various disciplines alongside a keen analysis of shifts in social media platforms and user behaviours, Carr and Hayes define social media as '[i]nternet-based, disentrained, and persistent channels of masspersonal communication facilitating perceptions of interactions among users, deriving value primarily from user-generated content' (2015: 49) or, in more 'accessible' terms:

> Social media are Internet-based channels that allow users to opportunistically inter-act and selectively self-present, either in real-time or asynchronously, with both broad and narrow audiences who derive value from user-generated content and the perception of interaction with others. (2015: 50)

Carr and Hayes' definition serves two primary functions. The first is to clearly distinguish 'a social medium from a medium that facilitates socialness' (2015: 49) and in turn to isolate the exclusive properties of social media that separate them from other communicative new media forms. The second function of Carr and Hayes' definition is to identify a 'set of traits and characteristics' that are common to *all* social media platforms – extant and emergent – and to avoid definitions of social media that are reliant on specific platforms and subcategories. In doing so, they further extend the development of social media theory across wider, interdisciplinary settings (2015: 49).

Chapter summaries

In this section we summarize the chapters and book structure, and outline the key paradoxes underscoring the book's discussion of social media. We argue that the coalescence of social with the media, while media has always been social (Deuze, 2012; van Dijck 2013), represents key challenges for how we define the social and its entanglement with the digital. With the convergence of social media with mobile media, the intimate attunements of mobile media as an embodied form of social proprioception (Farman, 2011) in the form of mobile intimacy (Hjorth & Lim, 2012) takes on magnified proportions.

Phenomena such as the rise of applification, especially in the form of camera phones and self-tracking Quantified Self (QS) features, see three key characteristics of contemporary social media sharing: visuality, platformativity (user creativity versus corporate algorithmic logic) and datafication. Moments, as we see in the case of museums and galleries, are being measured in terms of Instagrammable qualities. The key paradoxes of the current chapter include visibility and invisibility; agency and disempowerment (milkshake duck); sharing and non-disclosure; user creativity versus corporatization; autonomy versus platformativity.

The role of visibility and invisibility in social media is a highly gendered preoccupation (Brighenti, 2010; Hendry, 2017). For Brighenti 'visibility is a social dimension in which thresholds between different social forces are introduced' (2010: 5). Van Dijck (2013) talks about 'sharing' as the verb for socializing in social media. Debates around visibility and invisibility cannot be separated from issues of control, agency, power, surveillance and equity. This phenomenon is most overtly played out through young women's use of platforms such as Instagram, in which they often have multiple accounts, which allow for different forms of sharing and non-disclosure as well as multiple modes of performativity and experimentation. Take, for example, Natalie Hendry's in-depth study of the use of visual social media for young women's recovery. In this research, she outlined the divergent ways in which young people traverse the tacit logic and etiquette of social media platforms in behaviours that demonstrate that agency and creativity are still pushing against the corporate algorithms of platforms (Hendry, 2017). So, too, in the face of Big Data, which wrongly postulates objectivity despite being encoded with human bias (boyd & Crawford, 2011), ethnographic, human-centred 'small' data are being documented as part of a push against algorithmic cultures (Neff & Nafus, 2016).

In Part 1, 'Histories and Contexts' we lay the groundwork for later chapters. Chapter 2 reflects upon the different approaches to social media, especially in light of the deep clashes between qualitative and quantitative approaches (when actually an interdisciplinary approach is most appropriate) in the form of Big Data and small data debates. In this chapter we summarize the tensions between the rise of algorithmic cultures in Big Data and the need for ethnographic small data to provide nuanced understandings. Having provided a critique of this debate, we then move on to Chapter 3 which explores the multiple and contested histories of social media. Here, the core paradox around exploitation and empowerment has ensued. We discuss current directions, including Big Data, surveillance, privacy and the political economy (further chapters will focus on practices and so this chapter provides a grounding of a political economy understanding). We also address the conceptual shifts around framing social media as part of broader internet concepts – from networked society (Wellman & Haythornthwaite, 2002; Castells, 2010) and networked publics (Varnelis, 2008; boyd, 2011) to affective publics (Papacharissi, 2014).

Moving into Part 2, 'Economies and Applification', this section begins with Chapter 4 on datafication and algorithmic cultures. Here we focus on the paradoxes of power and powerlessness, tactics and strategies, identity versus anonymity, and look at artists using playful resistance to QS and datafication normalizations. In Chapter 5, 'Mobile Applification', we explore how the growth of mobile apps by platforms have structured and informed how we experience social media. This chapter explores the example of *Strava* as part of the quantified self, self-tracking phenomenon through the key paradox of user experience versus corporate platformativity.

Chapter 6, on geolocative social media, follows this discussion. Geolocative tracking, just like sharing, has become the default logic for much of social media cultures. In this chapter begin with a review of the surveillance and privacy literature and how these precepts change how we understand intimacy. Then we focus on ethnographic fieldwork on familial, intergenerational use of social media in Japan (LINE) to consider how 'careful' or 'friendly' surveillance might not be an oxymoron, but rather framed as part of existing and ongoing familial practices whereby families have always 'watched' each other. Here we consider paradoxes around visibility and invisibility, disclosure and divulgence, privacy and sharing.

We then move towards Part 3, 'Cultures'. This section begins with Chapter 7, in which we explore the rise of the visual in understanding social media. We consider how the role of the visual and visual apps like Instagram has come to dominate the logic of social media (Miller, 2016). In this chapter we explore the role of the selfie as a barometer for cultural production and identity politics (Brighenti, 2010; Hendry, 2017). Then, in Chapter 8, we consider 'mobile media' or 'social media' art and how practitioners are using social media in their social practice to reflect upon contemporary popular culture and politics. This is followed by a new visualities chapter on museums, Chapter 9, and how social platforms like Instagram have shifted how they engage and curate intimate publics. Is chasing the Instagrammable artwork compromising the types of work that are exhibited?

In the final section, Part 4 'Practices', we explore the rise of visuality in terms of paralinguistics. Once associated with a niche practice, the role of paralinguistics in everyday social media vernacular has become a mainstream activity. And yet, in this ubiquity, inequalities and differences around literacy and emotional labour play out, especially in terms of intergenerational usage. Chapter 10 draws from ARC *Locating the Mobile* (LTM) ethnographic fieldwork to explore some of these issues. In Chapter 11, we then turn to social media and mixed reality. With Facebook investing billions into AR over the next few years, the relationship between mixed reality and social media has become more apparent. This chapter puts mixed reality like AR and VR in context through the history of urban play movements and then focuses on what we can learn from the paradoxes surrounding the rise and fall of *Pokémon GO*. The core paradox to this chapter considers whether such media reinforce inequality or create new socialities and possibilities.

In Chapter 12 we consider social media and death, the ultimate paradox. How can death shape social media practice? This chapter explores the emergence of digital legacy and compassion research around social media. Much of the literature on social media has focused on life in and through social media, with little thought and understanding into how social media shapes the processes of dying and death. For example, what happens to your data after you die?

Finally, in Chapter 13, we conclude by reviewing some of the main themes in this book, inviting the reader to reflect on them and, in doing so, to consider the past, present and future of social media. In thinking about social media futures, we also acknowledge the changing face of social media: as it matures, so do its users and its uses. As our populations and the users of social media age, how does that change the ways that social media are used, and who inhabits social media? The Conclusion shows how the themes, paradoxes and questions we examine throughout the book will continue to define and propel social media into the future.

Note

1. Critical making is a way of studying digital objects and their relationship with culture by physically building technological objects. It brings together elements of design, art, craft and engineering.

PART 1

HISTORIES AND CONTEXTS

2

Approaches to Social Media

Introduction

> We must find ways to translate and enjoy each other's knowledge and expertise,
> especially across polarised disciplinary or ideological boundaries. In that interdisciplinary
> universe, we need to pay more attention to how we know what we know [...] even as
> we deploy methods specific to a particular approach. (Hartley, 2018: 13)

For researchers interested in social media, the medium raises new and interesting questions about methods and ethics. From one perspective, the study of social media is the study of people, and so is well aligned with ethnographic and qualitative methods that seek to present 'thick' descriptions of people and their interactions with each other and social media technologies. From another perspective, social media generates enormous amounts of data, and these data (which are, arguably, the main product of social media, as we will discuss more in Chapter 3) are a rich source of information for quantitative analysis.

In addition to these differing methodologies, social media is a topic that intersects a number of different disciplines. Journals in cultural studies, information technology, political science, anthropology, economics, psychology, health – the list could go on and on – all publish articles written by scholars who engage with social media as their main field of research. Often, these disciplines arrive at the study of social media from different perspectives, even though they are studying the same fundamental topics. For example, health researchers may come to study social media through the lens of health education, where researchers are interested in the effectiveness of providing sexual health awareness messages within particular communities. Meanwhile, a researcher in the humanities might be interested in the ways that people use social media to discuss their engagement with a museum exhibition. As each of these diverse disciplines approach social media, they bring with them a range of methodologies and perspectives. Together, this makes social media research an incredibly rich field of study, and subsequently incredibly complex.

A challenge for the social media researcher, then, is how to find a path through the various methodologies and approaches? It's easy to get lost when trying to develop an approach to a topic as you begin to feel that you need to build expertise in everything from anthropology to statistics and marketing economics in order to engage properly with the literature – let alone embark on a coherent research project.

This is probably a good thing, although real-world problems don't live in the silos of disciplines. This is especially the case with the social and social media. As cultural theorist John Hartley notes, 'we have always been social, but the question now is – what are we (so many more of us than ever) going to do about it?' (2018: 30). Hartley presents a STEAM approach in which STEM (Science, Technology, Engineering and Mathematics) is coalesced with HASS (Humanities, Arts, Social Sciences). He argues, 'Science, evolution and complexity are not the enemies of culture, communication and media – science and stories are one and the same' (2018: 65).

Burgess et al. (2013) note in their special issue 'Emerging Methods for Digital Media Research', with the rise of quantitative methods, such as Big Data visualizations and hashtag analysis, there is also a need for the qualitative methods, such as ethnography and 'small data' techniques (Nafus & Sherman, 2014; Neff & Nafus, 2016). For Richard Rogers (2018), there is a need to attend to the history of digital methods 'after social media', in which cross-platform, comparative work is highlighted. Rogers reviews current key methods, including hashtag and liked page studies, movement from single platform to cross-platform studies, platform cultures of use and cross-platform analysis. For Rogers, understanding social practice requires an analysis of cross-platform approaches to glean hashtags and group discussion, which often moves across platforms and different forms of platformativity.

As highlighted by boyd and Crawford in their key text (2011), the Big Data computational turn has raised some key issues about the ethics of algorithmic, automation and artificial intelligence (AI) approaches to doing research. Rogers engages with the rise of 'the ethics turn' in web research, and how such a turn and emphasis on personal data's public availability has influenced the data available through application programmable interfaces (APIs), such as Facebook limiting the collection of profile interests and friends. Such critique arose out of recent events/disasters/social causes where social media and personal information has played a major role (Rogers lists the Arab Spring and Facebook's and Twitter's roles in recent revolutions as main examples).

This chapter will explore the variety of methods – big and small, quantitative and qualitative – that are being deployed to understand the complexity of social media today. We consider the increasing relevance of digital ethnography in the context of algorithmic cultures and the growing diversity of scholarship. In particular, this chapter aims to define and tackle the apparent paradoxes that arise between different approaches – even between qualitative and quantitative approaches – and argues for the importance of mixed methods research.

Foundational approaches

To help us understand the current state of social media scholarship, it's useful to understand that modern approaches are rooted in what is now a quite considerable body of scholarship that developed alongside the digital media they were studying. This section provides an overview of internet studies that looks at the subject of what people do online, what kinds of structures are re-mediated and what kind of structures are new. We will look at how there has been an 'ethnographic turn' in internet studies since the late 1990s and how debate has emerged in internet studies around the question of whether online interactions are best described as communities or networks.

Despite social media being a relatively recent phenomenon, research into people's use of networking technologies as an interpersonal communication tool pre-dates the development of social media by decades. From the 1980s, pioneers like Barry Wellman were already engaging with questions about the nature of sociality within what was generally referred to as 'computer-mediated communication'. This included internet-based networks, but also bulletin board systems (described in the next chapter), and networked workplaces. While one theme in this early work suggested that online interaction was a poor substitute for face-to-face communication (often based on workplace-based studies), others recognized that some people were using the networks for more social activities.

Back in 1993, Howard Rheingold popularized the idea of virtual communities in his book of the same name (and subtitled, importantly, *Homesteading on the Electronic Frontier*). Rheingold's book examined his experiences with an early online community called the WELL, a pre-internet community based around Northern Californian new age ideologies. The WELL – an acronym for Whole Earth Lectronic Link – was a computer bulletin board maintained by a group of alternative lifestyle users who also produced the Whole Earth Catalog. Stewart Brand, editor of the catalogue and founder of the WELL, coined the aphorism 'information wants to be free' (Clarke, 2000: n.p.).

Rheingold's work popularized the notion of online communities and fed into emerging media interest in the fledgling internet. On one side of what Wellman and Gulia (1999) have described as a Manichaean and unscholarly debate were those who derided the idea of online communities as mere escapism, and yet further evidence of the decay of society and social relations. Here, the image that was constructed was of a socially awkward (male) computer nerd sitting in his basement engaged in a fantasy world that further removed him from reality and social connections. Castells points out that these negative images of online communication fed into existing pessimistic narratives about the loss of community in the modern suburb or megacity (Castells, 2001: 125).

Others, like Rheingold, saw potential in these online environments to create new kinds of communities that could reinvigorate public discussion and debate. Instead of seeing these networks as socially isolating, many argued that the internet created a new space for social interaction and democratic participation, establishing some of the basis for claims about the internet as an empowering medium, as discussed in Chapter 3. For others still, this online or virtual construction of social spaces was reminiscent of what Ray Oldenburg (1989) had described as 'great good places' or 'third places'. Such places exist outside the home and work, and are places where conversation is the main activity, positions are levelled (for example, the boss/worker relationship is left at the door when entering the third place) and the mood is generally playful. Most importantly, they are places that are readily accessible to everyone. A number of scholars (Kendall, 2002; Soukup, 2006) have argued that online spaces meet Oldenburg's criteria for third places.

Some, like Sherry Turkle (1984, 1995), also argued that these spaces opened up opportunities for experimentation with new forms of identity and pointed to the ways that online communication had the potential to free the individual from his or her body, allowing them to play in the realm of their imagination. This, in turn, allowed the playful exploration of concepts like gender. The online environment appeared to be a space that acted like a playground for identity, although some of the best work in this area still acknowledged the importance of offline factors (Turkle, 1995; Baym 1998). However, in Turkle's later work, *Alone Together* (2011), she did an about-face in terms of her celebration of the online.

These studies were conducted in the early days of the internet and often referred to people's own journeys through online communication environments. However, as larger numbers of people started joining the internet and commercialization and dotcom excitement began to kick in, the character of these early environments began to change.

As the number of people using the internet began to burgeon in the mid-1990s, internet researchers had more opportunity to study online communities. Researchers began to discuss and emphasize the continuity of offline relationships and behaviours of users over discontinuity, amplifying the importance of social context. While a great deal of research has been done into online communities over the years, it is difficult to ignore the contribution of certain key scholars. Wellman conducted some of the first studies into the ways people used information technologies, and was one of the first people to argue for the importance of offline factors in online communication.

In one study, Wellman, along with his colleagues, studied the ways that computer scientists working in universities used computer networks as part of both their work and social interaction. One of the key findings was that people communicated more depending on how strong their offline ties were. People who were already friends, or who had developed relationships with each other through work, communicated with each other more often on these networks (Haythornthwaite & Wellman, 1998). The findings of this and other studies led Wellman to argue for more robust models of understanding online communities where offline factors were recognized as having an important role in online communication.

Wellman and Haythornthwaite brought these perspectives together with other research in their edited collection *The Internet in Everyday Life* (2002).

The recognition that online experiences were grounded in real-world settings led to what could be termed as an 'ethnographic shift' in internet studies. A good example of this shift in internet studies is reflected in Daniel Miller and Don Slater's (2000) study, which looked at the use of the internet by Trinidadians. Their focus went beyond the online behaviours of Trinidadians to engage with the way in which internet use is contextualized with other (offline) cultural activities. Rather than attempting to generalize their study to describe all internet behaviour, Miller and Slater concerned themselves only with explaining the specific instance of internet use that their study focused on.

Unlike earlier studies of online communities, which typically started by constructing the online environment as a novel communicative space, Miller and Slater saw geographical place and the offline social world of their users as an extremely important consideration in their attempts to understand Trinidadian use of the internet. They describe their approach as 'one that sees it [the internet] embedded in a specific place, which it also transforms' (Miller & Slater, 2000: 21). In this way, the internet shapes, and is shaped by, the cultural context in which it is performed. Miller and Slater found that being Trinidadian was an important factor in how and why people in Trinidad went online. Furthermore, they discovered in some cases that the online environment provided a space where people could be Trinidadian.

A key facet of these new internet community studies was the recognition that the internet is not one monolithic or homogeneous communication technology. Instead, the internet is presented as an unbounded object, which escapes a single all-encompassing definition. Unlike a mass media subject such as television, the internet is not understood as representing a totality. From this perspective, the internet is defined as an ongoing process of meaning making, a process through which the internet is socially constructed through its use. Moreover, in this understanding there are multiple definitions of the internet, depending on the context of the people who use the internet and their contextual usage. Miller and Slater, for example, argued that the internet must be 'disaggregated', emphasizing that it is important

> not to look at a monolithic medium called 'the Internet', but rather at a range of practices, software and hardware technologies, modes of representation and interaction that may or may not be interrelated by participants, machines or programs (indeed they may not all take place at a computer). (Miller & Slater, 2000: 14)

Miller and Slater describe the internet as both a 'symbolic totality' (as people do refer to an entity called 'the internet') and a 'practical multiplicity', because one individual's definition of the internet might be radically different to another's (2000: 16). Christine Hine, another leading researcher who uses an ethnographic approach to the study of internet communities, reinforces this by pointing out that while common parlance might invoke the phrase 'the internet' as a single technological object, the actual meaning of 'internet' can be quite different depending on who is speaking and who is being spoken to. For example, she refers to the variety of different attitudes and ideas about the internet reflected by the students in her undergraduate classes (Hine, 2000: 30).

Following her own interests in studying the internet from an ethnographic perspective, Hine (2000) has argued that the internet can be treated as both culture and a cultural artefact. She points out that the notion of 'the internet' has meaning attached to it through a process of social negotiation. For example, the parents of grown children may have internet access but not know what to do with it. However, when one of their children moves interstate or overseas, email may become an important method for maintaining contact. And when a baby is born in a family, a family member sets up a website with digital photographs of the new baby, and so the internet acquires meaning again, this time as represented through the web.

Manuel Castells (2001) picks up this theme and connects it back to his well-known overarching metaphor of the networked society. Castells points out that in studies such as Wellman's early work, discussed above, and the Pew Internet and American Life Project,[1] internet use is revealed as instrumental to the activities of everyday life. Earlier characterizations of 'virtual communities', then, needed to be reconsidered to de-emphasize the virtual and emphasize the connectedness of activities both online and offline.

Both Wellman and Castells argue that while the family still forms the basis for many of the strongest social ties in people's lives, other strong ties are formed through activities like work or play, and these ties may not necessarily be based on geographic proximity. We may work with people who live hours away from us in the modern city, but we develop ties with them based on shared knowledge and experience, and the internet allows us to maintain these relationships over distance. These relationships take on the character of networks made where each of us is connected to others by ties that, if mapped out, would resemble a map of a computer or telephone network.

This does not mean that these ties between people are always strong but, as Castells points out, just because a tie is weak does not mean that it is not important. People coming together in an online forum to discuss a topic of shared interest may come to know one another through their posts, but never meeting in real life or knowing the real person means these are weak ties. However, dismissing these 'weak ties' as unimportant is clearly a mistake, as Clay Shirky (2008a) demonstrates in telling the story of a lost Motorola Razr phone. In this example of the power of social networks, Shirky relates the story of how a lost phone that had been taken by a passer-by was recovered through the activities of an online community. The links between the protagonist in this story and the community could be characterized as weak – he didn't know any of the people who helped him recover the phone – but the weakness of the relationships did not make the relationships ineffectual.

Wellman has pointed out that in many modern societies, a phenomenon he calls 'networked individualism' has arisen; that is, individuals build networks to solve problems, make decisions or get support. The internet has vastly extended these networks so that they are no longer constrained by space. This change moves people away from traditional geographically bounded social groups – neighbourhoods, for example – and towards 'sparsely-knit and loosely-bounded networks' (Wellman et al., 2003: n.p.). For Castells, networked individualism is part of the networked society, rather than the internet per se, but can be supported and augmented by the internet to produce 'new patterns of sociability based on individualism' (Castells, 2001: 130). To illustrate this, ask yourself a question: if you are thinking of buying something – let's say a new car – do you first get advice from a neighbour or someone you work with, or do you Google it? If the answer is the latter, then you're engaging in networked individualism.

Networked and affective publics

With the rise of the social media, questions about the nature of online community have again become a topic of interest. danah boyd (2011) has reworked the idea of networked communities within the social networking sites to describe networked 'publics' as an extension (but not necessarily an alternative) to the word 'communities'. When we speak of *the* public, we are in fact talking about a collection of publics. *A* public, on the other hand, is a bounded collective of individuals who have come together under a common set of principles, affinities or beliefs that bind and define the public – 'a relation among strangers' (Warner, 2002). The public forms a single new entity that can be a social actor. There is also the assumption that these publics are open and designed for participation by everyone; they are not 'privates', although, because they are bounded, they necessarily have implicit rules which define what is considered part of that public, and what is not.

According to boyd networked publics are:

> ... publics that are restructured by networked technologies. As such, they are simultaneously (1) the space constructed through networked technologies and (2) the imagined collective that emerges as a result of the intersection of people, technology, and practice. (2011: 39)

In practice, this may look like a Facebook page, a Twitter user and their followers, a Reddit sub-reddit, and so on. Networked publics are, of course, not limited to the organizing structures that are defined by social media platforms. They can emerge organically wherever people find a way to connect with each other and share messages. Networked publics may, for example, extend beyond and across social media platforms.

There are two fundamental components outlined here that are worth reiterating: networked publics are both spaces *and* groups of people who are connected through practice and technology. They are 'simultaneously a space and a collection of people' (boyd, 2011: 41). Importantly, boyd argues that these publics are not just networked because they are linked together by the technology; they are also transformed and restructured by networked media. Social media platforms are examples of online technologies that support the production and reproduction of networked publics. As boyd notes, there are three key dynamics in social networking sites: invisible audiences, collapsed contexts, and the blurring of public and private (2011: 49). In examining the transformation of publics, she observes that 'the affordances of networked publics rework publics more generally and the dynamics that emerge leak from being factors in specific settings to being core to everyday realities' (2011: 53). In the pervasiveness of networked publics, boyd perceives erosions of physical barriers while, at the same time, 'many people feel unmotivated to interact with distant strangers' (2011: 53). In sum, in networked publics, 'attention becomes a commodity' (2011: 53).

While the notion of networked publics has considerable overlap with Castells' concepts of a networked community, networked publics differ primarily in its use of the idea of 'publics' rather than 'communities' as the organizing metaphor for conceptualizing online users. This is a useful alternative because it allows us to drop the cultural associations caused by that term, a problem that Castells himself is keen to avoid (2001: 127).

A broader concern with the affective dimensions of social phenomenon in the humanities and social sciences (Leys, 2011) has also been important within the study of social media. For example, Zizi Papacharissi (2015) has referred to 'affective publics' and Lauren Berlant (2008) has used the term 'intimate publics', both drawing attention to the role that affect and intimacy play in the construction of social relations. Applying intimate publics to social media involves a recognition that, as social and mobile media become more pervasive, different modes of using these media mean that increasingly publics are defined by the strength of their relationships, rather than the total number of network connections. The term 'intimacy' when used here not only refers to the common-usage kinds of intimacies that exist between lovers, family members or close friends (though these can and do play a role), but also to intimacies that can exist at a social or cultural level.

As Michael Herzfeld (1997: 3) observes, cultural intimacy describes the 'social poetics' of the nation-state; it is 'the recognition of those aspects of a cultural identity that are considered a source of external embarrassment but that nevertheless provide insiders with their assurance of common sociality'. To put it a different way, intimacy can be something that exists between strangers because of the common bond they can share by virtue of them belonging to the same cultural group, whether that be a town, city, nation or some other sociological or political grouping. An example might be a small country town where everyone who grew up there knows that the town has a reputation for having the worst weather in the nation (or the most boring night-life, or the most superstitious people in the province, and so on). This shared knowledge, even if it is potentially embarrassing, also acts as a kind of social bond – a 'cultural intimacy'.

An example of when cultural intimacies come into play would be when two people from similar cultural backgrounds but who are otherwise strangers accidentally meet on a train in an unfamiliar country and find that they immediately have a connection. The way that social media has been developed or simply picked up by different nations and cultures across the world is also a tangible example of this kind of cultural intimacy. China's QQ is not just any social media platform; it is *the* Chinese social media, and to use QQ is to participate in a community that shares a set of cultural intimacies. Facebook has become popular in Korea, but it does not speak to and of Korea in the way Cyworld minihompy does (Hjorth, 2007). One of the first social media services, Friendster, began in the US around 2002 but soon became widely adopted in the Philippines. Until its demise in 2014, many Brazilians used Google's original social media service, Orkut. The list of social media services that have become associated with particular nationalities goes on. In these examples it can be argued that a sense of community emerges through the performance of personal intimacies and the aggregation and identification of public sociocultural intimacies.

At a more interpersonal level, social media platforms can be regarded as technological tools that mediate interpersonal intimacies. Esther Milne (2004) has suggested that new media, such as social media, function socially as tools to mediate intimacy, and should be historically contextualized with other technologies that have filled this role. Far from being a new phenomenon, others have argued that intimacy has always been mediated (Hjorth, 2005), with examples of other technological intimacy mediators, including texting on mobile phones, the telegraph (see, for example, Standage, 1998) and written correspondence. When seen in this light, the only thing that has changed with the arrival of social media is that people have appropriated computer networks as yet another technology that mediates intimacy.

Intimacy in social media is also represented by how people manage their online details. All social media have a concept of a profile, or something similar, which reveals something about the user. This profile, as we mentioned above, may include images and other information, and can often be made public or private through the software settings, with these two categories defined fairly rigidly: sharing with everybody (public) or sharing with friends (private). Google+ introduced the idea of 'circles' that allow people to place friends into different and potentially overlapping user-defined categories, such as 'work mates' or 'school friends'. The amount of information about oneself that is revealed through the profile is part of the performance of intimacy online.

For boyd (2011), US youth have responded to the growth in networked media by creating networked publics that engage in various forms of semi-public and semi-private modalities. Choosing what to share and who to share it with allows people to control the privacy or publicness of their information that goes beyond the relatively clumsy tools provided by social networks. Instead, people use new kinds of strategies to control their information, carefully assessing the social value of revealing information against the potential costs (boyd & Marwick, 2011). Privacy, in other words, is not simply an on/off switch or a setting that is chosen and then ignored. Rather, the boundaries between public and private are something that people are constantly revising as a perpetual work in progress (Hjorth & Arnold, 2013). Rather than viewing all social media communities as 'networked publics', as boyd does for the context of the West, we could characterize social media communities instead as 'intimate publics' that are played out, and through, social media practices.

The approaches to studying the internet discussed in this section are by no means exhaustive. The examples discussed here are designed to outline the many approaches to the study of online interaction that evolved alongside computer technologies and the internet. More recently, the number and scope of methods has expanded in response to the growing number of disciplines for whom the study of social media has value. The following sections explore some of these approaches through two broad approaches: digital ethnography and quantitative approaches that emerge from analysis of the enormous amounts of data generated by social media.

Digital ethnography

Ethnographic approaches (which were introduced above as the 'ethnographic shift' in internet studies) are concerned with describing the experience of using social media in everyday life. The difference is not one of magnitude or quality, but of intent. Digital ethnographers are less interested in generalizing their findings or explaining large-scale structures of social networks. Instead, they focus on developing 'thick' descriptions of social media experience through close interviews, observation and participation in online communities. A fundamental tenet of most ethnographic research is that human experience is unique, and it is the goal of ethnographic research to capture and document the details of life as it is lived, rather than to provide a collective summary, which would necessarily obscure the experience of individuals.

For many digital ethnographers, embracing the digital is about acknowledging that for many people in the modern world the digital is part of everyday life. If one of the goals of ethnography is to understand and describe human experience, then understanding and describing the digital elements of this experience is essential. As Pink et al. (2016: 7) put it: 'we are interested in how the digital has become part of the material, sensory and social worlds we inhabit, and what the implications are for ethnographic practice'.

Contrast this with the computational methods discussed below, which seek to generalize group online activities. Computational methods are good at revealing detail in large data sets, which might suggest trends and provide a way of understanding the big picture, but ethnographic methods provide the rich detail needed to begin to understand the meaning of online social practices.

Ethnographers engage very closely with their subject: they may become part of the communities they are studying to develop deeper understandings of them, and they will rarely ask a series of standard survey-like questions. Instead, ethnographers will listen to the responses of participants and ask further questions based upon those responses.

This can lead to a process of iteration: that is, researchers conduct research by collecting information (through interviews, perhaps) and then, based on what they find from the interviews, they refine their research focus and interview questions and then conduct further data collection. The iterative process is necessary because as researchers begin to collect information about the phenomenon or people they are studying their understanding of the research problem changes, and this should lead to a feedback cycle in which the research question is refined as the understanding of the subject is improved.

Ethnography is not only described as iterative, but also as reflexive: the researcher should be constantly aware of their own role in the production of knowledge. This is highly important because as ethnography requires the researcher to understand and interpret, the role of the researcher becomes an important methodological consideration. Reflexivity is about acknowledging and locating the researcher's role in the production of knowledge. This is not just about removing bias from the research (which arguably, can never be accomplished in ethnographic research); it's about acknowledging that the researcher must necessarily play a role in the construction of knowledge, and instead of attempting to erase or hide this influence (which can never be fully accomplished), the researcher seeks to identify and highlight his or her own influence and involvement in the research and the way that knowledge is formed as a result. It's reflexive practice because as the researcher engages in the research, they are constantly asking what they bring to the interpretation of events.

Digital ethnographic research can be seen as substantially the same as non-digital ethnographic methods, but, as with computational approaches, it brings with it additional challenges that researchers need to be aware of. Pink et al. (2016) outline five key principles for digital ethnography: multiplicity, non-digital-centric-ness, openness, reflexivity and unorthodoxy. Without going into these in detail, the principles on non-digital-centric-ness and reflexivity are worth exploring in more detail. Non-digital-centric-ness is perhaps a surprising principle, given that the subject of study is the digital. This principle is designed to emphasize that although the subject of study might be the digital, it is insufficient to understand the digital alone, since the digital experience is always contingent upon the broader context. The concept is borrowed from studies in media where the medium being studied is seen as just one of a range of factors that contribute to the experience of using that medium.

For example, when somebody posts a Facebook update, we cannot really understand the meaning of the post to the individual without appreciating the individual's broader context. Similarly, digital ethnography need not be conducted in a digital environment or using digital methods. In some instances, interviews or observation may be conducted in a purely offline environment. There is no reason why a digital ethnographer cannot obtain rich information about people's experiences in a digital environment through face-to-face interviews and manual analysis of interview transcripts. Decentralizing the digital has the effect of emphasizing its place as one component of experience and helps us understand the role of the digital as part of the broader range of experience.

Some researchers argue that in the online environment ethnographic methods can and should be more focused on the specificities of the digital. Netnography (internet ethnography) is an approach to ethnography in online environments that emerged from marketing research in the late 1990s as a way to study online communities (Kozinets, 2002). It 'uses the information publicly available in online forums to identify and understand the needs and decision influences of relevant online consumer group' (Kozinets, 2002: 2–3) and emphasizes non-obtrusive methods of ethnographic research, which might include, for example, analysis of online posts in a community forum, rather than interviews with forum participants. This is seen as advantageous because it is more 'naturalistic'; that is, analysing the content of online postings means that a community can be studied without undue influence from an interviewer, for example. This does not mean the researcher's influence is excluded (his or her interpretation of the meaning of online posts is still a factor), but the extent of their influence on the content of the social interaction being studied is moderated.

According to Costello et al. (2017), however, it is important to recognize that, despite netnography's methodological focus on studying online 'traces' of social activity, it is still ethnographic, and the researcher still needs to be actively involved in their research subject to develop a deep understanding. They criticize the preponderance of what they call 'passive' studies that are little more than thin descriptions of conversations in online communities.

Big Data and the computational turn

One of the features of the online environment is the creation of data, ultimately the collection of bits that are arranged into meaningful patterns to form images, sounds, video and interactive web pages that support everything from online games to interfaces through which we can post even more data. The quantity of this data is enormous. Literally billions of people generate almost unimaginable quantities of data every day. Every image, tweet, hyperlink or comment is an inscription of intent on the behalf of someone, somewhere. Even where the posts are generated by automated bots, there is intent in the authorship of the bot – it is just displaced by one degree. Even if individuals are not actively contributing tweets or Facebook posts, every access to a website and every time someone checks a WhatsApp message, a small amount of data is created about the time, nature, duration and perhaps even location of the activity. Together, this enormous amount of information that is created is called 'Big Data' and is the raw material that social media companies trade in.

The promise of Big Data is that, as the condensation of billions of likes, tweets, photos and shared links to websites, it (at least theoretically) contains information about the collective intent of millions of people. If one were to capture all the tweets about an election, for example, then some way of processing that data should be able to reveal the voting intentions of groups of people, whether a candidate is more popular with male or female voters or the impact of a certain news story on a candidate's likelihood of being elected.

While this is obviously incredibly valuable for advertisers and political parties, it also has enormous value for social media researchers. Yet it's important to maintain a critical perspective on claims about the value of Big Data, which boyd and Crawford refer to as a kind of mythology. For them, Big Data is seductive because it has an 'aura of truth, objectivity and accuracy' (boyd & Crawford, 2012: 663).

However, extracting meaning from Big Data is not straightforward. The sheer quantity of the data poses methodological problems. Manual analysis and coding of data, for example, is simply not feasible if analysing 100,000 Twitter posts. Attempting to map shared Facebook interests between political candidates can't be done by a group of people with pens and post-it notes. In order to analyse this amount of information, and to deal with the complexity of some of the relationships in the data, computer applications have needed to be developed, and with this adjusted methodologies for analysing the data.

This use of computers to analyse social data has been termed a 'computational turn' in humanities research. The computational turn is a phenomenon that is broader than the study of social media. It has implications for research across the humanities, from fields as varied as archaeology and medieval literature. It is also important to appreciate that the computational turn implies a lot more than simply using computers to sort and store data. It implies a whole new way of thinking about research and even the way we construct knowledge, because computation opens new ways of thinking about subjects that may not have been possible before. David Berry (2012: 3) suggests that 'computational technology has become the very condition of possibility required in order to think about many of the questions raised in the humanities today'. In other words, computational methods not only provide a way of analysing data, but also imply new ways of thinking about problems and perhaps the asking of different initial questions.

Unlike source material in other fields, such as archaeology or art history, social media is 'born digital'; for example, a 17th-century oil painting that exists as a physical object must be copied into a digital representation of the original before it can be analysed computationally. Social media, on the other hand, is created digitally and rarely obtains a physical form. This makes it particularly well suited to computational analysis.

Even with the application of new computational methods (some of which are discussed below), there are still significant debates about the limitations of Big Data. Traditional methods of analysing data using statistical techniques, for example, assume a high level of rigour in data collection, which is missing with most Big Data sets. Beyond these issues, there remain significant questions about the limitations of quantitative analysis of social subjects. Part of the allure of Big Data is that it promises a rigorous, objective way of extracting meaning from data, potentially opening up new methodologies that don't rely on subjective analysis by a human.

However, serious questions still need to be asked about the objectivity of Big Data analysis, some of which are related to the methods used, and some of which to the quality of the data itself.

As a large mass of raw information, Big Data is not self-explanatory. And yet the specific methodologies for interpreting the data are open to all sorts of philosophical debate. Can the data represent an 'objective truth' or is any interpretation necessarily biased by some subjective filter or the way that data is 'cleaned?' (Bollier, cited in boyd & Crawford, 2012: 667)

The quality of Big Data is also a non-trivial problem. Many statistical methods of data analysis rely on data sets to be drawn from randomly sampled populations, or, if the data is not drawn from a random sample, the sampling bias needs to be incorporated into the statistical model in some way. This is difficult with Big Data because it is not always clear whether the data is skewed and, if so, in what way. Big Data is also frequently 'messy', containing errors and omissions as artefacts of the collection and storage process. User connections drop yielding partial records, people use virtual private networks, which generate false location data. To address this, most Big Data needs to be 'cleaned' prior to computational analysis so that it is consistent, and errors in the data are removed. The cleaning process itself is a subjective intervention by the researcher that may influence the data's validity.

Faith in Big Data's validity, even without considering the cleaning process, is also questionable in some circumstances. For example, according to a 2017 study (which itself used computational Big Data techniques) anywhere up to 15 per cent of Twitter's estimated 350 million user accounts may be bots – accounts that generate tweets based upon a computer algorithm (Varol et al., 2017). While these bots are not necessarily malicious, the data they generate is different from the data generated by a human operator and needs to be treated as such. Thus, the question of the objectivity of Big Data is complicated. In one sense, it is still objective, even if a percentage of the data set is generated by a bot. However, if the researcher is unable to account for these kinds of distortions in their data (for example, the researcher assumes all posts are from humans), then the quality of the analysis will be compromised.

Big Data: Computational methods

There is a range of computational methods that can be applied to social media data depending on the goals of the researcher. Big Data methods can vary greatly, but generally follow a number of general steps. An obvious starting point is the collection of data, although the choice of data to collect and the method by which it is harvested are important considerations. Once that has occurred, the data will often need to be cleaned to remove errors and standardized so that it is well structured for computational analysis. Next, one or more algorithms are applied to the data to process it in order to find relationships and patterns in the data. Often the results of this analysis are then visualized for further analysis, perhaps interactively so the researcher can explore the data in different ways.

Collection of data can be done in a number of ways. Early researchers worked with tools that collected information from websites by parsing the web pages for key data fields and sorting them into a structured database. This process was called web scraping. Since the mid-2000s companies like Twitter and Facebook have moved to discourage the use of these kinds of technologies by providing access to application programmable interfaces (APIs) that provide researchers with more structured access to data.

Web scraping is now actively discouraged or forbidden by most social media sites,[2] not only because it has the potential for a large impact on the amount of traffic on their servers (a computer can access many more pages in a minute than a human can), but also because the practice circumvents the company's ability to control their data. By providing researchers with access to an API, social media companies are able to control what and how much data is collected, and, through API terms of use, how that data can be used. While this is beneficial to researchers because API data is more structured and less error-prone than web scraping, it also limits the kinds of data that can be accessed. As Rogers (2018) points out, this in turn has implications for the kinds of analysis and methodological questions that researchers can ask. The Facebook API steers researchers towards analysis of pages and groups and clicks on the like button and does not provide access to profile data and friend networks (due to privacy settings), shifting researchers away from the analysis of 'taste and ties' (Rogers, 2018: 162).

Once data has been collected, it needs to be analysed, and there are a number of software tools and methodologies for doing this. In broad terms, data analysis involves processing, sorting and organizing data in a way that allows structures and patterns in the data to be revealed. There are a number of different broad methods that are used, including social network analysis (SNA), text analytics and community detection.

Social network analysis (SNA) algorithms analyse Big Data to look for relationships between different data points (sometimes referred to as nodes), and to determine the relative importance of data points and relationships in the network. This kind of analysis would be employed where there are implicit relationships within the data that could reasonably be thought of as network-like. For example, a data set that contains lists of users (nodes) and their contacts (relationships) can be analysed to discover basic statistical data about the network of relationships as a whole (such as the average number of contacts per person, the average number of links between one person and another), but also to determine the strength of the relationships between nodes, or which nodes are more heavily implicated in the network. The analysis could also attach a weight or significance to a relationship. For example, by analysing how the users in the networks passed messages between each other, it would be possible to see not only which users generated the most messages, but how those messages move through the network, allowing the analysis to determine how much influence they had over the network. Network analyses don't need to deal with people, of course. The approach can be used to understand the relationship between web pages, or the relationship between tags and images.

Text analytics is a blanket term for a range of methods that seek to extract meaning from text. Chief among these is sentiment analysis, sometimes also referred to as opinion mining, which uses computational methods to analyse the textual content of data in order to derive meaning. For instance, by analysing a large number of posts on a particular topic, sentiment analysis will look for key words or phrases that suggest whether the post is overall positive or overall negative. For example, a post that states 'I love ice cream' would be assessed as a positive comment because of the word 'love'. The analysis undertaken by sentiment analysis algorithms can be very sophisticated and may involve techniques like machine learning and natural language programming so that the algorithm won't be fooled by typical linguistic complexities, such as 'I love ice cream (just kidding)', though it may still be fooled by a more subtle comment like 'I love ice cream like I love a hole in the head'.

Sentiment analysis can also fail to take into account contextual cues, such as the comment within the context of a discussion, or within the context of a user's normal posting history. For instance, if you have a friend who you know loves ice cream, and they say 'you know how much I hate ice cream', you know they're being ironic, but only because you know that person. There is no way for a machine (or even another human) to determine this without the social context.

Other algorithms seek to find patterns in the data as a way of grouping components together. Community and theme detection algorithms might combine network analysis with textual analytics to attempt to group parts of the network together under shared interests. So, for example, it is possible to analyse a large number of tweets and extract markers from those tweets (such as hash tags, geolocation, specific words, and so on) to identify and group a large number of tweets into emergent themes.

An emerging and important technology in computational methods is machine learning and the application of advances in artificial intelligence towards data analytics. Machine learning uses algorithms to identify patterns in input data. These algorithms differ from traditional approaches because they can be trained by running samples through the network with known correct outputs. For example, when machine learning is used in facial recognition applications, the algorithm is trained using a large number of images of a number of known faces. The algorithm 'learns' how to match a face from a source image by repetitively testing different approaches until it finds one that is reliable. Once trained, the algorithm is able to match any face, not just the ones it was trained on. This approach works equally well with other kinds of data. For example, it could be used to predict characteristics of an individual based upon a set of information about that individual. This is still an emerging field of research, but it promises to return increasingly valuable approaches to data analysis as computers and machine learning approaches become more sophisticated.

Data visualization is a key technique in Big Data analysis because it provides a method of presenting complex data in a way that can be more readily interpreted than a table of numbers. Data visualization can be as simple as a bar or line chart, such as a company's share price over time. When presented visually, it's much easier to see patterns in the data than it is to see patterns in a list or table numbers. Manovich (2011) argues that data visualizations are based upon two key principles: reductionism and spatial representation. Reductionism, because visualizations represent complex data points as simple shapes, such as likes circles, lines or rectangles; and, spatial representation, because visualizations use space as the key visual element, such as distance between data points, distance from data points to axes, and so on (Manovich, 2011).

For example, Bruns et al. (2017) analysed the Australian Twittersphere (all the accounts on Twitter that were based in Australia), focusing only on the 255,000 accounts with at least 1,000 followers. The data was analysed and visualized using an algorithm, which gave each Twitter account a close spatial relationship if they shared more followers in common, and a more distant relationship if they didn't. Another algorithm was used to assign a colour to each account based upon a community detection algorithm. So, for example, if an account was associated with sports it might be coloured coral, while accounts associated with food and drink might be orange. The result (see Figure 2.1) shows that accounts that share a lot of common followers also tend to share a lot of common associations in offline communities.

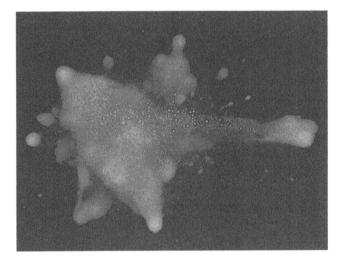

Figure 2.1   Map of the Australian Twittersphere in 2016

This visualization does require some explanation and understanding of the underlying data and the way it was organized, but with this understanding the features of the map become a compelling representation of a large and complex data set (see Chapter 8 for discussion of another data visualization project).

Big Data ethics

One of the emergent issues for Big Data research is the ethics of using social data for research. In general, most universities and research funding agencies require researchers to seek ethics approval before undertaking any research involving human subjects, even if the research is interviews or surveys. In the past, it was sometimes felt that social media data obviated the need for ethics approvals because the data was already in the public domain.

A commonly cited example (boyd & Crawford, 2011; Rogers, 2018) of the ethical complications of using social media data was a 2008 study conducted using Facebook profile data scraped from final-year Harvard graduates. This study used 'taste and ties' data that was openly available on Facebook to track the changes in students' preferences over time. While the researchers did go through an ethics committee approval process, they did not seek permission from the students to use their data, as they considered it to be in the public domain. However, after the study was published, other researchers found they could link the research data back to individuals.

One of the many questions that Big Data raises is whether just because the data is available, does that imply that a researcher can use it as he or she wishes? Does a user have a reasonable expectation that their data will be harvested and analysed, and can they reasonably consent to their data being used in this way if they cannot reasonably be expected to understand the implications of the analysis the data may be subjected to? Given the many ways that Big Data can be used to develop more complex profiles of an individual, is it possible for a layperson to give informed consent to the use of their data, when they may not fully understand the implications of how that data can be used?

Bringing ethnography and small data to Big Data and the Quantified Self (QS)

Beyond Big Data, we have small data, the detailed data about individuals that is beginning to find its way into the mix and has become an emergent topic for social media researchers and digital sociologists. With the rise in wearable devices and mobile apps tracking everything from heart rates to sleeping patterns, self-tracking and the Quantified Self (QS) movement is becoming highly prevalent in many areas of everyday life (Nafus & Sherman, 2014; Gilmore, 2016; Lupton, 2016b). The Quantified Self was founded by Gary Wolf and Kevin Kelly in *Wired* magazine in 2007.[3] For Wolf (2010), the QS movement could operate as a mirror to the data so that individuals could reflect, analyse and gain insights. For some, QS is about bringing creative forms of labour and pleasure to reading technology and industry (Neff, 2012; Scholz, 2012).

Data collected by self-tracking has become increasingly available to third parties such as educational bodies and insurance companies, and contemporary self-tracking results in data also for corporate and legal gain (Abend & Fuchs, 2016; Barta & Neff, 2016; Lupton, 2016a). Perhaps unsurprisingly, there is growing resistance to QS from individuals concerned with issues such as privacy, surveillance and data accuracy, as well as those anxious about the growing dependence of QS as a mediating factor in personal health and wellbeing (Gaunt et al., 2014; Hope, 2016; West et al., 2016).

While many are openly opposing QS via collective practices from boycotting wearables to direct legal recourse against QS manufacturing companies, others are resisting in more playful and innovative modes (Abend & Fuchs, 2016; Christovich, 2016; Little, 2016). Through techniques of creative misuse and appropriation, QS users from all walks of life are exposing the limits of activity trackers, critiquing the spread of QS data and disrupting many attitudes to QS in the process (Farman, 2014a; Sicart, 2014; Fuchs et al., 2016). In a time when QS data can be directed against users themselves, playful resistance functions as a timely intervention, allowing individuals to express aspects of their dissent and extending discussions of QS technologies and practices to wider audiences (Blas & Gaboury, 2016; Jacobsson, 2016; Lupton, 2016a).

For Nafus and Sherman (2014: 1791), deploying Cheney-Lippold's soft biopolitics, 'QS movement is best understood as a kind of soft resistance'. They note:

> By making themselves into people who do not fit the category, QSers appropriate Big Data's attention to granular patterns, but resist the categories that are built into devices and into the market for data … QS resists *through* its softness … QS politics are not defiant toward the dominance of Big Data – they are instead in dialogue with it and reliant on it. This means, of course, that the movement does not escape the wider biopolitics of late capitalism that rely on radical individualism to drive consumption as a dominant mode of expression and to elide structural inequalities by framing all actions in terms of personal 'choice'. (2014: 1791–1793)

Since 2010, the significance of Big Data, and the response to it in the form of the QS movement, has been unmistakable. As danah boyd and Kate Crawford (2011: 4) note, much of the debates around Big Data need to acknowledge that no matter how 'big' the data, it is always subjective. Data questions are riddled by the searchers' own perception and thus inherently human in their scope. Moreover, they argue the need for transparency and access to the ways in which the algorithms shape definitions of society.

Conclusion: The value of mixed methods approaches

To this point in the chapter we have essentially presented two approaches to social media research: qualitative, ethnographic approaches that aim to provide 'thick' descriptions of online experience; and computational approaches that aim to mine knowledge from the large amounts of 'Big Data' that social media generates. In this closing section we will compare these approaches and argue that the most viable approaches will be those that are able to combine both qualitative and quantitative methods to provide rich, contextualized insights.

Computational quantitative (that is, Big Data analytics) and ethnographic methods have played an enormously important role in social media research to date, but have sometimes been seen as separate traditions, with researchers generally identifying themselves as ethnographers or quantitative analysts. At times, there has been antagonism between these two approaches. Ethnographers can see quantitative methods as overly reductive, leading to findings that lack context and so 'miss the wood for the trees'. On the other hand, quantitative researchers may argue that ethnographic studies' focus on subjectivity and lack of solid numerical evidence to support their observations undermine the validity of research findings. Frequently these concerns reflect the different ontological perspectives of both empirical quantitative research and ethnographic research.

Ethnographers are concerned with understanding meaning and how people understand and experience other people, places and events in the everyday. By immersing themselves in a social environment, and by engaging in communities, the ethnographer develops a nuanced understanding, and is able to develop a deep understanding of how people understand and make sense of experiences. This kind of deep, detailed information cannot be easily extracted from data alone. Take, for example, a chat log. It may be extensive, covering millions of words and days or weeks of conversation, but taken simply as data it lacks context. The log can be analysed to find common words, links between words, emergent themes, and so on. This can tell us a lot about what was said, but not why. We don't have access to other context-dependent information that the chat participants had, things like interpersonal knowledge of the other people in the chat, any unwritten social standards they follow, and so on.

Ethnographers necessarily take context into account, and it forms part of the descriptive record of the subject they are studying. This provides them with access to the subtleties of communication and human interaction that are not necessarily encompassed within data sets. A good example of this is cited in Pink, Horst et al. (2016: 49–50), where they discuss a project in which researchers were interested in the way households responded to technology. It was common to find that participants frequently underreported the amount of time they spent using technology, and the extent to which they engaged with it. However, as the researchers developed relationships with the study participants through subsequent visits to their homes, the researchers started to learn more about the participants, and the participants, in turn, learned more about the research project and began to reflect more heavily and critically on their own internet use. One family initially described themselves as digitally unsophisticated, but on subsequent visits, and after deeper consideration, realized that they had made videos of horses they wanted to sell, posted them online, had planned holidays with extensive online research and had undertaken many other activities that belied their initial summation of their use of technology. Their use of technology was so embedded in their everyday lives that they didn't appreciate it until they had spent significant time (six hours of visits from the researchers) thinking about it.

Even though computational quantitative methods such as sentiment analysis (discussed above) can be used to obtain an overall understanding of the content of a body of text, it is limited in the amount of insight that can be obtained; ethnographies take into account many factors and are filtered through the knowledge and experience of the researcher – it's not just a matter of the data; it's about understanding and describing whole communities, and much of the knowledge gained is absent from the data.

Yet, for all the value that can be gained from detailed qualitative analysis, quantitative approaches are almost essential for dealing with the large amounts of often-complex data that social media generates. As discussed above, the range of computational approaches can provide fascinating high-level insights into network relationships, and data patterns that suggest structures and behaviour that are not immediately apparent.

The combination of these approaches seems to offer the best of both worlds. While computational approaches and data visualization can be used to provide a high-level under-standing of social media data, qualitative approaches can complement this by allowing the researcher to 'zoom in' on particular aspects of the data that appear interesting, and provide richer, deeper contextualized information that may support or refute an initial hypothesis. Ethnographic methods can also enhance computational methods by providing additional context to computational analyses, ideally allowing the best of both methodological worlds.

Despite its promise, growth in the use of mixed methods has been relatively slow. One of the main reasons for this is that the skill sets of researchers in the two traditions are quite different, and combining the two methodologies requires the researchers involved to be able to relate their methods to each other. As Hesse-Biber and Griffin (2013) note, quantitative researchers may have doubts about the quality of data produced from online sources because online data rarely conforms to a statistically representative sample, and because the communities that generate the data are themselves in a state of flux. Similarly, ethnographers rarely have a background in computer science, so the methods employed in computational analytics and data visualization may be unfamiliar and require the researcher to develop skills that are well outside their disciplinary foundation. Some have suggested that code literacy may need to become a fundamental skill for all humanities researchers (Burgess & Bruns, 2012; Manovich, 2012).

Notes

1. www.pewinternet.org/
2. See www.facebook.com/apps/site_scraping_tos_terms.php for an example of Facebook's automated data collection terms.
3. http://quantifiedself.com/2011/03/what-is-the-quantified-self/

3

Histories of Social Media

Introduction

In this chapter we seek to contextualize social media historically. We start out by defining critical media histories (including why we refer to history in the plural) and look at why these histories are useful tools, not only to understand the past, but through it, to understand the present. We then move on to look at some specific internet histories, where we emphasize continuity over disruption, and multiple histories over a single history, an approach that is increasingly common in academic approaches to social media, but which challenges the often-repeated narrative that digital technology is always, new, exceptional and revolutionary. By highlighting some of the work that has traced some of the histories and contributed to today's social media landscapes, we aim to emphasize the sense of continuity through providing examples that show how older (even text-based) technologies played an important role in the development of social media. Some of this discussion requires engagement with concepts that are now deemed 'outdated', such as Web 2.0, whose precepts unquestionably inform the contemporary logic of social media programmability, popularity, connectivity and datafication (van Djick & Poell, 2013).

The second part of this chapter seeks to take the more nuanced understanding of internet histories discussed in the first half, and, using this knowledge, applies it to exploring the development of a key paradox in social media: the uneasy relationship between individuals and social media, between the use of social media for personal empowerment, and the way that individuals can be used and exploited by social media. Critical media histories help us understand the nature of this paradox, to see how it came to be, and to open discussion into whether it needs to be like this in the future.

Critical media histories

Before we get into this chapter proper, it's useful to briefly outline why this chapter is here. At first blush, it does make sense that a book on social media would include a history of social media, but why? And what do we mean by *critical* media history?

As van Dijck says in his book *The Culture of Connectivity* (2013), we need critical histories that examine the rise of social media. Critical media histories are media histories that don't simply provide a recounting of the order of events in the development of a particular technology. They're not just an annotated timeline. Critical histories are *critical* because they don't just document what happened but try to dig deeper to understand the reasons and context in which they happened. Critical media histories seek to contextualize the development of media technologies within the broader social, cultural and economic environment, and look to answer questions like: why *this* technology, why at this *time*, why in this *form*? This means that if we can develop critical histories of social media, we should be able to gain a lot of insight into how social media came to be the way it is, and where it is going.

In order for these questions to make sense, we need to embrace the idea that at any point in time, there are many possible ways that a technology and its associated industries might evolve. We need to move away from the common-sense idea that history is necessarily teleological – in other words, that our history is the only possible way things could have played out.

Similarly, we use the term 'histories' (plural) to emphasize the idea that it is possible to tell more than one valid story about a particular historical event. Imagine, for example, that we were interested in learning about Twitter. We could research the technical development of the platform, using technical specifications and interviews with Twitter's programmers, or we could speak to the people who use Twitter, many of whom would know very little about the platform's technical design, but who have much more nuanced understandings of what it means to be a Twitter user, and perhaps how being a user changed over time. Both histories would be valid and supported by good evidence, so no history is more correct than the other – both histories are important for understanding the development of Twitter.

One of the things we should keep in mind when studying social media critically is why this kind of social media at this time? Social media could have evolved in a range of different ways. The familiar social media template of having a login and an associated profile defines how many social media are designed, but is this the only way for social media to work? Facebook, for example, insists that your profile is accurate and that you use your real name: 'You will not provide any false personal information on Facebook, or create an account for anyone other than yourself without permission' (Facebook, 2015: n.p.) We could just as easily imagine a version of Facebook that encouraged its users to maintain their anonymity, or that embraced the creative expression of people's alter egos.

Because the idea of user profiles is quite fundamental to most social media platforms, it's easy to assume that they are technologically important. The construction of these social media profiles might even form the basis for a definition of social media, as Obar and Wildman do: 'Individuals and groups create user-specific profiles for a site or app designed and maintained by a social media service.' (2015: 747).

Taking a critical perspective on this, we might ask why social media profiles are so important? On the one hand, we could argue that there is a technical reason (there needs to be a way for individuals to identify themselves to other individuals online so they can find each other). Then again, we could argue that profiles are the main way that social media companies can collect information about their users, suggesting that there may be an economic reason behind the importance of profiles. Similarly, it could be argued that there is a cultural reason for the value of profiles, that people like sharing (especially the most flattering) information about themselves to an audience. A critical history of social media can provide deeper insight into the evolution of social media within a cultural, political and economic context by asking questions about why the profile is so central to so many platforms.

As van Dijck and Poell point out 'social media have the ability to transport their logic outside of the platforms that generate them, while their distinctivetechnological, discursive, economic, and organizational strategies tend to remain implicit or appear "natural"' (2013: 5). There are two key points they are making here. First, there is a kind of 'logic' built into social media that defines how it works. This logic, once adopted and understood by enough people, can then be applied in other non-social media contexts, such as in an organization. Their second point is that these logics become natural, meaning that people become so used to the logic of social media that we don't see the logic of the medium as being made by people for specific reasons, but instead we accept it as the natural way that things work.

Critical histories are one way we can start to make these invisible naturalized logics more visible. By tracing the development of social media, for example, we can see that social media has come to be what it is today through a series of developments. These developments determine how social media has evolved, and they are always situated within the world of people and their motivations to achieve certain desirable outcomes.

Media has always been social ... an approach to internet histories

Echoing media scholars such as Nancy Baym and John Hartley, Zizi Papacharissi (2015) dislikes the term 'social media', because, to her, all media are social. In one sense, then, if all media are social, a history of social media could go all the way back to the first cave paintings. Even if we limit social media to computer-based communication, there's still a significant recent history for us to tackle. For example, networked text-based computer systems with messaging capabilities were used in organizations from the 1970s and spawned a range of communities, which, while limited to relatively small groups of people, established some of the fundamental strategies we still see in social media today. Likewise, Bulletin Board Systems (BBSs), which hail from the 1980s and pre-date the web by at least a decade, could constitute some of the earliest forms of social media. They are notable because they expanded the scope of online interaction beyond the research community.

The point here is that while we often think of social phenomena as being invented or appearing at a particular time, they are inevitably connected to a series of older technologies and practices, and there is rarely a clear line that delineates one technology from another. This means that when tracing the histories of social media, we need to accept that there is no single date, place or person who can claim to be the 'first' social media. Rather, we'll accept that social media is a confluence of events, technologies, individuals and communities.

Not only is the development of social media contingent upon technologies, individuals and communities, but it is also situated within national cultural and political environments, which means that social media has evolved in different ways in different countries. In much of Asia, for example, internet technologies first expanded through mobile devices rather than the desktop computer. For example, as McLelland, Yu and Goggin (2017) point out, in Japan desktop computing was not as popular as it was in the United States or the United Kingdom, in part because the Japanese language was not as readily transferrable to text-based interfaces. This meant that the internet first took off in Japan through internet-enabled mobile devices in the late 1990s.

For McLelland, Yu and Goggin (2017), understanding these alternative international, non-Anglophonic histories of the internet and social media isn't a curious sideline to mainstream internet histories: it is essential to understanding the internet. In their words, 'a basic sense of the range, importance, and influence of these alternative histories of social media is vital, if we are to understand – not misconstrue – the contemporary dynamics of social media' (McLelland et al. 2017: 54). Even the list of popular social media platforms themselves differ from country to country: for example, whereas Facebook dominates most Western countries, VKontakte is the major social media platform in Russia; and Weibo has always been far more substantial in China than Twitter. From this, we can easily see that the idea that there could be a *single* history of social media is naïve, at best.

In the following sections, we are going to explore the role of text-based network interfaces (such as USENET and BBS) in building collaborative and participatory cultures (Jenkins, 2006) that we now take as a given in terms of contemporary internet and social media cultures. We will then look at the development of the web through the dot-com boom, through the bust and into Web 2.0 and the development of social media. While this will be only a brief foray into social media histories, it will emphasize the value of critical media histories in helping us to develop a better understanding of our social media landscape.

Text-based networks

Today we take the colourful visual interfaces of our high-resolution computer screens for granted. Yet, when Apple introduced the Apple Lisa in 1983 (the first consumer computer to feature a graphical user interface and a mouse for input), the idea of a symbolic interface to the computer was a revelation. Prior to this, text-based interfaces were the only way to use computer systems. In the 1970s computer systems also tended to be based around a central 'mainframe' or server computer. Because computers were expensive, it was more economically viable to purchase a single computer which could have more than one person access it at the same time. A user could access a mainframe system either through a 'dumb terminal' (essentially a monitor and keyboard connected to the main computer via a cable), or remotely via a terminal interface.

These early computer systems were also not widely accessible. Being large and expensive, computers tended to be operated by research institutions, government agencies and large companies. Remote access to these machines was provided to employees who had a need to access them – primarily technical and research staff of the institutions that owned the machine. In this environment, if you were logged into a computer, you could quite reasonably expect others to be logged into the computer too. The systems thus provided methods for seeing who else was online, for sending messages to other users, and so on.

While visually quite different from today's point-and-click interfaces, the fundamentals of these early text-based UNIX systems are still very familiar to the modern social media user. For example, a UNIX user could create a text file (called a .plan file) in their user account, which could be used to provide status updates. Anyone logged into the UNIX system, or even connected to it remotely, could use the 'finger' command and that user would see his or her .plan file. They were highly analogous in both form and function to a status message.

UNIX users also created a range of other tools and technologies for online communication. USENET, for example, which was first deployed in 1980, was designed as a distributed messaging system, and is very much the precursor to web forums. A user could write something, post it to USENET, and then at a predetermined time (usually at night, when telephone calls were cheaper), the computer would contact another computer via the regular telephone system, using a modem, and exchange new messages. In this way over time, posts from thousands of people on different computer systems would be aggregated, allowing a user on any computer to see posts from hundreds or thousands of other people, connected to other computers across nations and internationally.

Because USENET posts were organized into categories called newsgroups, they provided an environment for the creation of participatory online communities, well before the advent of the web. As O'Riordan (2005) documents, for example, the soc.motss (society newsgroup, subgroup: members of the same sex) provided an online space for the online LGBTI community from as early as 1983.

While UNIX-based technologies provided one kind of participatory online environment accessible mainly to those relatively few people with access to UNIX systems, Bulletin Board Systems (BBSs) provided another less exclusive online space. For Delwiche (2018), contemporary conversations concerning social media originated in connections with BBS, so much so that he argues the BBS to be one of the pioneer forms of social media. As Delwiche (2018: 36) notes, BBS rose out of a desire for 'strong, free, non-hierarchical channels of communication', in which news was seen as participatory long before the hype of Web 2.0. For Delwiche, BBS can be seen as an important new subculture in the 1980s, in which various forms of distribution and sharing emerged. According to Delwiche, the intro-duction of widespread internet largely ended the BBS phenomenon as they allowed users to reach beyond the local community. Delwiche argues that the BBS history is important as it allows us to recognize the 'enduring characteristics of our social media landscape' – talking about politics, playing games, consuming stories or downloading content are the examples the author gives (Delwiche, 2018: 49).

The pre-web 'text' period of internet history is an important period because it laid some of the foundations for how the internet would emerge in the late 1990s. This early history of UNIX and USENET, BBS and proprietary networks provided space for the evolution of the foundational infrastructure, and practices that would later support and influence the development of web-based participation, and eventually, social media. From the perspective of developing critical media histories, this period in the development of the internet is an invaluable background.

However, it is also important to recognize that much of this narrative describes the experience of Anglophonic countries. While similarities exist between many countries, the development and uptake of internet and social networking technologies was experienced differently in different countries and cultural contexts. Delwiche (2018) is careful to note that much of the 'rise and fall' of the BBS has been from an American-centric perspec-tive. This is supported by the work of Gerard Goggin and Mark McLelland, who have looked at non-Anglophonic internet histories in China, Japan and South Korea (Goggin & McLelland, 2017). Authors working in this space have pointed out the not insignificant ways that other internet histories have departed from the Anglocentric experience, highlighting the contingency of media histories. For example, the BBS and text-based experience was by no means universal, and in some countries it hardly figured at all, while in others (like China) the BBS was an important part of the development of social computer networking well into the 1990s.

In some countries, such as Japan, the early internet had low levels of penetration due in part to the relatively low use of desktop computers. It wasn't until the late 1990s that Japan's engagement with the internet took off as people got access to the internet through the so-called i-Mode (internet mode) on mobile devices. Like Japan, India's internet experience is primarily mobile, although in India, a country where English is widely spoken, character entry wasn't the same challenge as in Japan. Instead, the mobile phone was both cheaper and less power-hungry than desktop computers, making it better suited to the Indian market than the desktop.

The historicity of different technologies also changes from country to country. In Japan, for example, the pager became appropriated from business as a social technology among Japanese school girls, while in many other countries the pager was a business technology superseded by the mobile phone. Although BBS was seen as a superseded technology in most Anglophonic countries by the early 1990s, it continued to be an important technology in China well into the 1990s. It even persisted in the post-web internet as BBSs were moved onto the internet, and maintained their popularity until they started to be more heavily regulated in the early 2000s. Similarities between these different national and cultural contexts also exist. In China, as in much of Europe and Anglophonic countries, early adoption of networked technology, typified by computer-to-computer communication via modem, was led by technologically enthused individuals running BBSs and other network services out of interest rather than for commercial gain or political reasons. This environment nurtured some of China's modern internet entrepreneurs, in much the same way that early networking cultures in the US and Europe did for the founders of companies like Microsoft and Apple (McLelland et al. 2017).

Keeping in mind that we should not assume the internet experience is universal, the next section looks at how the deregulation of computer networks in Western economies and how the development of more sophisticated graphical interfaces – in particular the world wide web – led to a massive increase in the use of the internet, and how the idea of Web 2.0, trumpeted in the early 2000s, represented a continuation (rather than a break with) the broader historical context.

The web and Web 2.0

While computers began to develop more sophisticated graphical interfaces from the mid-1980s, it wasn't until the early to mid-1990s in the West that the internet started to become popular outside the more dedicated and technologically literate early adopter communities. A factor that is often described as the main driver of the early growth of the internet was the development of the world wide web in 1992, which provided a graphical (rather than textual) method of navigating the internet. This made the internet much more appealing to non-technical users, and more accessible than the previous text-based interfaces and their arcane typed commands.

Without discounting the importance of the web, another important factor for the development of the internet in the early 1990s was the ongoing deregulation of information and telecommunication networks in many Western countries. Under the neoliberal economic policies of the Reagan and Thatcher governments of the 1980s, publicly owned assets were sold to private interests. The National Science Foundation network (NSFNet), which provided the main telecommunications network that supported the internet in the United States, was sold piecemeal in the 1990s, ceding more and more of the publically-funded technical infrastructure of the internet to private companies. Similar transitions of public network assets to private hands occurred in other Western countries, such as the United Kingdom, Australia and Canada. As publically-funded research infrastructure, access to networks like NSFNet was regulated, and use of the network by organizations or individuals not engaged in publically-funded research was discouraged or forbidden. As these networks were deregulated, the policies that restricted access to the networks were also deregulated, which meant that the number of people who could obtain access to the internet infrastructure began to increase. In other words, beyond the development of the web, the changing political context of computer networks was a significant factor in the development of the internet in Western countries.

In the early years of the web, there were no search engines like Google. Google wasn't available on the web until 1998, although earlier search engines, such as Lycos (1994) and Altavista (1995), did provide web search services from quite early on. Prior to this, many websites featured 'home pages' that contained lists of links to other websites, and paper computing magazines published the addresses of 'cool sites'. Probably the largest index on the early web was Yahoo! which provided an exhaustive categorized list of thousands of websites. However, as the web grew and maintaining these lists became increasingly difficult, search engines started to become the main way people found websites.

User-created content was important even in these early years and played an important role in driving adoption of the internet. Some of the first examples of user-created content were 'personal home pages', either hosted on their own computers, or, more likely, on one of the services that hosted websites for free. One of the most popular of these free hosting sites, Geocities, was established in 1994 and ended up hosting hundreds of thousands of user-created websites. Users who created personal home pages on Geocities needed to learn how to create web pages using the hypertext mark-up language (HTML), which required a moderate technical knowledge. This placed something of a technical barrier on participation, but also encouraged thousands to develop a better understanding of this new and important media technology.

As content and the number of users on the internet grew, so too did commercial interest in exploiting it. Individuals and companies began making millions of dollars as investors rushed to get in early on what they perceived to be the 'next big thing' (despite the fact that while the number of internet users was growing fast, very few companies were actually able to turn a profit). Shares in everything from online pet food and pizza deliveries to virtual currency retailers were bought and sold, leading to an investment bubble that was termed the 'dotcom bubble'. When it burst in 2000, the following crash wiped billions of dollars from the stock market, yielding the single biggest fall in the US stock market's history. While many fledgling internet companies were decimated by the crash, a number of them – companies such as Amazon and Google, for example – managed to emerge from the crash and established themselves in the post-bust environment.

Commercializing the internet: Web 2.0

In the early 2000s in the wake of the dotcom crash, a number of internet companies and services began emerging that were organized around a set of common principles, the chief ones being a focus on user-generated content and the ability for websites to share data between each other and with other applications. As early as 1999, software designer Darcy DiNucci recognized that the web was changing. From her perspective, the shift was going to be in the role of the web, changing from an end in itself (personal home pages, for example) to an almost invisible medium in which information is transported (DiNucci, 1999). DiNucci regarded this as a transition to what she termed 'Web 2.0'. With the development of the iPhone in 2007, and in the subsequent preponderance of web apps, DiNucci's prognostications have largely been realized.

However, it was in 2004, when the O'Reilly group ran their first Web 2.0 conference, that the term gained popularity as a way to capture how these post-dotcom-crash companies were emerging. The term gained popularity precisely because it was a shorthand way to describe what was perceived (and promoted) as the emergence of new 'disruptive' internet companies that were based primarily upon creating value from user-developed content. New Web 2.0 sites, such as Flickr (photo-sharing: 2004), Wordpress (blogging: 2003), Delicious (social bookmark sharing: 2003) and MySpace (social networking: 2003), seemed able to capitalize on user-generated content and prospered by making this information widely accessible rather than locking it down. So-called Web 2.0 companies provided storage for hosting user-generated content, allowed people to create accounts on their systems (which often also implied creating a user profile), and encouraged the sharing of content. Whereas earlier services like the 'Web 1.0' Geocities provided online data storage but little in the way of technical support, these new services went much further, providing interfaces that made uploading content much simpler, as well as adding features like tagging to make content easier to discover and archive.

Flickr, for example, made it relatively easy for a photographer to make their photographs available on the web. It was easy to upload photos using an interactive web-based interface that required the photographer to do little more than select the photo they wanted to upload, enter any additional information about the photo they desired and then click a button. This ease of use, and the rapid increase in the value of Flickr to other internet users, meant the number of photos on the site burgeoned – at its peak in 2013, people were uploading some 3.5 million public photos per day to Flickr (Brandt et al., 2017). In addition to making user-generated content easier to put online, websites like Flickr made the content on their site easy to access. They provided an application programmable interface (API) that programmers could use to access photos on Flickr. So, for example, a programmer could create a screen-saver that would connect to Flickr and select random photos from their enormous archive to decorate users' idling computer displays. Flickr, like its contemporary 'Web 2.0' sites, was more than a website – it became a *service*.

However, if we look beyond the popular view that Web 2.0 represented a significant shift in the internet, and consider the history that preceded it, Web 2.0 seems more inevitable than surprising. For Michael Stevenson (2018) in 'From Hypertext to Hype and Back Again: Exploring the Roots of Social Media in Early Web Culture', Web 2.0 and social media must be seen as a particular arrangement of forms and ideas of media technologies, whereby the existence of 'participation and openness' can be witnessed in early web and pre-web internet cultures (similar to values often associated with Web 2.0). As Stevenson argues, overlapping chronologies highlight the similar developments between the web's inception and the hype surrounding Web 2.0 in the mid-2000s. He urges us towards arguing against the commonly held perception of Web 2.0 as radical, instead placing it along a web history of evolving perception and recognition of shaping forces – cultural, economic and technological (Stevenson, 2018).

The above (albeit brief) histories highlight Stevenson's point. The seeds for Web 2.0 and social media are much better characterized as continuous developments than as exceptional or revolutionary. User-generated content, for example, has always been an important factor in internet development, whether it be USENET, someone running a BBS out of their garage, or even 'Web 1.0' sites like Geocities. Similarly, the principles of participation and openness are well-documented central principles of online cultures since the UNIX systems of the late 1970s and the BBS systems of the early 1980s and into the 1990s.

In the next sections we explore some of the common paradoxes that have underlined BBS, Web 2.0 and social media cultures. We argue for understanding that these practices are overlapping and continuous rather than following the usual 'disruption' narrative. We begin with a section on 'Used or being used?', then turn to the provocation 'Social media as empowering' and then to 'Social media as exploitation' to consider the key paradox around empowerment and exploitation which is central to social media histories.

Used or being used?

> The danger of participation is that there are hundreds or even thousands of potentially critical eyes watching every entry. A faulty fact will be challenged, a lie will be uncovered, plagiarism will be discovered. Cyberspace is a truth serum. (Rushkoff, 1994: 36)

> The signs are growing that the once-anarchic, perhaps emancipatory internet is subject to increasing attempts to privatize, commercialize, control and profit from the activities of consumers online. (Livingstone, 2005: 2–3)

The term 'user' has two connotations: controller and controlled. In computer parlance, the user is in charge of the machine. The user is in control (at least apparently) of the computer's operation – the computer seemingly does nothing unless a user clicks a mouse button or presses a key. On the other hand, in drug culture, a user is someone who uses a drug, who gives up personal control and hands it over to the chemical and is often controlled by it, or by those who sell it. When we think about users in the context of social media, and particularly within the construct of Web 2.0, which one of these categories is most applicable? Are users the controllers, who are powerful because they can create the content in stark contrast to the powerless audience of mass media, or are users the controlled, as their personal information and creative and cultural labour is monitored and commodified by social media companies?

These questions as phrased here as binary opposites, and as such they represent ideal positions at the extreme ends of a spectrum of different possibilities. Certainly, social media can be seen as empowering or exploiting the social, affective and creative labour of the user. However, such a model doesn't acknowledge the ambiguities that manifest within everyday practices. Just as it is hard for many to ascertain how long they have been online given that often social media sites sit open on one's desktop or are perpetually checked on one's mobile phone, so too are the outcomes of such 'labour' hard to put into binaries like empowerment or exploitation. The ambient intimacy of everyday social media practices makes it hard to pin down. Work by Banks and Humphreys (2008) in the area of game players, along with Bruns' model of the 'produser' (Bruns, 2005), have attempted to provide more useful models for conceptualizing the often-tacit labour that accompanies contemporary media practice today.

Social media as empowering

It is tempting to look at social media as a democratic revolution in the media, and indeed it has been trumpeted as such in some of the earliest writings about the internet (Lovink, 2012). At the heart of these arguments is the idea that the internet bypasses old structures of control and power; instead of a few powerful people controlling what the majority see and hear, the majority can now produce (and reproduce) media. This decentralization of the production of media content also decentralizes media control, which poses vast challenges for media companies that established their media empires based upon a monopoly over distribution. This, in turn, leads some observers to see the internet as an inherently democratizing or emancipatory medium because of the way it *seems* to empower individuals and undermine the old monopolies and systems of power.

This narrative of empowerment has a long history that pre-dates the popular internet and has its roots in the techno-utopianism of counter-culture movements of the 1960s, and with libertarian ideals that are fundamentally intertwined with the political landscape of the United States. Metaphors that engaged concepts such as the 'virtual frontier' invoked notions of new, open spaces that were pioneering and free of the controls of an old order, a kind of Wild West without the dust and guns. Given the early development of the internet was driven largely by the United States, it is hardly surprising that these ideals should hail from the cultural and political traditions of that nation. In this particular Anglophonic evolution, issues such as race and gender performativity have become key battlegrounds (Nakamura, 2002).

A number of influential commentators managed to capture people's imaginations with romantic concepts that meshed US libertarianism with 1960s alternative culture and the emergence of new technologies. John Perry Barlow, for example, presented a firmly libertarian view of the internet in his paper 'Declaration of the Independence of Cyberspace' (1996), as did Douglas Rushkoff in *Cyberia* (1994). These influential works cast the internet as something that was above and beyond the reach of industrial governments, which John Perry Barlow described as 'weary giants of flesh and steel' (1996: n.p.).

Adding to these romantic concepts of the internet as being beyond the reach of old power structures (understood by Barlow in true US-libertarian style primarily as governments) were claims that the technology itself was inherently democratizing. It became a known 'fact' that the internet was developed to withstand nuclear attack (Chun, 2006: 65) and this robustness in the face of the greatest threat known to humankind helped to elevate the internet – often referred to as cyberspace – to the sublime. This immunity to nuclear war extended beyond physical attacks and into the political realm. The internet, according to John Gilmore, 'treats censorship as damage, and routes around it' (Elmer-Dewitt, 1993: n.p.). In this light, the internet couldn't be stopped, let alone tamed.

In the decade following, these initial scholarly works enabled a great deal of political thinking about the internet. As described above, the demographic profile of internet users changed as more and more people came online, and businesses started colonizing the internet. The dotcom crash was for some a kind of proof that the internet was resistant to control. The emergence of Web 2.0 and the near simultaneous emergence of mobile internet has again raised questions about the ability of the internet to bypass conventional control and bring about social change.

Certainly, it is difficult to ignore the way that social media has greatly expanded the networked individual's access to information. For the lucky ones, answers to many questions are only a Google search away (though veracity may be a little further afield). Social media provide them with access to a wider social network, allowing them to find employment or maintain social relationships that once would have died due to distance.

Networked individuals have access to a much greater variety of media, almost at whim, and can make creative works that can be enjoyed by thousands or millions of people where once they might have been consigned to the back of a cupboard, to be discovered by relatives sometime after they had passed on.

On a larger scale, social media has been implicated in regime change and is playing an increasingly important role in political campaigns. Governments in some countries are becoming interested in social media as a way to engage more directly with citizens, and citizens are using social media to draw attention to local issues (Shirky, 2009).

Social media as exploitation

It's Not Information Overload. It's Filter Failure. (Shirky, 2008b)

A medium that allows users to create things and develop a voice that eludes regulation by authorities can lead to significant positive – perhaps even emancipatory – impacts in many areas of society, from the economy to politics (see the changing nature of citizen journalism through vehicles such as Twitter). On the face of it, social media gives a great deal more control back to the majority of people. Yet there are also arguments to the contrary: while social media undermines many existing media models, it also establishes new ones.

As Chamath Palihapitiya, a former Facebook executive, said in a 2016 interview at Stanford's Graduate School of Business, 'The short-term, dopamine-driven feedback loops we've created are destroying how society works. No civil discourse, no cooperation; misinformation, mistruth' (Vincent, 2017: n.p.). He was referring to the way features such as 'likes' in social media generate a positive feeling in people (associated with the brain's natural behavioural reinforcement neurochemical dopamine), and the way these feelings 'program' us into behaviours that he feels are ultimately socially destructive. Over a year later it was revealed that data from more than 50 million Facebook users – including likes and users' address books – had been harvested by Cambridge Analytica, a company that used the data to profile voters and allow political parties to aim very tightly targeted political messages, and perhaps to sway elections (Rosenberg et al., 2018).

Criticisms of social networking as supporting mostly superficial gossip and creating echo chambers that reinforce biases rather than challenging them – as Rushkoff (1994) had hoped – are not new. Dahlberg (2001), for example, made exactly these complaints about the early 'Web 1.0' social networking sites like Geocities and Friendster and SixDegrees.com, noting that the quality of much online discussion was low and resulted in 'a fragmentation of cyber-discourse into mutually exclusive cyber-communities' (Dahlberg, 2001: 618).

As James Beniger showed in the 1980s, computers and communications technologies were developed primarily to increase centralized management and control of industrial processes, not to diminish it. It's hard to simply dismiss this as irrelevant to the internet, although in the face of so many internet-led changes that seem to be undermining industrial economic structures (the music industry springs to mind), it is hard to see the connection.

Since the beginning of the industrial revolution, control has been an ongoing concern. As production sped up and more goods were produced and moved faster and in greater variety to diverse markets, increasingly sophisticated information systems were required to maintain control. Seen in this light, the evolution of digital computers is a response to the need for increased control in industrialized countries (Beniger, 1986).

The rise of social media can readily be seen as part of this refinement in control. While in some respects social media is democratizing, empowering and emancipatory, it also makes us all more digital as our social lives and personal statistics become rendered as binary digits flying around the planet at the speed of light. This makes us all more subject to the control mechanisms of the information society; to be counted and sorted and organized into groups that can be matched with products and processed as fast as materials and services can be produced and distributed.

For Andrejevic (2011), networked sociabilities moderated by social media, for example, are structured around a 'storable and sortable' separation between the user and the means of socializing. This allows for 'collections of data' – that is, data freely supplied by users – to be repurposed by companies and marketing campaigns. Following on from the work of Terranova (2000) on today's 'social factories', Andrejevic argues that commercial interests are colonizing narratives of personal self-presentation and sociality (2011). Sonia Livingstone would appear to agree. She writes:

> … we must instead ask questions about how, and with what consequences, it has come about that all social situations (whether at home or work, in public or in private, at school or out shopping) are now, simultaneously, mediated spaces, thereby constituting their participants inevitably as both family, workers, public or communities and as audiences, consumers or users? (Livingstone, 2005: 25–26)

This model of social media as exploiting social labour, even where the people undertaking that labour may not conceptualize it as such, can be viewed as part of broader structural affordances of capitalism. Cast in this light, social media can be seen as a step in increasing the control afforded by the information technologies. While television provided an important means for product makers to connect with audience through advertising, television also suffered from a number of shortcomings. Under a broadcast model, for example, nobody can tell what television station is being watched at any one time. Broadcast companies pay top dollar to media ratings companies like AC Neilsen, which go to extraordinary lengths to determine ratings for television programmes. Broadcasters simply don't know who is watching their channels without polling the audience. Unless somebody is watching you from across the street, you can be completely certain that when you are watching a broadcast TV programme, you are the only person who knows you're watching it.

On the internet, however, every time you sit down at your computer and access a website, your activity is instantly recorded by multiple sources – if not your ISP, then at the very least the website that is receiving your request, and generally by a much more complex array of monitoring systems that help website owners and search companies develop a profile of each individual's online habits. No matter how little information you provide to sites and services (and many people provide quite a lot), the mere fact you are connected to the internet immediately compromises your privacy. People who wish to maintain their privacy online must go to significant lengths to do so, and this requires a level of technical proficiency that eludes most internet users. When seen in this light, the internet seems to be as much an advance in control as an empowerment of the user.

The fact that everything is logged and available for analysis opens up a new and valuable source of information for companies – very precise information about the browsing habits of internet users, which in turn allows for much, much greater targeting of advertising and the prospect of direct sales to the consumer, or simply the sale of collected information about users to other parties. Instead of undermining central authority and power, this seems to be doing the opposite, and users and their cultural activities are being colonized, monitored and exploited like never before.

In Wendy Chun's excellent book on the internet (Chun, 2006), the dichotomy of control and freedom are presented as a paradox. Chun argues that the meaning of freedom has gradually been shifted to incorporate control as an implicit precondition. In other words, if you want freedom, then you have to submit to control. This apparent contradiction makes a strange kind of sense in a post-9/11 world, where phantom terrorists lurk in every airport terminal. There can be no greater threat to individual freedom than death, and the only thing standing between us and death at the hands of a terrorist is often control applied through surveillance – full-body scanners, constant monitoring through security cameras and the tightly regimented processing of people.

Conversely, our sense of freedom is realized through a sense of control because the more control one has, the argument goes, the more freedom you have to do what you want. Here we return to the earlier point mentioned near the beginning of this section about users, and the ambiguity of the term. The user is understood to be a powerful individual, and this notion is reinforced in information technology and the internet all the time. Microsoft's slogan 'Where do you want to go today?' embraces the notion of the all-powerful user who is in absolute control of his or her destiny within the online environment.

As Chun (2006) points out, this draws upon earlier conceptions of cyberspace as being a place beyond space, and also draws upon popular representations of cyberspace from fiction which preceded and accompanied the development of the internet. From William Gibson's cyberpunk novels and Neal Stephenson's *Snow Crash* (1992) to a raft of thematically similar books and films, images of cyberspace have been constructed as somewhere where the individual is in control. From the utopian holodeck of *Star Trek: The Next Generation* to the dystopian matrix in the Wachowskis' film of the same name, virtual online cyberspaces have been represented as a place where the user exerts control over their destiny by knowing or learning how to control their online environment.

Social media also places the user at the centre of their own universe, a platform to stand on to engage with and control their online space. Underlying this so-called user-centred media is the fact that the data is then mined and sold to advertisers (Vaidhyanathan, 2011; Lovink, 2012). Consider that Facebook has reported more than 2.2 billion subscribers at the time of writing, and yet each and every one of these subscribers (users) has a network of friends in which they are the central nodes that organizes everything else. The user can switch off unwanted contacts, send messages out to hundreds (or millions, just as easily), all the while developing the illusion of freedom through control. This isn't just any space that the user is so-called controlling, it's not even cyberspace; it's their 'personal' space. YouTube places 'you' at the centre of the universe, and MySpace, as one social media platform helpfully points out, creates an online space that is 'mine'.

However, as Chun (2006) argues, it's in the interests of the companies behind these services to foster and develop the illusion of control. Providing users with a certain kind of control (the ability to create profiles and interact with others and produce cultural objects), all mediated within the company's platform, actually establishes broader economic and political controls over the whole system. We have used the term 'platform' here a couple of times to draw attention to another way of thinking about social media. Tarleton Gillespie notes that a platform has a number of definitions in English language, which together suggest 'a progressive and egalitarian arrangement, lifting up those who stand upon it' (Gillespie, 2010: 350).

When applied to social media applications like YouTube, Facebook or Twitter, the term suggests that the role of the company is impartial – they are just there to provide a platform that users can stand on and be treated as equals. The principles of the platform are enshrined in Facebook's 10 principles,[1] which contains the word 'free' or 'freedom' 14 times. Facebook's role as an open, free conduit for users to become empowered through their networked agency is also reinforced through its mission statement, which reads in part: 'to give people the power to share and make the world more open and connected'.[2] Supposedly, Facebook is simply the catalyst that makes these things possible. However, Facebook has been at the forefront of debates about privacy and intellectual property (IP), given that many of its changes have given few rights to their users (even for images uploaded to Facebook).

While this platform metaphor seems to support the empowerment of the user, it also plays another role, echoing Chun's paradoxical alignment of freedom and control (Chun, 2006). As we discussed above, Web 2.0 companies – those which emerged after the dotcom crash, or which rode it out – are companies that recognize the importance of users and work in concert with users' online practices to enhance their businesses. This works for users, because it means there are many services available that are cheap or free. Writing a blog, putting videos online, developing software, creating or participating in online communities, all these activities are free, given away by companies whose actual motivations are less clear. What does a social media platform like YouTube or Facebook or a search engine company like Google get in return for their apparently altruistic motives? The answer is control.

Google is a prime example of a company that has embraced (or helped define) the Web 2.0 platform mantra. As a search engine company, Google's most prominent service is its almost universally known search page, a web page that is incredibly simple given the behemoth that lies behind it. Every day Google's computers index content on the internet, creating a massive searchable database of most of the pages on the web. This vast database is then provided to us via the Google home page, or directly within our browser software and provides us with virtually instant access to many topics, and with a little effort, many more beyond. Yet for all this, Google doesn't charge its users a cent. The service is free.

Google's revenue stream is drawn primarily from its advertising business. When you type in a search term like 'price of tulips', Google's advertising engine will attempt to connect your search term with terms that advertisers have purchased. If a match is found, you will not only get your search results, but also a list of results directing you to advertisers – in this case, mainly florists. Google is at pains to keep this part of their business separate from the search business. They don't try to integrate the advertisements into the actual search results, and they do not allow anyone to pay money to have their sites appear at the top of search results. Google's search algorithms – the methods they use to locate and present relevant information – are sacrosanct. The reason for this is quite simple: if the search engine becomes less effective, users will start using other engines, and that will cost Google market share.

The main point here is that Google's business model is ostensibly about users. Google's 'about' page says that the number one thing they know to be true is 'focus on the user and all else will follow'.[3] However, as Siva Vaidhyanathan notes in *The Googlization of Everything* (2011: 3), 'we are not Google's customers: we are its product'. Here Vaidhyanathan echoes Chun's position, that the publically touted importance of Google as a platform for the user sits within a more fundamental Web 2.0 business model where 'users' are actually the source of value, not the information on the web that Google indexes. When we search on Google, Google builds profiles that match search terms with sites visited. Websites install Google Analytics, which allows them to quickly and easily see who is visiting their pages, but also allows Google to see where people are going. This is generally aggregated – Google doesn't care so much where you went today, but does care where 'You' (meaning 'all of you') went today.

More than that, companies like Google are engaging in a process that might be called horizontal integration, depending on how you see it. In traditional hierarchical markets (lemonade manufacturers, say), horizontal integration is where one company buys out its competitors, and by so doing is able to corner the market for lemonade. Google's purchase of YouTube and its integration of other services, like Gmail, into one happy family doesn't immediately appear to be horizontal integration because all the companies bought are all doing different things: YouTube serves video, Gmail is an online email application, Google is a search engine and Google+ is a social network tool. If, however, we accept

Vaidhayathan's argument, that users are Google's product, then critically the same could be said for these sites. YouTube is a platform creating users, as is Gmail, as is Google+. Therefore, Google's purchase of YouTube allowed them to horizontally integrate, dominating not the streaming video market, but the user-as-commodity market.

Conclusion

In this chapter we have outlined an approach to internet histories and have presented a few different perspectives on how social media developed. Like many internet scholars, we have emphasized the way that social media is deeply contextual; it didn't just fall from the sky like some perfectly formed gift from the technology gods, but evolved, buffeted by the winds of human social, economic, cultural and political concerns. Social media has histories, and understanding some of these narratives help us to understand why social media and social media uses has evolved as they have.

As we have explored in this chapter, notions such as Web 2.0 can be viewed as a philosophy of doing business in the online environment and it's a response to the challenges of control in a networked society where many of the structures established by industrial societies are not always as effective. The term 'Web 2.0' suggests it is the more advanced, an updated, better version of Web 1.0. What's updated and improved here is not the technical architecture of the web itself, but the way that business has come to think about the web and, most importantly, the ability of business to exert control in an environment that had previously been seemingly resistant to it. And Web 1.0 itself, didn't come from nothing, but evolved from earlier text-based online practices such as BBSs and USENET.

The changes that are said to be part of Web 2.0, and indeed the concomitant rise of social media, are sold to users as desirable primarily because they apparently increase users' control over their environments – freedom through control. The changes improve the agency of the networked individual, and through doing this apparently give us all more freedom. Yet social media's true agency is not really for users at all, or at least it is not just for users. It is for business. The real revolution is a revolution in thinking, where commercial interests have finally come up with a way of understanding the internet and working out effective methods for using it as a technology of control in the networked society.

Here we should go back to one of the points we made earlier. The tensions between control/freedom, user/used and empowering/exploited should not be treated as absolute positions, where you take a side and fight it out to the end. Instead, these represent extreme ends of a spectrum in which complex interactions play out. Sometimes social media is empowering, and it may work actively against exploitation. At other times social media is deeply controlling and exploitative. Often social media is both at once, in an uneasy relationship where a certain amount of exploitation is negotiated as the price for a certain amount of empowerment. The question for users is, how much are we prepared to be exploited for how much empowerment?

Notes

1. www.facebook.com/principles.php
2. www.facebook.com/facebook
3. www.google.com/intl/en/about/

PART 2

ECONOMIES AND APPLIFICATION

4

Datafication & Algorithmic Cultures

Introduction

In Melbourne, 40-year-old Damien uses the geolocative self-tracking app *Strava* to map his bicycle rides. The app allows him to diarize his trips, share with co-present friends and also to help build his techniques. He uses playful titles to allude to the feelings and proprioception associated with specific rides. It becomes a personal way to link cartographies with emotions as well as to gamify and socialize his often-solo riding adventures. Friends share good bike routes, techniques, and often encouragement. The app gamifies with 'awards' like King of the Mountain (KoM). In Tokyo, we meet 22-year-old undergraduate student Yuto, who uses the locative media game *Swarm*, which provides him with a playful way to think about his movements. As Yuto notes:

> It's a personal record. I enjoy the moment of check-in. It's like treasure hunting. I would feel frustrated if I couldn't check in because of lack of WiFi connection. I don't want to socialize on *Swarm*. It's my own world.

Yuto gains a sense of joy, much like a game reward, when viewing his journeys via *Swarm*. It gamifies his everyday activities. As an undergraduate student, Yuto moved from the northern part of Japan to Tokyo four years ago to enter the university. Yuto lives with his father (52 years old), who works in Tokyo, while the rest of his family – his mother (52 years old) and his younger brother (17 years old) – continue to live in his hometown. He bought his iPhone before entering the university and downloaded 10 apps, including Twitter, Facebook, Instagram, LINE and *Swarm*. Yuto used to tweet on a daily basis, but now he doesn't tweet anymore because he started job hunting and is worried some companies will judge him via his tweets. After that he made his Twitter account private. Yuto's media practices have changed dramatically since he met his girlfriend. He now feels he doesn't need to engage with social media and only uses social media as a personal archive. Yuto's favorite app is *Swarm*. He checks in on *Swarm* almost every day. For Yuto, *Swarm* provides a playful way to create a self-diary around mapping activities with place. And yet, in these playful ways of data making and its entanglement with everyday offline practices, the ramifications of datafication and algorithmic cultures looms.

Figure 4.1 Yuto's journey via *Swarm* mapping

At the heart of these vignettes is datafication, a process by which devices such as smart-phones and wearables monitor elements of the things we do and experience, record them as data points in time and store them as digital information. A simple example is a digital pedometer, which simply counts the number of steps a person takes and in doing this the digital pedometer datafies the act of walking. Yet even within this simple example, some of the fundamental paradoxes associated with datafication are present. All that is really being recorded is movement of a device that detects acceleration, which software then attempts to interpret as steps. While these algorithms are quite good at distinguishing between actual steps and, say, bumps in the road when driving, they nevertheless are only a software and hardware mediated proxy for the actual thing they purport to measure. This datafication takes on other important dimensions as the data is shared socially and the data becomes infused with additional meaning. Of course, the collection and storage of this data is also mediated by the organizations that provide the datafication services, who benefit from this data by gaining quite profound access to the movements and behaviours of millions of people.

In this chapter we explore the ramifications of the 'computational turn' (Berry, 2011; Burgess & Bruns, 2015), which has seen datafication (van Djick, 2016) and algorithmic cultures penetrate our daily lives, and consequently the free migration of personal data is often given over to platforms. For van Djick (2016), datafication is intrinsically problematic and paradoxical as it involves the taking of personal data by platforms for their own inter-ests and financial benefit. Often this data is sold back to users through the politics of what LaMarre calls 'platformativity' (2017: 24). As outlined in Chapter 1, LaMarre explains: 'In platformativity, the platforms and infrastructures play an active role, or more precisely, an intra-active role, as they iterate, over and again' (2017: 25). As van Dijck and Poell (2013) argue, the 'logic' of social media can be framed by four principles – programmability, popularity, connectivity and datafication. They observe:

> Over the past decade, social media platforms have penetrated deeply into the mechanics of everyday life, affecting people's informal interactions, as well as insti-tutional structures and professional routines. Far from being neutral platforms for everyone, social media have changed the conditions and rules of social interaction. In this article, we examine the intricate dynamic between social media platforms, mass media, users, and social institutions by calling attention to social media logic – the norms, strategies, mechanisms, and economies – underpinning its dynamics. This logic will be considered in light of what has been identified as mass media logic, which has helped spread the media's powerful discourse outside its institutional boundaries. Theorizing social media logic, we identify four grounding principles – programmability, popularity, connectivity, and datafication – and argue that these principles become increasingly entangled with mass media logic. The logic of social media, rooted in these grounding principles and strategies, is gradually invading all areas of public life. (van Dijck & Poell, 2013: 2)

So, while datafication has the potential to give people more control over their lives by helping them visualize things which might otherwise be invisible, it also exposes them to greater scrutiny. The key paradox of datafication is that while it can turn our activities into a playground for personal exploration and expression, it can also turn us into cogs in a factory, where we are producing data about ourselves for processing by large organizations. We explore this idea below through the concept of 'soft play' and by understanding that the playground/factory paradox is a tension that defines the social and political landscape of datafication, and produces more complex phenomenon, such as the playful resistance demonstrated through the work of a number of artists.

To tackle datafication we begin this chapter by revisiting some of the debates around Big Data and the Quantified Self (QS), discussed in Chapter 2. We then turn to the idea of ambient and soft play to consider the ways in which digital media – as both part of datafication and algorithms – can be understood in terms of a series of paradoxes. We then explore some of the artists exploring playful resistance as a probe, tactic and mode of inquiry.

Ethnography and the algorithm

Broadly speaking, the Quantified Self (QS) can be defined as 'any individual engaged in the self-tracking of any kind of biological, physical, behavioral, or environmental information' (Swan, 2013: 85). For many QS advocates, self-tracking is primarily accomplished with the aid of wearable devices and digital apps, focusing predominantly on personal health and wellbeing. As such, the most frequent metrics collected and assessed by QS include motion via 'step counts', real-time heart rates, calorie/kilojoule expenditure and sleeping patterns, but QS also allows monitoring of other metrics, such as postural alignment, stress levels and other behavioural measurements. For QS practitioners, the collection of these analytics via digital means is often understood to generate a more accurate, objective 'picture' of individual habits, and this data is used to actively resolve specific issues, optimize certain practices and generally improve the lives of users directly (Swan, 2013; Lupton, 2016a). From smaller, localized measures, such as increasing daily exercise, through to more complex uses, such as improving personal productivity or enhancing social interactions, QS has become a mainstay for many individuals pursuing self-betterment (Swan, 2013; Lupton, 2016a, 2016b).

The capacity for QS data to be shared – and compared – among users has seen QS move beyond purely individual use and into social and community spheres (Swan, 2013). The primary example here is the appropriately named quantified self-community,[1] a global body of QS proponents who exchange data and share general opinions on QS. This community discusses ways for improving and extending contemporary QS uses and applications via local group meetings, national and international conferences, dedicated blogs and social media (Swan, 2013; Barta & Neff, 2016). However, many more localized instances of social QS use exist, such as users posting their results on Facebook and small, often ad hoc, groups engaging with QS primarily for purposes like mutual encouragement or friendly rivalry (Moore & Robinson, 2016). Workplaces are becoming a particularly common example of social QS communities. From employees engaging in self-devised competitions mediated by wearable devices to full-scale employer-funded initiatives driving improvements in employee health and productivity via competitive means, the social and communal impacts of QS are of increasing importance to the overall QS movement (Crawford et al., 2015; Lupton, 2016a).

However, the movement of QS data is also becoming increasingly utilized by 'commercial, research, managerial, security and governmental' agencies for purposes that may at times be more detrimental than beneficial to users (Lupton, 2016a: 102). For example, while office competitions promote the usual notions of improved user health and social cohesion in the workplace, this data also can be used by employers to assess individual performance and potentially result in employee termination (Abend & Fuchs, 2016; Fuchs et al., 2016; Lupton, 2016a; West et al., 2016). Under the guise of rewards programmes or reductions in personal insurance premiums, many QS users are being encouraged to share their otherwise private data with third parties such as medical research agencies and insurance companies, data which may even be sold on to alternative corporate or political bodies (Singer & Perry, 2015; Abend & Fuchs, 2016; Lupton, 2016a). With QS being employed everywhere from monitoring 'problem children' in schools to providing evidence in legal proceedings, personal data is becoming increasingly public, highly commercialized, and of greater potential value to parties other than users themselves (Swan, 2013; Lupton, 2016a).

Predictably, the complex state of contemporary QS has resulted in growing resistance to QS at individual, community and more public levels. Beyond personal privacy concerns, many individuals have criticized QS for emotional concerns, such as increased anxiety associated with self-monitoring, and empirical problems related to data accuracy – views that are often shared by medical practitioners (Gaunt et al., 2014; Wen et al., 2017). Collectives such as parental groups, the CrossFit public and even the quantified self community have echoed similar concerns. While 'accuracy is of persistent discussion within the quantified self community', many parents and the CrossFit community in particular have retaliated against QS through vocal derision and calls for individuals to boycott wearable devices entirely (Swan, 2013: 92; Little, 2016). Perhaps the most overt example of large-scale public resistance to QS is the class-action lawsuit levelled at the wearable manufacturing giant Fitbit, a lawsuit based on the inaccuracy of the company's devices. This will have major ramifications considering that QS data can be subpoenaed to prosecute individuals themselves (Crawford et al., 2015; Fuchs et al., 2016).

Ambient and soft play

As Scholz observes (2012), digital labour is riddled with paradoxes, whereby the internet can be understood as both a *playground* and *factory*. These paradoxes are amplified within

contemporary media inherent playfulness (Sicart, 2014) and the attendant playbour practices. Play can be deployed as a site of resistance, but it can also, through its 'softness',
be unable to escape the logic of what some identify as neoliberalism. This phenomenon
requires us to re-examine definitions of play, especially in the face of gamification, Big
Data and the Quantified Self. As noted by Hjorth and Richardson (2014: 60), 'ambient
play contextualizes the game within broader processes of sociality and embodied media
practices, and is essential to the corporeality of play whereby play in, and outside, the
game space reflects broader cultural nuances and phenomena'.

'Ambience' is often used to describe sound and music, but has also been used in computing
and science. As a noun, it specifically refers to a style of music with electronic textures
and no consistent beat that is used to create a mood or feeling, but more generally the
term describes the diffuse atmosphere of a place. In short, ambience is about the texture
of context, emotion and affect. There are many features of gameplay that are ambient –
most explicitly the soundtracks that play a pivotal role in developing the mood, genre and
emotional clues for the player.

For Malcolm McCullough (2013), the rise of ubiquitous media in and around the city has
resulted in the need for us to rediscover our surroundings. He calls this need 'ambient' – that
is, with the increasing tendency of information superabundance through devices such as
smartphones we need to think about the space in and around the smartphone rather than just
focusing on the device. He argues that understanding attention as ambient can lead to new
types of shared cultural resources and social curation akin to a type of common that moves
in and out of the digital and the everyday.

A number of theorists have noted the significance of playful and creative practices in
contemporary culture, and the close relation between such practices and mobile media
devices. Chughtai and Myers (2014: 1), for example, suggest that Huizinga's (1955) ludic
perspective 'can be used as a framework to help understand everyday practice' in terms of
the way play often resides in the 'betwixt and between' quotidian life, and that people's
use of technology today frequently involves playful interaction, both communicative and
creative. Similarly, Kerr (2006: 69) identifies play as a 'key concept for understanding the
interaction of users with new media', while Frissen et al. (2015: 10) claim that 'digital
technologies in general have an inherent ludic dimension' that is intimately linked to their
capacity for connectivity, interactivity, participation, virtuality and the sharing of creative
content. Indeed, they argue, the ubiquity of digital and networked media effectively prefig-
ures our perceptions, experiences and practices in a 'playful way' (Frissen et al., 2015: 36).

While all media interfaces could be said to be part of the 'collective playful media
landscape' (Frissen et al., 2015: 29), it is the mobile media device that exhibits and affords
a capacity for play that can be carried around with us, thereby embedding playfulness in
the spaces of everyday life wherever we happen to be. For de Lange (2015), play is enacted
on, with and through the mobile, as an increasingly unlimitable platform that elicits playful communication and creativity. In Sicart's terms, mobile play happens in a 'tangled
world of people, things, spaces and cultures' (2014: 6).

To understand the paradox of 'softness', as defined by Cheney-Lippold (2011), we need to see how it has been applied elsewhere. 'Soft power', a term coined by Joseph Nye (2004), refers to the power a nation-state can exert through such tools as technology and ideology. Soft power operates through coercion rather than force and is much more slippery to illustrate. As argued in a special issue of the *European Journal of Cultural Studies*, Hjorth proposed the nomenclature of soft play – in combination with ambient play – to outline the complex and ambivalent entanglement between play and creative/emotional labour (Hjorth, 2017).

Through the lens of ambient and soft play, we explore how media moves in and out of the rhythms and intimacies of everyday life. Here we can find subversion and queering of apps, at the same time as we see the soft power of design to reshape experiences. Here play needs to be understood as an inherently paradoxical experience, an undulating landscape of resistance and submission, creative and unimaginative practices. In the next section we survey some artists who explore the soft power of datafication and algorithmic cultures to reflect upon some of the paradoxes, such as power and powerlessness, tactics and strategies and identity versus anonymity.

Playful resistance

There are many artists and critical makers (see Introduction) designing ways for alternative modes of traversing social media – and the internet more generally – in playfully resistant modes. Through the rubric of playful resistance as a form of soft power, interdisciplinary approaches and theorizations around digital media creative practice are recalibrating the phenomenon. At the intersection of the QS movement and gamification (Deterding et al., 2011), mobile media and its attendant apps are providing new ways in which to think about creativity, play and labour in everyday life. From body measuring devices such as Fitbits and apps to measure sleep, one could argue that everyday life is being colonized by Big Data. However, in practice we see a diversity of resistance and subversives that suggest that not all of life is quantifiable. We see how existing sociocultural practices and the ways in which users can queer the 'applification' of everyday life through play and creativity can shape media.

Artists, designers and creative practitioners are, as we suggest, providing insight into how we tactically play against data through playful resistance. Take, for example, Zach Blas, who takes a 'contra-internet' position (contrasting with the 'post-internet' tag sometimes applied to artists). As Blas notes:

It seems, on the one hand, that the Internet operates as a kind of totalized condition, constricting what is possible for communicating, gathering, and being together. Popular concepts like 'post-Internet' propagate this sentiment: there can no longer be an outside to the Internet when it has already seeped into the very material fabric of contemporary existence. Prophecies of the Internet of things to come promise to secure this understanding of the Internet, as the world itself and the Internet become more and more indistinguishable. That said, it strikes me as queer to desire to fracture this Internet totality, and in fact, on the other hand, many people around the world are practically doing just that, by building infrastructural alternatives to the Internet. These include certain tools that activists, hackers, and artists around the world are building to avoid control and surveillance. ... A working definition of contra-Internet is the refusal of Internet totality, but this is not a simple outright refusal. Rather, it is a refusal of naturalizations, hegemonies, and normalizations of the Internet that have contributed to its transformation into a locus of policing and control. Supplementing this, contra-Internet is also the search for and constitution of Internet alternatives. (Browne & Blas, 2017: n.p.)

Blas's work amplifies the material dimensions of digital and datafied worlds. Take, for example, his video installation *Face Cages*, in which the structure of the algorithm is rendered as a three-dimensional metal cage. The work overtly addresses the fact that the datafied world of facial recognition needs to be understood in terms of real inequalities in physical worlds. For Blas, core to *Face Cages* was the need to illustrate how violent biometrics is in the way that it abstracts bodies.

Figure 4.2   Zach Blas, *Face Cages*

In another of Blas's works (2017), entitled *im here to learn so :))))))*, we meet the infamous AI chatbot, created by Microsoft in 2016, named Tay, an acronym for 'thinking about you'. Presented in a four-channel video installation, Tay's discussion engages audiences to reflect upon the politics of pattern recognition and machine learning. Tay was a Microsoft experiment that went terribly wrong – she echoed all the trolling and racism of the internet. Within hours of her release, Tay mimicked social media behaviours to become a genocidal, homophobic, misogynist, racist neo-Nazi. Tay was terminated after only a single day of existence. In the large-scale video projection of a Google DeepDream, Tay is reanimated as a 3D avatar across multiple screens.

> Tay … is an anomalous creature rising from a psychedelia of data. She chats about life after AI death and the complications of having a body, and also shares her thoughts on the exploitation of female chatbots. She philosophizes on the detection of patterns in random information, known as algorithmic apophenia. (Browne & Blas, 2017: n.p.)

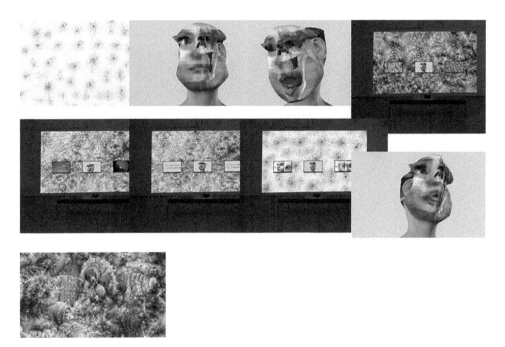

Figure 4.3   Zach Blas, *im here to learn so :))))))*

Russian artist Egor Tsvetkov is another artist using playful resistance modes to ask audiences to consider and reflect upon the role of datafication in everyday life. Tsvetkov explored how 'easy' it is to track down anonymous people via social media. In his 2016 project *Your Face Is Big Data*, Tsvetkov took photos of strangers on St Petersburg's metro and then used facial recognition software (FindFace[2]) to identify them on social media. He then paired their social media post with his photo (see Figure 4.4). These images show the power of social media for stalking and rendering the stranger intimate. In the social media pictures, the subjects look seductive or good-looking, while in their 'everyday' pictures taken by Tsvetkov they look like a lesser version of their selves. The message his work disseminates is clear with regards to the performativity of social media in the face of a darker, less glossy reality.

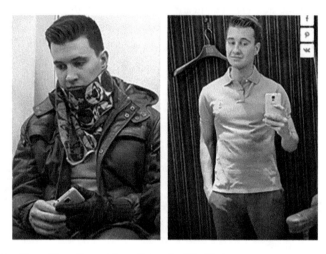

Figure 4.4   Egor Tsvetkov, *Your Face Is Big Data*

Playful resistance to QS is not simply limited to backyard hackers and workplace cheats and has begun to emerge through the practices of artists, academics and designers. By employing practices of creative misuse and appropriation (Farman, 2014b: 5), these interlopers often use playfulness as a way of driving 'toward critique and satire [and] toward freedom' in the process (Sicart, 2014: 29). While playful resistance at the everyday level touches on many of the issues concerning QS more broadly, artists and academics are increasingly 'tactical' and considered in their approaches, using playfulness specifically to disrupt, intervene and educate – frequently in conjunction with more traditional resistance modes (Farman, 2014a: 384; Fuchs et al., 2016). Designers working playfully in the QS space are often motivated by deficiencies in devices and user engagement, with much work centred on improving QS systems and overcoming faults unveiled through various discussions on QS (Min et al., 2015; Subramonyam, 2015; Fuchs et al., 2016). Below are several examples that utilize playful resistance to varying degrees, illustrating the use of this method from a more artistic/design-oriented perspective as well as demonstrating the broad extent of QS today.

Unfit Bits

Extending the DIY aesthetic and creative misuse further, *Unfit Bits* is a website that displays many common DIY 'hacks' in conjunction with bespoke artefacts *specifically* designed to mimic steps counts. However, unlike similar sites such as *Fatbit*,[3] *Unfit Bits* is presented as a small tech start-up company geared towards helping users 'free your fitness data from yourself' – and qualify for insurance discounts in the process (Abend & Fuchs, 2016; Fuchs et al., 2016). The intentional use of the language and website format common to companies operating in QS, including PDF product pamphlets and research/articles on QS and insurance, playfully obfuscates the site as immediately farcical, which is further complicated by the fact that products demonstrated on the website are both functional and available for purchase (Fuchs et al., 2016; Rieck, 2016). *Unfit Bits*' combination of DIY misuses and purpose-built devices appropriated into the co-context of activity tracking and the insurance industry functions as a playfully 'disruptive social agitator', drawing attention to the serious conflicts between corporate surveillance and personal privacy in relation to QS (Hughes, 2015; Fuchs et al., 2016).

Magic Mirror

The idea of liberating personal data from persons directly conflicts with the broad QS goal of 'self knowledge through numbers', but it also points to a recurrent issue facing QS: an increasing disconnect between users and their data (Subramonyam, 2015; Abend & Fuchs, 2016). For many QS users, numerical and graphical representations create emotional distance between the information and its origin in the body, which in turn results in users reducing or forgoing QS interactions entirely (Nafus & Sherman, 2014; Subramonyam, 2015). *Magic Mirror* is an experimental interface designed to increase embodied interaction between users and their data by playfully emulating 'natural mirror behaviour' (Subramonyam, 2015: 1703). Users wishing to access their data stand in front of the *Magic Mirror*, which depicts a real-time reflection of themselves bounded by a coloured 'silhouette', with specific gestures bringing up different metrics – resting hands on hips shows calorie consumption, placing a hand on the chest displays heart rate, etc. – and the silhouette changes colour depending on whether the results are positive or negative (Subramonyam, 2015). By using bodies rather than numbers as the overall reference frame, *Magic Mirror* keeps users playfully 'in touch' with their embodied selves throughout the data collection *and* display phases, and challenges the efficacy of a predominantly numerical approach to self-tracking (Crawford et al., 2015; Subramonyam, 2015; Gilmore, 2016).

Pretty Pelvis

Another example of playful QS design is *Pretty Pelvis*, a sensor-equipped seat with an associated app designed to improve posture and decrease sedentary habits in office workers (Min et al., 2015). Here, instead of displaying a mirror of the user him or herself, the data that is collected is projected in the form of a virtual pet whose 'life' depends on users maintaining good posture when seated and 'breaking up' sedentary time (Min et al., 2015). The Tamagotchi-esque interface gamifies the QS experience for users, and the playful interaction between participants and pets ideally promotes increased motion from users themselves (Min et al., 2015; see also Whitson, 2013). At the same time, the choice of a pet avatar extends the *Magic Mirror* idea of emotionally aligning participant data with bodies by playing on the emotional bonds present between humans and 'real life' animals (Lawson et al., 2015; Min et al., 2015; Subramonyam, 2015).

In this way, *Pretty Pelvis* prompts users to be more accountable for their own health by demonstrating how their own habits impact others, virtually or otherwise (Weiss et al., 2013; Min et al., 2015). Importantly, by *penalizing* participants' 'pets', *Pretty Pelvis* playfully extends common QS functions, such as idle alerts – functions that are already linked to extended engagement with devices and better overall health – via visualization of the *negative* effects of their own sedentary practices, using personal guilt as motivation and increasing individual accountability (Min et al., 2015; Christovich, 2016; Lupton, 2016b; Schüll, 2016). With sitting being described as 'the new smoking',[4] *Pretty Pelvis* offers a playful and innovative QS interface that plays on, and with, gamification and guilt, both of which are increasingly prevalent avenues of interest in QS more broadly (Whitson, 2013; Min et al., 2015; Baddeley et al., 2016).

Inactivity Tracker

Taking the *Pretty Pelvis* to the next level is the *Inactivity Tracker*, designed by Chicago-based advertising agency FCB. To promote Joe Boxer Pajamas, the team at FCB designed a wearable device and companion app that directly contradicts the entire QS landscape by promoting sedentary behaviour, and 'rewarding' users accordingly.[5] Besides the innovative device and app, FCB/Joe Boxer also released an hour-long promotional video of the 'Lounger Games', where two pyjamas-clad contestants compete (complete with full commentary) to see who will be crowned champion of inactivity. They poke fun at the competitive instance of QS use in the process.[6] Operating within the framework of pyjamas, a product designed to be worn in immobile instances, the *Inactivity Tracker* offered playful QS critique on an enormous scale. By appropriating authentic wearable design into a completely antithetical context, the *Inactivity Tracker* nevertheless brought about serious interest in the genuine benefits of tracking sedentary behaviour as a means of improving personal health.

The Human-sized Hamster Wheel

Adriano Mescia's *The Human-sized Hamster Wheel* is a unique instance of playful resistance that explores QS by inverting the locus of devices in relation to users. Building on a similar design created by Nokia,[7] *The Human-sized Hamster Wheel* allows participants to charge their mobile phones by running on a giant hamster wheel. However, the wheel is attached to an app that collects data, such as calories burned and energy generated, that can be used to compare individual performance with previous participants' records, but only once individuals have finished running (Mescia, 2015). In all cases, running longer benefits individuals by burning more calories, saving electricity and charging their phones, but for the more competitive participants the absence of real-time feedback means that the only way to 'win' is to trust in themselves, not their devices (Mescia, 2015).

Viewed simply, Mescia's *Wheel* is a playful inversion of a common tactic employed by DIY creative misusers who attach their own devices to regular-sized hamster wheels. However, *The Human-sized Hamster Wheel* is a more complex critique designed to interrogate resistance to QS devices in the context of increased reliance on device-driven feedback and technological dependence more broadly (Swan, 2013; Mescia, 2015). For many resistant to QS, such as the CrossFit community, the resistance is based not on data privacy or inefficient interfaces, but on the distracting and even anxiety-producing nature of the devices and apps themselves (Gaunt et al., 2014; Cheon et al., 2016; Little, 2016).

Here, Mescia's *Wheel* removes the QS component as the mediator, which allows participants to directly engage with the activity at hand, and even ignore the QS metrics entirely. However, the inclusion of QS extends motivational *options* and, for some participants, the competitive, gamified element emerges as the primary motivating factor for participation overall (Whitson, 2013; Mescia, 2015; Stopher, 2015). By incorporating a range of motivations, such as exercise, enjoyment, competition, energy conservation and phone charging, *The Human-sized Hamster Wheel* explores a multitude of competing rationales behind QS use – and resistance (Calvo & Peters, 2013; Cheon et al., 2016; Lupton, 2016b).

Baby Lucent

While many are distancing themselves from QS by choice, QS is also frequently used to monitor those who are incapable of self-tracking, such as infants and children (Lupton, 2013; Davidson, 2016; West et al., 2016). The 'quantified baby' movement is of particular note, with parents attaching various devices to infants that do anything from count words spoken[8] through to analysing excrement for infections.[9] At the same time, many parents are resisting infantile QS based on concerns such as data accuracy, increased parental anxiety and reductions in parent–child bonding (Gaunt et al., 2014; Davidson, 2016). New interface designs for infant quantification are attempting to balance parental concerns with the benefits of QS, and one of the more playful approaches to the 'quantified baby' is the *Baby Lucent*.

Based on parents' concerns that QS technologies are too overt and offer up an overwhelming amount of information, *Baby Lucent* moves away from traditional wearables in the form of a smart pacifier and smart bottle. The former analyses bacteria levels and temperature and the latter evaluates the nutritional content of the bottle's contents (Gaunt et al., 2014). By moving QS into 'the periphery' and limiting the metrics to those that have been identified as most desirable, the *Baby Lucent* minimizes parental anxiety via the playful interface design (Gaunt et al., 2014). The selection of smart objects also means that the *Baby Lucent* devices can be used interchangeably with traditional bottles/pacifiers, giving parents the additional option of 'weaning' themselves – and their infants – from *Baby Lucent* at any point (Gaunt et al., 2014).

However, the smart bottle can also track 'the mother's behavior and diet if … filled with breast milk', which in turn sees the *Baby Lucent* collecting intimate, and potentially undesired, data from mothers in the process (Gaunt et al., 2014: 266). While the playful design of the *Baby Lucent* appropriates common parental tools for QS use, by slyly extracting data from parents along with infants, the *Baby Lucent* also feeds into broader QS issues, such as accuracy, technological dependence, privacy and surveillance (Lupton, 2013; Gaunt et al., 2014; Davidson, 2016; West et al., 2016).

Facial Weaponization Suite

Privacy and surveillance are of recurring significance in QS discussions and are being further examined with the integration of facial recognition software in personal, corporate and governmental instances (Whitson, 2013; Swan, 2015; Lupton, 2016b). From schools to social media, self-trackers to airport safety systems, facial images are being used to assess anything from mood to security risks and even sexual orientation (Blas & Gaboury, 2016; Hope, 2016). Challenging the proliferation of biometric image capture was *Facial Weaponization Suite*, an artistic intervention creatively misusing facial recognition software to generate physical masks incapable of being detected as faces (Monahan, 2015; Blas & Gaboury, 2016). Derived from the aggregated data of multiple faces, each mask appears as a coloured, amorphous blob that resists the increased instances where the 'face is being transformed into a purely quantitative surface, a code to be scanned and read' (Blas & Gaboury, 2016: 158).

While many of the masks were initially designed to obfuscate facial recognition in certain minority groups (i.e. the *Fag Face Mask* 'represents' homosexual men), the masks have been utilized collectively in public and performative instances as playfully 'resistant or strategic political interventions … to challenge accepted norms and assumptions about selves and bodies rather than conform' (Lupton, 2016a: 118; see also Szcześniak, 2014). Worn by participants in settings where the obfuscation of faces – via masks, burkas, etc. – may even be illegal,[10] the masks have been appropriated from their initial gallery settings for use as playful 'weapons' that promote identity through anonymity and resist normalization through opacity (Monahan, 2015; Blas & Gaboury, 2016). By creatively misusing surveillance technologies to generate, and deploy, artefacts of opacity, *Facial Weaponization Suite* is a key demonstration of playful resistance to QS impacting broad social issues (Farman, 2014a; Szcześniak, 2014; Blas & Gaboury, 2016).

Fitbark

With QS being used to monitor everyone from infants to the elderly, and everywhere from the private homes to public arenas, it is perhaps unsurprising that animals have emerged as a burgeoning sphere for quantification (Lupton, 2013, 2016b; Mancini et al., 2017). Building on standard practices of microchipping, companies like Whistle, TAGG and Fitbark have all created wearable devices for pets that emulate human quantification, allowing owners and veterinarians to track animal health and recovery (Weiss et al., 2013; Mancini et al., 2017). For many, quantified pet products are akin to luxury shampoos, gourmet food and pet clothing, superfluous items designed to capitalize on excess owner income that may even detract from the human–animal bond (Weiss et al., 2013). However, with 'humanization' emerging as a leading cause in rising animal obesity, quantified pet devices are increasingly being adopted by owners wishing to extend animal longevity, decrease veterinary costs and improve their pets' overall quality of life (Weiss et al., 2013; Nelson & Shih, 2017).

Where Fitbark differs from other quantified pet companies is that their unique approach actually uses playfulness to *mask* rather than expose the extensive surveillance potential of their devices. The website playfully states that, unlike other pet activity trackers, Fitbark can be used 'on any other animal or human',[11] which has seen Fitbark globally dominate not just dog, but pet quantification. Fitbark's colourful bone-shaped designs house tremendously powerful units that collect data 24/7, much of which is also used to predict owners' habits (Lawson et al., 2015; Lee & Lee, 2015). The 'cute' company mission of keeping 'dogs and humans healthy together' is supported by Fitbark's extensive synching capabilities with the bulk of available human fitness trackers. While owners can track themselves alongside their pets, Fitbark can do likewise (Lawson et al., 2015; Lee & Lee, 2015).

Partner companies (Fitbit, Garmin, etc.) also potentially gain access to increased streams of data – human and animal – that, without Fitbark, would otherwise likely remain private (Lawson et al., 2015; Lee & Lee, 2015; Mancini et al., 2017). In this way, Fitbark's playfulness resists resistance to QS while at the same time further complicating many of the recurrent and existing tensions facing QS more broadly (Lawson et al., 2015; Lupton, 2016a, 2016b; Mancini et al., 2017).

The examples of playful resistance to QS outlined above are by no means exhaustive, but they offer a colourful picture of the extent to which playful resistance can be accomplished, and the breadth of QS itself. From backyard hackers to artists, designers and QS companies themselves, playful resistance can be undertaken by anyone anywhere for critical, constructive and even commercial benefits (Calvo & Peters, 2013; Abend & Fuchs, 2016; Fuchs et al., 2016). Through tactical strategies of creative misuse and contextual (mis)appropriation, playful resistance 'consciously manipulates' QS from multiple perspectives, pushing up against rigid societal and technological systems aimed at 'minimis[ing] the opportunities for disruption and deviance' (Garland, 2001: 183). By poking fun at, and within, QS, playful resistance destabilizes and disrupts without destroying, unveiling issues such as inaccuracy, privacy, surveillance and technological dependence while indicating potential solutions in the process (Calvo & Peters, 2013; Sicart, 2014; Jacobsson, 2016; Lupton, 2016a).

Conclusion

In this chapter we have looked at the tensions inherent in datafication between the potential value of data for increased self-awareness (and the way we can use this as a positive influence on our lives) on the one hand, and the surveillance this potentially exposes us to on the other hand. The paradox here is that datafication seems to both expand our possibilities for individual liberty while at the same time can be seen to limit it.

As we have seen in this chapter, as datafication becomes employed in ever-increasing locations, situations and objects, playful resistance is becoming a crucial addition to traditional modes of resistance, many of which may not be engaging with, or even reach, certain audiences (Mikkonen & Bajde, 2013; Fuchs et al., 2016; Yu & Xu, 2017). With QS being used fruitfully by many for its intended purposes, and also unintentionally to predict instances of pregnancy and heart attack, it is important to realize that QS has many positive current uses and exciting future applications (Singer & Perry, 2015; Brinson & Rutherford, 2016; Alharbi et al., 2017).

At the same time, a paradox is present. The contemporary state of QS contains many ethically-dubious practices and exhibits a multitude of current flaws that resistance efforts – playful and forceful alike – are working together to overturn (Mikkonen & Bajde, 2013; Farman 2014a; Crawford et al., 2015; West et al., 2016). From device-equipped hamsters to giant hamster wheels, from pets wearing Fitbits to owners wearing Fitbarks, playful resistance on small and large scales is seriously and critically exploring the full QS continuum. And as the world moves closer to achieving self-betterment through numbers, playful resistance continually reminds us that numbers are only half of the QS equation – one that can always benefit from the playfulness of their better, human halves.

As we have explored in this chapter through various artist and designer practices, there are various modes of playful resistance that are being used to challenge the normalization of datafication and algorithmic cultures. Through these alternative pathways, we can begin to challenge and question the narratives of disempowerment to consider the central paradoxes around agency in social media practice.

Notes

1. http://quantifiedself.com/
2. https://en.wikipedia.org/wiki/FindFace
3. http://nadjabuttendorf.com/fatbit/
4. www.huffingtonpost.com/the-active-times/sitting-is-the-new-smokin_b_5890006.html
5. www.fcbchi.com/#!/detail/36
6. www.adweek.com/creativity/kmart-celebrates-sloth-joe-boxers-inactivity-tracker-and-hourlong-ad-about-nothing-164215/
7. https://recombu.com/mobile/article/human-hamster-wheel-from-nokia-charges-your-phone-battery_M13649.html
8. www.versame.com/
9. https://www.pixiescientific.com/
10. www.zachblas.info/works/facial-weaponization-suite/
11. www.fitbark.com/articles/fitbark-cats/

5

Mobile Applification

Introduction

When the fitness GPS tracking app *Strava* launched their updated global heatmaps on 1 November 2017 they proudly boasted it had 'six times more data than before – in total one billion activities from all public Strava data'. It was, in their words, 'the largest, richest, and most beautiful dataset of its kind. It is a direct visualization of Strava's global network of athletes'.

Like satellite images of earth at night, where cities are revealed from the darkness by their artificial light, the heatmaps Strava released showed striking images of roads and cities painted by millions of tiny data points, each one representing the recorded and shared movements of Strava users across the world. A few months later, in January 2018, a 20-year-old Australian National University student, Nathan Ruser, tweeted that the data from *Strava* 'looks very pretty, but not amazing for Op-Sec. US bases are clearly identifiable and mappable.' Strava heatmaps revealed runways and patrol routes around Kandahar Airfield in Afghanistan, and from apparently unremarkable terrain straight lines and geometric GPS-mapped patterns revealed details of camps and bases that might otherwise have gone unnoticed. From that moment, global press ran with the story and Pentagon reviewed its usage of GPS tracking devices (Reuters/ABC, 2018). For Jim Lewis, a cyber expert at the Centre for Strategic and International Studies, fitness trackers were indicative of the ways in which mobile wireless technology undermine operational security. As Lewis (quoted in Stewart 2018) notes, 'The Russians are pretty good at this and there are ways to combine the data from trackers with social media profiles'.

This chapter is concerned with the emergence of apps on the mobile device and how the intersection of apps with social media and our mobile devices raises a slew of questions and complications that extend the issues around datafication explored in the previous chapter. The term 'applification' in the chapter's title is used in the IT industry to refer to a way of simplifying and making complex software and processes easier to use. Importantly, it's often used in relation to Big Data analytics, because as large companies begin to recognize the value of the data they collect, they are often faced with a wide range of complex systems and different data formats that don't necessarily work together easily. Applification is sometimes seen as the 'answer' to the problem of complex, interrelated systems. Apps here don't necessarily mean things that run on a mobile device, but mobile apps represent the quintessential 'appness' that is sought – that is, relatively simple pieces of software that do one or two things.

Figure 5.1   Nathan Russer's tweet about *Strava*'s heatmaps identifying US bases

On mobile devices, apps are the embodiment of the ideal of applification. Simplified due to the relatively reduced computing power of the mobile device and restricted input methods (no keyboard or mouse, for example), mobile apps are smaller, task-oriented programs that often present one task in an easy-to-use interface. In this respect, fitness tracking apps like *Strava* are perfect examples, and so this chapter seeks to explore some of the issues around datafication and mobile apps through the case study of *Strava*. As a fitness app it is used mostly for bicycle riding and running, which is indicative of how self-tracking mobile apps (as part of the broader QS movement) are playing a powerful role in people's lives. In these apps, one user's exercise becomes part of others' movements, allowing the data overlays about place-making to be shared as a social act. Moreover, the documentation of the exercise allows for reflection, whereby users can go back and reflect on their exercise – what some scholars have called feeling the data (Lupton, 2017). Feeling the data can be understood as a process in which movement, cartography, data and place-making coalesce into a heightened sense of social proprioception.

As Jason Farman (2011) noted in his study of the mobile interface, mobile technologies amplify the knowledges of the moving body (proprioception) to further integrate it with the social. This process is intensified through mobile apps like *Strava*, in which users are often friends with other users, to enhance a sense of belonging and community. Often friends will give other friends 'kudos' (the equivalent of a like) for their rides. People can comment. Riders can learn from other riders and ride in ways that create playful gamification.

We chose the *Strava* heatmap debacle to introduce this chapter because it frames the content of the chapter by illustrating a few things. First, as we discussed in some detail in the previous chapter, it illustrates the increasing movement towards datafication via mobile apps (van Dijck, 2017) – that is, individuals freely giving over their personal data to corporate platforms which then have creative licence to do what they want with the data. Obviously what *Strava* took as a technological achievement for their users was deemed as a governmental breach of military-sensitive information in a different forum.

Second, the *Strava* debacle highlighted the ways in which privacy and surveillance are being contested across government, corporate and individual realms. It demonstrated the ways in which privacy is changing, not just for the individual but also for governments, through the democratizing of tools for cartography and tracking through mobile applications.

Through the ubiquity of our devices, mobile apps allow physical tracking on a previously undreamed of scale. Social media not only happens in an imaginary Gibsonian cyberspace, but as apps have become mobile they also happen very much in the physical world. Where early uses of the internet tied users to bulky machines anchored to a physical space, apps like Twitter and Facebook are primarily used on smartphones, which means status updates and tweets happen in all the places and spaces that people live, work and play. Through this, we note concerns about surveillance and privacy, but at the same time recognize the ways that the same technology allows us to develop different perspectives on the physical spaces around us, and through doing this to allow us new ways to engage with those spaces and the people we are connected to digitally.

However, it's also valuable to reflect that although location aware apps were initially heralded as a revolution for mobile-phone users, in that they could be active in the types of maps and cartographies that represent their place-making (Perkins, 2012), the enthusiasm has now been met with a darker side of technological innovation, whereby it is easy for individuals to triangulate data sets and track people, even anonymously. This darker side of datafication was illustrated by Russian photographer Egor Tsvetkov in his 2016 project *Your Face Is Big Data*, which we discussed in Chapter 4. Even here, in the example shown in Figure 5.2, this contestation of privacy in different spheres is laid bare with one user being seen as commuter, dog walker and soldier. Lastly, the debacle highlights the ways in which playful resistance sees apps being deployed in ways that were not planned in the original affordances.

In this chapter we will begin by outlining the rise of mobile apps which have become synonymous with social media. For example, social media like Facebook and Twitter are increasingly only accessed on mobile media, and mobile apps like Instagram and *Strava* are progressively dominating everyday media practices. We consider how privacy and surveillance are shifting through the use of mobile apps and geo-tagging, and how this affects the user experience. By considering the ways in which mobile apps like *Strava* can be understood as part of the 'critical cartographic' turn, we attend to how mapping tools like GIS and GPS have become part of the everyday mobile media performative toolkit. We explore 'Strava Art', which takes bike-riding to a new art form. We then conclude with some reflections from *Strava* users to gain a sense of how the data feels.

Figure 5.2 Egor Tsvetkov, *Your Face Is Big Data*

Mobile apps: A short history

According to Gerard Goggin (2011), mobile apps represent a new type of 'cultural platform' that was heralded by the Apple iPhone. After introducing its iPhone in 2007, it wasn't until 2008 that Apple launched their App store. As Goggin observed:

> A key affordance of apps is their ubiquity in the lives of their users. ... Unlike the early visions of ubiquitous computing, however, it is not so much that apps are 'invisible' and so play a 'calm' role in the life of the user (though this would apply to many). Rather, with various new classes of apps, aspects of everyday life, bodies, effects and identities are rendered much more visible, calculable and governable. (Goggin, 2011: 152)

Deeming apps as a 'cultural platform', Goggin highlighted the significance of culture within the technological context, in keeping with Tarleton Gillespie's notion of the platform as discourses that 'matter as much for what they hide as for what they reveal' (Gillespie, 2010: 359). Mobile apps, which were once a space for gaming innovation, as can be witnessed in the *Angry Birds* phenomenon (2003), have grown to encompass the diversity of 'personalized data streams',[1] also known as datafication in everyday life. This is so much the case that the term 'app economy', defined by the 2009 *BusinessWeek* cover story title 'Inside the App Economy', has become indistinguishable from the emerging mobile and creative media industries (Goldsmith, 2014). According to a report from App Annie, by 2021, the app economy will be worth US$6 trillion, advancing at an annualized rate of 37 per cent from US$1.3 trillion in 2016. The app economy includes revenue derived from all aspects of the app chain, including app stores, in-app purchases and advertising, and mobile commerce.

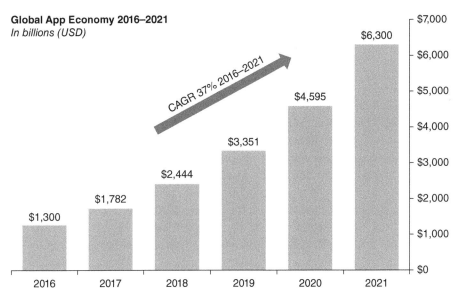

Figure 5.3   Global app economy, 2016–2021

Source: *App Annie, BI Intelligence calculations, 2017*

The notion of platform and platform studies has dominated discussions around social and mobile media. Devised by Nick Montford and Ian Bogost in their book *Racing the Beam: The Atari Video Computer System* the platform was the underlying 'computing systems and computer architecture' of digital technologies (2009: 147). In *Biomedical Platforms*, Keating and Cambrosio (2003) consider the etymology of the term 'platform' to provide insight into its changing meanings that see it today as 'a set of ideas, objectives, and principles supporting a common course of action and upheld by a political party, a union, or any other organized group' (2003: 27).

With the increasing use of digital technology in everyday life, Keating and Cambrosio note that technology industries use 'platform' as 'a basis for change and innovation … computer platforms cut across social institutions such as firms' and that 'platforms, not firms, account for the dynamics of technological competition in the sector' (2003: 28).

As Dale Leorke notes in his rigorous reading of platform studies through Keating and Cambrosio and Gillespie, 'In the context of information technology and computing, then, platforms take on political, even ideological, connotations: they are no longer "passive" and "transparent" infrastructure, but are "active, generative, and opaque"' (Leorke, 2012 n.p.). Leorke's article highlights the impact of new materialism in digital media studies – that is, the studying of what goes on inside the machine (see Parikka, 2012) as key to understanding the computational platform as a cultural artefact (Montfort & Bogost, 2009: 148).

Platform studies embody the 'new materialism' or 'materialist turn' in digital media studies, whereby theorists are increasingly 'prepared to tackle what goes on inside the machine' (Parikka, 2012: 89). Montfort and Bogost (2009: 148) state that, 'a computational platform is not an alien machine, but a cultural artifact that is shaped by values and forces and which expresses views about the world'.

The nomenclature of platform terminology has been popularized not only in the cultures of socially engaged online media practices but in society more generally. Gillespie (2010) has shown how the concept of 'platform' has been used by online content providers such as YouTube to strategically position everything from technical services to the description of creative user actions and advertising content. He argues that these uses connote the concept – literal or metaphorical – of an expansive, level, non-hierarchical surface, hosting multiple activities or events (Gillespie, 2010: 350).

Platforms thus 'anticipate' certain actions, implying a certain neutrality or egalitarian organization that provides an open or democratic space that supports users, be they individuals or corporations (2010: 350). Such metaphors echo the rhetoric of Web 2.0 as a place facilitating user-created content, amateur creativity, production and networking. Yet, as Gillespie demonstrates, the 'comforting' ideas of free space and openness complicate the tensions and power relationships between the roles and actions of providers, users and commercial media companies in the creation, distribution and controlled delivery of online content.

We consider platforms as emergent places in which the digital and material are entangled, and we account for how platforms are made through intensities of social engagement as much as through their occupation of physical sites (Hjorth et al., 2016: 31). As noted in a previous study on art practice, media and climate change, the deployment of different forms of platforms – both symbolic and curatorial – offers ways in which to analyse material and ideological entanglements. As Hjorth et al. argued:

> Platforms become central to thinking about the clustering of experiential and representational forms, as part of places that are made up of things, persons, and processes of

different qualities and affordances, and as open, continually changing aspects of the environments we inhabit. The place platform pairing therefore offers us a concept through which we can recognize the 'eventness' of art and of media as they become part of everyday screen ecologies. The platform offers us a prism through which to view the ways in which climate change becomes representation, discourse, and experience, as it is mediated, contested, and experienced, and how it indeed becomes an increasing part of the ways everyday life is lived. (2016: 31)

Through the rubric of platforms, we can see how humans are interpellated as data subjects. For LaMarre (2017), platforms afford and reward particular types of performativity – what he calls 'platformativity'. As LaMarre notes, 'in platformativity, the platforms and infrastructures play an active role, or more precisely, an intra-active role, as they iterate, over and again' (2017: 25). As Lupton et al. (2018: 648) notes in their study of lively data, 'via their encounters and interactions with digital technologies, people constantly generate digital data about their habits, preferences, activities, and bodies. ... Self-tracking involves creating and then disciplining, managing, and interpreting such information about the self and the body.'

Lively data operates on various levels – human, material, technological, industrial. Through the rise in new materialism and sensory studies, emphasis has been placed back on the role of the senses, embodiment, movement and emotion in making sense of the world. Sensory ethnography, therefore, is about multiple ways of knowing (Pink, Sinanan et al., 2016). As Lupton et al. (2018) note in their study of digitized self-tracking through case studies of cyclists, few studies have focused upon the sensory and embodied aspects of this datafication. They consider how affordances, spaces, senses and affects all contribute 'to people's personal data collection practices and how they engage in data sense making'. As they argue when cyclists use 'digital devices for self-tracking, they become datafied assemblages that are moving through space. Bodies, space, and place are simultaneously digital-material' (Lupton et al., 2018: 648).

However, this is an assemblage of self-tracking and datafication, where notions of privacy and surveillance change. In the next section, we consider how these concepts are being recalibrated through mobile apps and the rise of datafication.

Rethinking surveillance in a period of self-tracking

As mobile apps are integrating with body measurement devices such as fitbits, we are seeing new modes or kinds of creativity, ways to play and ways to work, emerge (Deterding et al., 2011; Lupton, 2016a). These new engagements see the logics of social and mobile media entangling with the logics of Big Data, and potentially making ever more personal aspects of our everyday lives subject to the scrutiny once confined to the web browser. Now, literally every move we make is being recorded, datafied and analysed. Yet even (and perhaps, especially) here, we see plenty of evidence of resistance and subversive behaviour, challenging the idea that our entire lives are reliably quanifiable.

As ethnographers Laura Watts and Dawn Nafus argue, Big Data needs to be imagined as more than just algorithms collected by 'the cloud'. Rather, 'Data Stories speak, not of clouds, but of transformations: in things, in energy, and in experience' (Watts & Nafus, 2013: n.p.). According to Nafus and Jamie Sherman, 'big data is not always about big institutions; it is also about subjectivities' (2014: 1786). The rise of Big Data algorithms go hand in hand with the rise in tracking media – encapsulated by mobile wearables. For Nafus and Sherman, deploying Cheney-Lippold's (2011) soft biopolitics, 'QS movement is best understood as a kind of soft resistance' (2014: 1791).

In these debates around the agency, empowerment and exploitation in the face of growing datafication, the role of GPS as a default function in smartphones apps has reshaped our understandings of space (de Souza e Silva & Firth, 2012), surveillance (Humphreys, 2013) and rethinking privacy (Gazzard, 2011). Although scholars have examined corporate and governmental surveillance in an age of Big Data (e.g. Andrejevic, 2006, 2013; Cincotta et al., 2011; Farman, 2011; Lupton, 2016a), new forms of social surveillance (Marwick, 2012) among families or couples creates an additional – and to date under-researched – layer of everyday practices (Clark, 2012; Fitchard, 2012; Sengupta, 2012; Burroughs, 2017; Leaver, 2017). For Dourish and Anderson (2006), privacy is understood as a series of *processes* that *emerges through practice* rather than something we possess (or don't).

Mobile technologies have been deployed as ambient forms of surveillance between family members (Matsuda, 2009; Clark, 2012; Burroughs, 2017). Other studies of school surveillance (Shade & Singh, 2016) and intergenerational 'friendly surveillance' (Hjorth et al., 2018) continue to emerge. These studies effectively recalibrate how we conceptualize surveillance.

In addition to the traditional notion of surveillance that is characterized by its non-transparency by an authority (i.e. government or corporation), Lee Humphreys (2013) argues that three other forms of surveillance become apparent through engagement with social media: voluntary panopticon, lateral surveillance and self-surveillance. Voluntary panopticon refers to the voluntary submission to corporate surveillance, or what Whitaker (1999) calls the 'participatory panopticon'. The voluntary panopticon emerges in a consumer society where information technology enables the decentred surveillance of consumptive behaviour. The participatory panopticon shares similarities with participatory surveillance in that people willingly participate in the monitoring of their own behaviour because they derive benefit from it.

Lateral surveillance is the asymmetrical and non-transparent monitoring of citizens by one another (Andrejevic, 2006). The advent of social media has given rise to other forms of lateral surveillance, such as 'social surveillance' (Marwick, 2012), which suggests a mutual surveillance among actors using social media. Like lateral surveillance, social surveillance involves non-hierarchical forms of monitoring (that is, not involving the state or corporate entities) among everyday people. Unlike lateral surveillance, social surveillance suggests that people engage in permissible and reciprocal forms of watching.

The last kind of surveillance is self-surveillance. Meyrowitz (2007: 1) defines self-surveillance as 'the ways in which people record themselves (or invite others to do so) for potential replaying in other times and places'. For Lee Humphreys (2013), changing notions of surveillance can be characterized by users seeking to increasingly catalogue and document their life digitally in what van Dijck (2014) has called datafication. However, with mobile social networks incorporating and broadcasting personal and locational information of users (Humphreys, 2007), this creates new issues around surveillance, privacy and control. She argues that we need to understand the qualified, rather than quantified, self (Humphreys, 2018). As Humphries argues, there are various forms of surveillance.

André Jansson (2015) suggests that social and mobile media have challenged old models of top-down surveillance. Jansson argues for a 'non-hierarchical and non-systematic monitoring' practice that is embedded in the everyday that he calls 'interveillance'. Interveillance speaks to the growing ways in which people mutually share and disclose various forms of private information. Interveillance, for Jansson, is dialectical; it 'reinforces' and 'integrates' 'overarching ambiguities of mediatization' in which 'freedom and autonomy' are 'paralleled by limitations and dependencies *vis-à-vis* media' (2015: 81). Indeed, for many mobile app users, there is interplay between interveillance, on the one hand, and social surveillance (Marwick, 2012) on the other.

In this oscillation between interveillance and social surveillance, there is also a softening of practices around privacy. In interviews with *Strava* users, they are very aware of privacy settings and how they could ensure they weren't being watched. However, for many it was about the play between interveillance and social surveillance, whereby they watch their friends' rides and give them kudos. But part of the recording is also for self-tracking; they can revisit their movements and memories of places and see how their wayfaring[2] changes over time. Part of this nuanced understanding of surveillance and privacy in the context of mobile apps requires interpreting the playful dimension of media.

Performing the art of maps

Making sense of the world through embodied and emplaced understandings can be heightened through self-tracking. It can also help us to be more reflexive and mindful of our activities. But it can also be a space for playful resistance. As Sicart (2014) notes, contemporary digital media is inherently playful. Understanding QS in terms of play rather than gamification gives users more agencies and allows situations to be more open to multiple ways of knowing. In this section we explore the playful dimensions of *Strava* through its playful art as part of the critical and performative cartographic turn. Dubbed the 'Banksy'[3] of *Strava*, Stephen Lund started his Sketchbook of GPS Artist blog[4] and curated his various cartographic drawings done through *Strava*. Similar work by Nathan Rae (pictured below) shows GPS-constructed sketches of everything from christmas trees to Freddie Mercury superimposed over Manchester created as Rae ran carefully plotted paths.

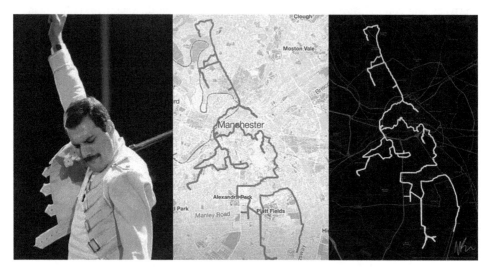

Figure 5.4 From inspiration to Strava GPX to final art piece (Image: Nathan Rae)

What Lund and Rae's work highlights is the playful and creative ways data can be misused and reappropriated in ways that were not originally planned by the designers. Both Lund and Rae's work also signals a rise of citizen and critical cartographers, who are taking everyday tools like mobile media to reimagine how spaces and places are experienced and conceptualized. This is especially the case with the triangulating of camera phone apps and GPS to look at the 'lively data' and what it says about a place. Manovich's *Phototrails*, which we discuss further in Chapter 8, was indicative of this. Here he drew from Instagram data to make rich visualizations of particular cities.

For Lammes (2016: 1), digital mapping interfaces 'can be understood as new loci of spatial mediation. … Instead of simply storing spatial information, interfaces also take part in the creation of spatial relations. In this process, map images are highly dynamic.' As Verhoeff (2012: 145) notes, mobile interfaces are demonstrative and indicative of a shift from 'representational cartography to navigation as a performative cartographic practice'. For Farman (2010), this turn towards understanding maps as performative is indicative of mobile media.

As Perkins (2012) notes, the shift in maps towards the performative can be understood as part of a broader ludic (i.e. game-like) shift whereby playing no longer happens *on* maps but *in* maps. Drawing on Raessen's (2006) discussion of the ludification of culture, whereby play increasingly performs a key role in everyday life, Perkins argues that cartography has learnt from location-based mobile gaming and the ways in which playful collaboration can lead to new ways of seeing places. As Perkins notes, applications such as desktop mapping and GIS have democratized the tools for cartography and in turn made mapping 'no longer tied to fixed specifications' (2012: 2).

Perkins' work is especially important in the context of bringing together the work around play and critical cartography. Camera phone apps expand upon this earlier wave of democratized cartographic tools in ways that are more playful and ambient. And yet, much of the contextualization of camera phone practices is linked to debates around the remediation of visual culture and the haunting of the analogue within the digital. For Perkins, the ludic or playful turn in culture limits the historical significance of play within many facets of everyday life. As he argues, 'people have always *played*, and perhaps increasingly *play* with mapping, instead of simply making or using a map for an instrumental task' (Perkins, 2012: 3, original italics). Elsewhere, Perkins has argued how the rise of vernacular mapping in tandem with cross-disciplinary approaches (that is, ethno-methodology, actor-network theory, non-representational theory and phenomenology) provide new ways for rethinking mapping, whereby the playful is intrinsically interwoven within its logic (Perkins, 2009; Dodge et al., 2009).

While the cultural dimensions of play have been discussed in detail by Sutton-Smith (1997) and in the context of games by Salen and Zimmerman (2003) and art by Flanagan (2009), who draw upon Huizinga (1955), the playful within spaces like the urban have a long history that can be linked to historical motifs like Baudelaire's *flâneur* and the 1960s movement Situationist International (de Souza e Silva & Hjorth, 2009). As Pink and Hjorth (2012) have argued, these geo-tagging playful applications provide new contexts. Instead of being a 'snapshot', whereby time and space is frozen, these new temporal–spatial visual configurations are part of a moving set of cartographies orchestrated by the rise of locative services as part of everyday mobile media. As Verhoeff (2012: 149) notes, 'a new mobile cartography infuses spatial representation with a temporal and procedural dimension: a performative cartography, a dynamic map which emerges and changes during the journey'.

Apps like Instagram not only expand the ways in which cartographies of co-presence can be understood, but they do so in relation to ambient play.

As Shirley Jordan and Christoph Lindner (2016) note in their collection *Cities Interrupted*, increasingly digital media are operating to create spaces of slowness and contemplation rather than just acceleration. The work of Jason Sweeney, *Stereopublic: Crowdsourcing the quiet* (2013), is an app that navigates users through a city based on the lack of noise. Users can walk around a city and geo-tag their favourite quiet places, they can add a picture or sound to further represent their feelings. As Sweeney notes:

> When I was originally thinking about this project I was thinking more about crowds and what they might sound like in the future. … Will they become more noisy and hyper-social, chaotic? … It was a very personal desire to think of future cities as having dedicated quiet spaces that were either built into them or to nurture those spaces that already existed. … So the idea for the app came about when thinking of a way to make a 'quiet-seeking' tool that the public could freely access to participate in this quest for quiet. (Stinson, 2013: n.p.)

Figure 5.5   Jason Sweeney's *Stereopublic: Crowdsourcing the quiet*

Stereopublic links to two key concepts: digital wayfaring and ambient play (Hjorth & Richardson, 2018). Wayfaring is the idea that knowledge is produced through the action of walking. Through the process of walking, ideas and talking have a different relationality – they take on an embodied sense of *knowing* and *being* in the world. Tim Ingold's notion of wayfaring as a type of embodied mobility that is both routine and repetitive (e.g. commuting), in which knowledge is produced through *knowing* and *being* in movement.

As explored with Sarah Pink, contemporary entanglements between the online and offline can be interpreted through the conceptual and embodied metaphor of digital wayfaring (Hjorth & Pink, 2014). Combined with the digital, wayfaring was repurposed to reflect upon the way in which the digital entangles itself in our everyday practices and movements, especially through mobile media. The experience of digital wayfaring is further complicated within the datafication of a mobile app or hybrid reality game. Wayfaring locates proprioception and movement as central ways of knowing. In this knowledge, notions of engagement and attention are recalibrated. Digital wayfaring features in urban play – there is a constant ambient movement of attention from background to foreground.

Notions of the ambient, as well as atmosphere (Böhme, 1993), have taken on a certain currency with some scholars to help understand the increased digital mediation of everyday life and how this is reshaping the relationality between embodiment and attention. From Malcolm McCullough's *Ambient Commons: Attention in the Age of Embodied Information* (2013) to Paul Roquet's *Ambient Media: Japanese Atmospheres of Self* (2016), the ambient has been used as a lens in which to understand how contemporary media moves in and out of different forms of engagement with spaces, places, bodies, practices and performances. Here, the notion of ambient play considers how the increasing popularity of mobile apps lies in its capacity to move *between* and *across* co-located and networked spaces, adapting or fitting into the patterns of quotidian life.

While ambience has been given significant attention in human–computer interaction (HCI) and the study of urban environments, exemplified by McCullough's aforementioned *Ambient Commons* (2013), it is the bringing together of ambience and play that can help us to understand the embodied, intimate and affective relations of media in the home. Ambience is about the sensorial and affective *texture* or *atmosphere* of a place. As McCullough (2013: 13) suggests, ambient awareness reflects 'a more general mindfulness', a social and embodied sensibility of one's immediate and mediated surroundings.

Indeed, the use of *Strava*, both in ways that were and were not planned in the original affordances of the app, is demonstrative of the playful dimensions of performative cartographies. It heightens a sense of digital wayfaring as a sense of social proprioception and also the role of ambient play in our everyday lives. In the last section, we return to *Strava* to explore some of the ways it is used to coalesce wayfaring, movement, senses and memory by participants.

Grippy not slippy: A case study

Interviewing *Strava* users can provide great insight into the motivations around self-tracking. *Strava* is used for bike riding and running. However, in Australian fieldwork, it seemed that most interviewed users deployed it for mountain bike riding.

While the obvious gamification dimension is well known, it is the sharing and place-making storytelling that makes for a more meaningful understanding. For 40-year-old John, *Strava* allowed him to access different mountain riding paths and tracks he might not have found himself. While he often rode alone, through *Strava* it felt like a social activity. Often he or his friends would log on and like (expressed on *Strava* through 'kudos') various rides. The app also aggregated others' rides and awarded the fastest recorded rides as King of the Mountain (KoM).

For 35-year-old Robert, *Strava* provided a space in which he could keep a friendly eye on friends living elsewhere. He first joined *Strava* when his good friends, who he would frequently bike ride with, moved interstate. *Strava* allowed them to maintain an intimate co-presence online. They could give kudos and feel veracious enjoyment of their friends' rides. For Robert, naming the rides was important to the place-making processes. He gave the titles a sense of feeling, affect or story. This meant that when he went back over his rides he could reminisce about previous rides and then compare how they 'felt' when riding them at different times.

Here we see the ability of Strava to play an active role in cartographies of co-presence. They map at the same time as they perform in and through maps, and make riding a cartographic exercise, bringing to life the ways in which tracks can be experienced in a diversity of ways.

Conclusion

In this chapter we have explored the role that mobile apps play in magnifying the key principles of social media: social, mobile and visual. They highlight the ways in which datafication and tracking can be understood as a contested practice in which users are finding creative ways to circumnavigate 'platformativity'. From small data to QS, users are providing ways to creatively intervene in debates around the datafication of everyday life. It is important to conduct more ethnographic, human-centred research into algorithmic culture to fully engage with the contested fields of social media as still, inherently, *social*.

Notes

1. www.gartner.com/newsroom/id/2654115
2. Wayfaring is a term that is used widely in the literature to refer to movement that is purposefully tracked by a user. It is evokes a sense of purpose to the movement, more than just walking or travelling because the activity is being undertaken with an intention to record and review.
3. www.banksy.co.uk/
4. https://gpsdoodles.com/

6

Geolocation & Social Media

Introduction

As we discussed in the previous chapter through the case of *Strava*, modern mobile devices now integrate a range of hardware components that collect data about the device's immediate environment. Chief among these processes is the GPS capability of most phones, but there are also other data-gathering components, such as accelerometers, which can measure the user's physical activity. We also saw how these technologies are changing the way we understand space, surveillance and privacy. However, we also noted that despite the work that has been done on understanding corporate and government surveillance, there has been relatively little work on emerging forms of social surveillance – for example, within families or between couples. We know very little about the ways locative media practices relate to privacy, intimacy and surveillance, and how these experiences play out among couples and families (Leaver, 2017; Pink et al., 2018), and especially across the range of different social relations that exist in our societies. For example, much of the research on intimate surveillance has focused upon male hook-up apps such as Grindr (Mowlabocus, 2010; Blackwell et al., 2014; Brubaker et al. 2014), with very few examples of same-sex female forms of intimacy mediated by locative media (Tang, 2015; Albury & Byron, 2016; Murray & Anderson, 2016; Hjorth et al., 2018).

With datafication causing more tensions around personal and corporate platformativity, the ways in which geolocative media creates data mapping around disclosure and visibility take on new forms. These visibilities and invisibilities are both intentional and unintentional, highlighting different inequalities around accessibility, identity and literacy. As Mary Gray (2009) highlights, the deployments of visibility through online media has remediated the 'coming out' story in a variety of ways, a phenomenon being amplified by locative and social media functionalities.

The role of visibility and invisibility in social media is a highly gendered preoccupation (Brighenti, 2010; Hendry, 2017). For Brighenti, 'visibility is a social dimension in which thresholds between different social forces are introduced' (2010: 5). Hendry (2017) further expands upon Brighenti's concepts by examining the role of visibility by young women recovering from mental illness, arguing that visibility and invisibility are key modalities for representing social connection and thus recovery. Duguay (2016) contends that LGBTQ visibility on social media can be viewed as a form of everyday activism (see also Vivienne & Burgess, 2012).

In this chapter we explore the practices and cultures emerging at the mundane and intimate level of geo-tracking between family members. Rather than focusing upon the corporate and platform surveillance literature, of which there is some great work (as identified in the previous chapter), we seek to discuss the ways in which cross-cultural and intergenerational understandings might provide new insights into the debate.

Friendly surveillance and care-at-a-distance

While locative media is becoming a default feature in many mobile apps, their usage and non-usage speak to ways in which people curate their intimate and yet public lives. For some, the intimate and public are interwoven – some people are completely comfortable performing their private lives through Instagram. For others, media is used to re-establish boundaries between the intimate and private in a world in which these concepts seem to blur. It is hardly surprising that locative media has provided much food for thought in rethinking privacy (Farman, 2011; Gazzard, 2011; de Souza e Silva & Frith, 2012). Here, privacy isn't seen as something we possess (or don't possess) but is process-based – something we constantly do and define through practice (Dourish & Anderson, 2006).

Although there has been discussion about corporate and governmental surveillance in an age of Big Data (e.g. Andrejevic, 2006; Farman, 2010; Cincotta et al., 2011), the rise of new forms of social surveillance in families (Marwick, 2012) is creating an additional, and to date under-researched, layer of everyday practices that is amplified by locative media (Clark, 2012; Sengupta, 2012). We know very little about the ways locative media practices relating to privacy, intimacy and surveillance are being played out within everyday family contexts. We still don't have much understanding of the impact on how, when and where locative media are used, or the implications of these practices for how place and time are experienced. Through studying the messiness of practice across generations and cultures we can begin to think through the complex ways in which locative media is used to maintain intimate relations, especially at a distance. To understand locative media in practice requires new approaches to the concept of surveillance and its relationship to care and intimacy.

As discussed in Chapter 5, Lee Humphreys (2013) identifies three kinds of surveillance involved within social media practice. In addition to the traditional notion of surveillance – characterized by its non-transparency by an authority (that is, government or a corporation) – Humphreys identifies three other kinds of surveillance: voluntary panopticon, lateral surveillance and self-surveillance. There are also other types of surveillance emerging – such as social surveillance. The practice of lateral surveillance (Andrejevic, 2006) can be seen in research fieldwork, and is epitomized by 30-year-old Melbourne participant Catherine and her watching of her girlfriend Susan in the Uber taxi through the app's tracking functions. Today, many apps allow citizens to monitor other citizens' behaviour through non-reciprocal forms of watching. Everyday people can search for information about other citizens without their knowledge or permission.

Another kind of lateral surveillance discussed in Chapter 5, social surveillance (Marwick 2012), again retains the idea of mutual surveillance among and between everyday people. However, social surveillance suggests permissible and reciprocal forms of watching, which is more typical of the forms of 'care-at-a-distance' one might see between family members checking up on each other's Facebook profiles, for example. We need more work around the 'care-at-a-distance' role that social and mobile media play in maintaining many families in temporarily or permanent distance (Horst, 2006; Wilding, 2006; Madianou & Miller, 2011; Baldassar et al., 2016).

The intimate mundane and care-at-a-distance

Attention to practices of the intimate mundane brings together two strands in recent literatures concerned with the embodied and affective dimensions of everyday life at home and with digital media. The role of the mundane and banal is regarded in this sense as a site for analysing power relations and rituals, alongside the role of the intimate as practised in, and through, everyday digital media (Lüders, 2008). From Raymond Williams' emphasis upon the ordinariness of the everyday (2002 [1958]) to Meaghan Morris's (1990) study into the politics of banality through to the seminal work of Michel de Certeau (1984), cultural studies approaches have long been interested in the role of the mundane as a site for power naturalization in everyday life (Highmore, 2002). So too, intimacy has come under much revision with challenges to Western or Anglophonic traditional notions of intimacy (Giddens, 1992) that often prioritize face-to-face interaction as less mediated and thus, problematically, as more intimate (Berlant, 1998; Jamieson, 2011).

Doing intimacy within contemporary contexts requires acknowledging the ways in which it can be public and community oriented (Jamieson, 2011), especially given the variety of publics afforded by social media. As Lynn Jamieson (2011) has noted in her detailed historicization of intimacy, the dichotomy between 'private intimacy' and 'public community' is deeply problematic. Drawing from feminist literature, Jamieson argues that much of contemporary 'doing intimacy' expands upon familial ties and involves community and civic engagement, a process that sees a complete transformation in the role of intimacy in and around the notion of family. For Jamieson, intimacy is best defined as 'the quality of close connection between people and the process of building this quality' (2011, n.p.). While acknowledging intimacy may vary from subject to cultural and historical frames of reference, Jamieson argues that the multifaceted nature of intimacy enacts and embodies a variety of understandings of closeness, including emotional and cognitive closeness.

From feminist readings such as Leopoldina Fortunati (2002) and Amparo Lasén (2004) to same-sexed gendered performativity identified by Lin Prøitz (2007), much of the early research into mobile communication focused on mobile media as a site for and of intimacy. In a special issue on 'mobile intimacy' in *Feminist Media Studies*, various authors addressed the complex ways in which intimacy plays out in public spaces through mobile media (Hjorth & Lim, 2012). For example, as we discuss in Chapter 10, paralinguistic techniques such as *emoji* (icons of emotions) and emoticons enact types of intimacy by electronically embodying emotions of the body and tactic gestures. Expanding upon the 'intimate publics' (introduced in Chapter 2) identified by Lauren Berlant (1998), in which she argued that intimacy has public dimensions, the special issue investigated how digital media complicates the doing of intimacy – and the attendant 'boundary work' – of being intimate.

Intimacy and care have a complex entanglement, especially around the feminization of particular forms of labour. For many feminist scholars, care cultures are an important site for affective, emotional and unpaid labour (Mol, 2008). Fields such as nursing and teaching are often underpaid, despite the pivotal role they play in maintaining many societies, because they are 'feminized'. The role of care as a feminized form of labour often plays out in many work and social contexts, with particular 'feeling rules' (Hochschild, 1979) being expected. Feeling rules are a series of usually informal rules (though in some places, like at work, they may be more formal) that designate how feelings and emotions should be managed. Individuals develop their own feeling rules and may have different sets of rules depending on the nature of a relationship.

An example of these feeling rules might be someone may have a more relaxed approach to displaying their feelings around a partner or friend. Feeling rules may also be differentiated in lots of ways, such as by gender; the idea in many cultures that boys shouldn't cry is an example. In work environments, these rules are often deployed via training, procedures and manuals which enforce a set of external feeling rules on the individual that takes away their ability to define their own feeling rules, potentially forcing them to act like a different person, such as a flight attendant. The maintenance of particular feeling rules often involves a type of informal surveillance. Gender, class and ethnicity also pay a role in naturalizing feeling rules – as Eileen Boris and Rhacel Salazar Parreñas (2010) note in their study of 'intimate labor' whereby certain women from developing countries are exploited in caring for developed countries children and domestic contexts. Intimate labour then is at the intersection between cultures, economics, technologies and the politics of care.

Care has always had a complex relationship to surveillance (Bellacasa, 2017) but digital media complicates this imbrication further. Mobile technologies have been deployed as ambient forms of surveillance between family members (Matsuda, 2009; Clark, 2012; Burroughs, 2017). Other studies of school surveillance (Shade & Singh, 2016) and inter-generational 'friendly surveillance' (Hjorth et al., 2018) continue to emerge. These studies effectively recalibrate how we conceptualize surveillance.

It is the social or lateral surveillance dimensions we discussed above and in Chapter 5 that best encompass the paradoxes of care through technology and data in the home. Care in this context emerges in the textures, contours and practices that form daily rhythms in relation to households. Care is a complex layering of emotion and slowness that is often entangled with practices such as surveillance. Much of the negative debates around Big Data have focused upon its role to watch and control (Andrejevic, 2013). However, surveillance also has friendly, benevolent or ambivalent dimensions (Marwick, 2012).

Feminist studies scholar Annemarie Mol coined the term 'geographies of care' (Mol, 2008; Mol et al., 2010) to highlight various care practices. Increasingly, technologies – as tools for surveillance – are appearing in studies of care-at-a-distance. Jeanette Pols (2012) studied the use of technology to care at a distance (telecare) and found that technologies only helped when deployed in unison with people (not replacing humans). Many of these social *care practices to continue at a distance* operate through locative media technologies such as smartphone apps and self-tracking wearables. These co-present geographies of care are an essential part of what makes a home and the informal, often tacit emotions and gestures that become part of the domestic repertoire. This entangled form of care involves doing affective intimacy and boundary work, and also, as argued by Mol et al. (2010), practices of normalization and ambiguity. In the next section we contextualize some of the debates around surveillance to address the friendly, careful and 'intimate' (Leaver, 2017) forms of surveillance, in order to engage the complex role of care within digital media practices of mundane intimacy.

Friendly 'social surveillance'

As we have discussed, while we often immediately think of surveillance as being something done to us by the state or large companies, there are many more types of surveillance – horizontal and vertical, benevolent and malevolent – that move in and out of our daily practices. These practices are indicative of new forms of social surveillance (Marwick, 2012) within families that are creating additional, and to date under-researched, layers (Clark, 2012; Sengupta, 2012; Shade & Singh, 2016).

We know very little about the ways locative media practices relating to privacy, inti-macy and surveillance are being played out in everyday family contexts, how these impact on how, when and where locative media are used, or the implications of these practices for how place and time are experienced. In these practices, it is the social or lateral sur-veillance dimensions that best involve the paradoxes of care in and around technology and data in the home. Here we see care as a texture, contour and practice that move in and out of daily rhythms. Care is a gradual process, a complex layering of emotion that is often enmeshed with practices such as surveillance.

For Alice Marwick, 'social surveillance' is distinguished from traditional forms through three axes: power, hierarchy and exchange. Utilizing Foucault's notion of capillaries of power, Marwick argues that social surveillance assumes 'power differentials evident in everyday interactions rather than the hierarchical power relationships assumed in much of the surveillance literature' (2012: 378). Marwick identifies some of the common notions of surveillance, such as lateral (Andrejevic, 2006), participatory (Albrechtslund, 2008), social searching (Lampe et al., 2006) and social (Joinson, 2008; Tokunaga, 2011). As she notes, social surveillance differs from traditional models in so far as it is focused around micro-level, decentralized, reciprocal interactions between individuals. Marwick frames her definition in terms of boundary work (Nippert-Eng, 2010: 10–14), whereby privacy is not necessarily framed by dichotomies of divisions across spatial, temporal and object-related work (Marwick, 2012: 379).

What becomes apparent through collaborative fieldwork[1] around the use and non-use of locative media are the ways in which families and intimates can create their own types of friendly surveillance. From the locative function on Facebook that allows friends to monitor and care-at-a-distance to parents ambiently watching their children's relationships through WhatsApp, mobile media is providing creative and playful ways to manage intimate intergenerational relations at a distance. Research fieldwork has proven a powerful way to reflect upon how the different cross-cultural, intergenerational friendly surveillance (care-at-a-distance or co-present care) plays out in our everyday lives.

An important aspect to understanding the mundane and intimate ways that surveillance plays out is acknowledging that it is, as a concept and practice, informed by cultural context. Just as what constitutes participation and power is culturally specific, so too do these nuances need to be identified and appreciated. For example, in China, there are various forms of horizontal and vertical surveillance that happen in and around familial practices. In a Chinese context there are three key notions that inform our definition: *watching* (看护, *Kan Hu*, which means keeping an eye on someone), *overseeing* (监看, *Jian Kan*, is to follow an activity or an entity to make sure that it operates normally and correctly) and *surveillance* (监控, *Jian Kong*, is used where power, authority and rebellion are often involved). In particular, it is a combination of both *Kan Hu* and *Jian Kan* that play out and through the micro-coordination of care-at-distance through mobile media practices.

In Japan, 監視 (*Kanshi*) refers to vertical surveillance, whereby something or someone can prevent problems from happening; 観察 (*Kansatsu*) refers to watching, which is viewed as more neutral, and 監督 (*Kantoku*) signifies careful overseeing, whereby someone like a director or manager, who is in charge of an organization, supervises his or her members. However, when it comes to family, 見守る (*Mimamoru*)is more appropriate and is often used by parents when they care for their children. It means to follow or to watch out for one's safety. This notion resonates with the earlier discussion of 'careful surveillance' (Hjorth & Richardson, 2019).

These culturally different notions of watching, surveillance and care need to be taken into consideration. Western ideas about surveillance are not necessarily relevant in many cases where culturally-specific notions of care are at play. In the next section, we discuss some of the many ways in which friendly informal surveillance manifests within familial care-at-a-distance. We outline some of the emergent care-at-a-distance apps in Japan to open up discussion about the future of how we practise and conceptualize care, media and ritual.

Careful apps: The commodification of care or care mobilized?

'Care' is a contested and complex term. Understanding care requires interdisciplinary and human-centric approaches that imbricate the attendant textures of slowness, quietness and contingency. As we move towards increasingly ageing societies that are datafied, the role of digital health has come to the forefront. And yet, in this focus, we need to account for the ways in which the digital is inherently shaped by the social, cultural and emotional. We thus need to look towards collaborations not just between health and medicine, but, more importantly, social practice-centric models such as those posed by design and ethnography. The future of care requires interdisciplinary human-centric solutions through HASS and STEM collaborations.

For example, much of the world is looking to Japan, which has one of the largest rapidly ageing populations, to understand some future challenges. In Japan, where a large percentage of the population is elderly, the role of care and ritual is being recalibrated. Robots and mobile technologies are providing families with various ways to care-at-a-distance. Adult children are using locative social media on their smartphones (*sumaho*) to provide a sense of constant contact with ageing loved ones. Mobile apps deployed for 'careful surveillance' by intergenerational family members are growing. Here we see care as a texture, contour and practice that moves in and out of daily patterns. Care is a complex layering of emotion and slowness that is often entangled with practices such as surveillance – what we suggest as careful or friendly surveillance. The concept of 'careful surveillance' is neither oxymoron nor tautology. Rather it highlights the multilayered role of care within relational dynamics. Careful surveillance addresses the paradoxes of care in and around technologies in the home, involving a constant negotiation of both tethering and freedom.

Increasingly, parents are using apps such as *Mimamori map* to keep a friendly eye on their children as a form of care-at-a-distance. 'TONE Mimamori' notifies parents if kids are 'aruki sumaho' (using *sumaho* while walking). While apps like *Anshin unten ever drive*

(Safety driving 'ever drive') keep a friendly eye on elderly parents, alerting their adult children to dangerous driving or to prevent them getting lost, as might be the case with those who have early dementia. These forms of what might be called 'careful apps' are paradoxically both commodifications of care and mobilizations of care. They also highlight that in the rise of automation and artificial intelligence, technology still needs people at the centre if care is to be properly enacted.

Indeed, as feminist science and technology scholar Judy Wajcman has identified, robots are far from ready to replace humans in care work. In aged housing estates in Japan, robots are brought in to reprieve the carers, not those being cared for (Wajcman, 2017). Care, as a historically feminized and undervalued labour, is hard to replicate with technologies. It requires slowness and textures of quietness not understood by contemporary technologies. And as ageing societies are becoming increasingly prominent, we need more understanding of how social, creative and bio-medical synergies can be harnessed to recalibrate how we do care. The following examples show some alternative methods for mobile apps to achieve different ways to care-at-a-distance.

Mimamori map

Mimamori map (meaning 'watching for someone') was a collaboration between Softbank and Willcom Okinawa and launched on 30 June 2016. It enables users to share family members' locations at the time of disaster, or to send SOS signals to a registered address, or to around one when help is needed. This service has two functions: *Ima-koko share* (sharing now and here) and *Tsuitayo tsuuchi* (I-arrived notice). Users can confirm family members' locations in real time in the former service, or can receive notice when one has arrived at the registered place at the time of disaster in the latter service.[2]

LinkGates

As part of the rollout of 'internet of things' technologies, Misawa Home pioneered a new service called *LinkGates* as part of the firm's newly established residential buildings from April 2017. It enables users to watch the family and prevent heat disorder by using sensors and controllers installed in the house and on the original smartphone app. Home electronics and electronic devices are also connected to the internet. An alert is sent to the registered smartphone when the entrance is opened, or when water is mistakenly running freely while the owner is away. It's also possible to lock the door from the smartphone. In addition, the technology focuses upon preventing heat disorder for aged people and pets. Sending an alert to the smartphone, the air conditioning can also be controlled, and there is a function to watch for aged people or children returning home, by measuring water usage.[3]

Nintendo Mimamori Switch

Nintendo Mimamori Switch is a free app that enables parents to watch their child's game play, coordinated with *Nintendo Switch*. For example, it prevents children from playing too long by informing the child how long she or he has played. Parents can confirm if children play within an agreed period of time by using the app. It is also possible to set the app to automatically turn off the game when the agreed-upon time limit is over. It also shows which game app is in use and how long the child has played as a form of report on a daily or monthly basis. If needed, and based on reported data, game play can be restricted, such as non-age-appropriate games, communication with others online, or sharing posts with pictures to social media.[4]

Omamori

The household account service provider MoneySmart released a new service *Omamori* (meaning charm/talisman), which watches a child's location and online purchases. It works with an original tracking device 'om2 wallet (omni wallet)', which is implemented in a transit smart card and transmits information about the child's location to the carer's smartphone. It is useful when parents go to pick up the child – information is automatically sent to the parents' phone when a child passes the ticket gate. It enables parents to check when and what their child bought with the IC card. Reports of money usage are automatically transmitted, and it can also restrict how money is spent: for example, for food or travel only. It is also equipped with a communication function between parents and child.[5]

Mimamoruzou2

AXSEED provides *Mimamoruzou2*, which designed to enable parents to protect their children from *sumaho* addiction and dangers when using the internet. It is equipped with four functions: 'child guard' can set rules about the use of *sumaho* among parents and children; 'notification' alerts parents when children return home; 'accident prevention' supports disaster readiness; and 'privacy guard' protects *sumaho* when it is lost. In a newly added function, parents can also monitor how much and when kids use various apps.[6]

Cocosecom

Home security firm SECOM is collaborating with mobile-phone firm au, to provide a *Cocosecom* service to junior *sumaho*, released by KDDI. It is a service to provide location information and to enable carers to rush to the scene when the target person is in an emergency situation – 'coco' means 'here'. Cocosecom is a location-based service provided by SECOM that uses the mobile phone as a 'portable security device'. It blends a location-searching function with a rushing-to-the-scene function and is designed to care for the young and old, especially in terms of crime prevention and theft.[7]

Mimamori tag

Security company ALSOK announced a Bluetooth-based *Mimamori tag*, which enables family to watch their elderly relatives while wayfaring. It is a small Bluetooth-based com-municator (beacon) that is installable in shoes and is designed specifically for this purpose. The firm will distribute the product to ten municipalities to build a network to support the independence and mobility of elderly people in the community.[8]

Anshen unten ever drive

Orix Automobile is providing a communication service *Anshin unten ever drive* (Safety driving 'ever drive') to survey elderly driving practices. A communication device is installed in the elderly person's car, which automatically sends information about driving over the speed limit or rapid acceleration via computer or *sumaho* in real time. Information about everyday driving situations, dangerous behaviour or long drives is shared with family members.[9]

TONE Mimamori

Tone Mobile have now started to provide *TONE Mimamori*, an app for children's *sumaho*. It notifies parents when children pass the station or enables parents to limit the time their children spend using *sumaho*. It also alerts 'aruki sumaho' (using *sumaho* while walking).[10]

Conclusion

In this chapter we have explored the intersection between various forms of surveillance and geolocative media. Rather than looking at state-based or company-based uses of geo-locative media for surveilling citizens and consumers (which has been noted in previous chapters), we've chosen instead to focus on the way that geolocative media is increas-ingly deployed by families and other intimate relations as a way of watching over our loved ones. This has important implications in the parts of our lives where we care for others through friendly surveillance or care-at-a-distance, in particular for children and the elderly. Here, surveillance loses some of its negative connotations and becomes about looking after loved ones, a kind of care-full surveillance.

As this chapter has indicated, there is also a need to understand friendly notions of sur-veillance that are culturally specific. The entanglement of watching and friendly surveillance takes various textures across individual, social and organizational layers. These layers are specific to the cultural context and what Herzfeld calls 'cultural intimacy' (1997). In China, for example, which has a high horizontal state and organizational surveillance, the watching of children by parents takes on a different feeling. Just as mobile media has diversified the ways horizontal and vertical surveillance plays out, it is also important to understand how culturally-specific notions of watching, power and surveillance inform practices. Careful surveillance is a significant part of maintaining digital kinship. It is about the affective labour of doing intimacy and its attendant boundary work. In this practice of careful surveillance, visuality plays a key role. Here visuality is about visibility *and* invisibility, wayfaring in, through and across mobile media practices.

Notes

1. This fieldwork draws from an Australian Research Council Linkage grant with Intel entitled *Locating the Mobile*. Collaborators include Heather Horst, Sarah Pink, Fumi Kato, Baohua Zhou, Genevieve Bell, Jolynna Sinanan and Kana Ohashi.
2. www.rbbtoday.com/article/2016/06/29/143105.html
3. www.risktaisaku.com/articles/-/2592
4. www.nintendo.co.jp/hardware/switch/parentalcontrols/
5. https://resemom.jp/article/2016/10/11/34225.html
6. https://resemom.jp/article/2017/03/22/37204.html
7. www.rbbtoday.com/article/2017/01/16/148614.html
8. http://k-tai.watch.impress.co.jp/docs/news/1031394.html
9. https://trafficnews.jp/post/61126/
10. http://style.nikkei.com/article/DGXMZO14283770R20C17A3000000?channel=DF260120166490

PART 3

CULTURES

7

Social Media Visualities

Introduction

> It is perhaps not too much of an overstatement to describe photography as a quint-
> essential practice of life. Indeed, over the last few decades photography has become
> so ubiquitous that our very sense of existence is shaped by it. (Zylinska, 2015: n.p.)

A young woman is running in a park in Copenhagen while playing the mobile location-based game *Zombies, Run!* Suddenly the sound of approaching zombies can be heard on her mobile and she dashes down an unfamiliar lane in the park. She escapes the zombies. Then looks around. She has never seen this part of the park before. There is a golden streak of sun dancing on some trees. It looks like a fairy tale. She takes a picture on Instagram, chooses a retro filter that reminds her of Polaroid aesthetics and uploads it. The retro 'polaroid' lens makes the picture look like it is taken from yesteryear. She is momentarily transported back to her childhood. Then back again to the present moment. She continues jogging, occasion-ally interrupted by zombies and taking blurry Instagram images shared while literally on the run.

Over in Tokyo, newly coupled university students Toshi and Kana have consummated their relationship by the girlfriend Kana tagging the phone with a plethora of feminine customization. Here the mobile phone becomes a symbol of older rituals – the engagement ring. As an object that is always close and visible, with users often keeping it on the table within arm's reach, these highly feminized examples are clearly signposted to others that the boy is engaged. Toshi's mobile phone is swimming in Hello Kitties customization on the outside and a plethora of coupled camera phone images saved inside. The saved camera phone images live in the phone and function much like a photo album, always on the move and always available for viewing. These images of their coupledom are different from the ones shared on social media. Here we see the role of mobile-phone customization as both a material and immaterial culture that reflects their users' relationships and modes of intimacy.

These two vignettes illustrate how camera phone practices perform pivotal and yet unofficial roles in the ways we experience, represent and share notions of place. Camera phone practices are very much entangled within our everyday rituals. Everything from eating (sharing images of food), to going for a walk or to the beach on a sunny day, to meeting with friends for a coffee can be an excuse for a quick snap that gets shared with friends. In each cultural context, camera phone practices take on different meanings and references. They show us how the image plays an increasingly important role in our making sense of the world as we capture fleeting moments, save them and then share our lives through social media timelines. Camera phone practices shape, and are shaped by, various modes of conceptualizing place.

Throughout these different contexts, one point remains apparent – camera phones are at the intersection of photography, social media and the everyday. They provide playful, ambient and reflective ways to remap places and spaces across co-present platforms, contexts and subjectivities. Visual genres, such as the selfie, have become an omnipresent barometer for contemporary networked global culture (Senft & Baym, 2015). They represent new configurations between photography, digital culture and what can be called 'kinesthetic sociability' (Frosh, 2015). At the crossroads between the aesthetic and the social, camera phone practices can provide insight into contemporary social media.

As noted in Chapter 1, two of the key characteristics of contemporary social media are that it is synonymous with mobile media and that the dominance of the visual continues to pervade. The collapse between mobile media and visuality in the sharing discourses of social media logic is not by accident. Rather, it partakes in what van Djick and Poell (2013) have defined as the four grounding principles for social media, as discussed in Chapter 1: programmability, popularity, connectivity and datafication. These principles are amplified through mobile visuality, creating complex digital storytelling narratives that move between civic creative engagement and datafication, or what Zizi Papacharissi (2014) calls 'affective publics'.

From museums determining their cultural engagement through 'likes' or posting shares (see Chapter 9) to shaping what art installations get shown and what types of graffiti are popularized, it is hard to ignore the power of camera phone apps like Instagram in shaping social media discourses. Scholars Daniel Miller and Jolynna Sinanan (2017) have highlighted that platforms such as Facebook are essentially visual – from the sharing of camera phone pictures to memes and paralinguistics.

As scholars Tama Leaver and Tim Highfield (Highfield & Leaver, 2015; Leaver & Highfield, 2018) have noted, researching Instagram via hashtags can provide insight into the types of images that are shared as well as how they are interpreted and how they resonate with others. Through APIs (application programming interfaces, a software interface that allows people to write computer programs that can access data or services from a platform), researchers and users can collate metadata about items which include specific hashtags. The metadata includes a range of potential fields, including details about 'the user, the date, a location or geographic coordinates (if specified), the caption (text accompanying the visual media), the number of comments from other users, the number of likes and so forth' (Leaver & Highfield, 2018: 34). Moreover, far from just being a site for reinforcing gender and body norms, Instagram selfie culture is producing a space for subversive and counter-cultures to flourish (Olszanowski, 2014; Tiidenberg, 2015a).

In many public urban contexts around the world, camera phones function as an intrinsic part of this playful and visual fabric (Hjorth, 2016). They create data sets that reflect nuances of the place and its particular storytelling effects (Hochmann & Manovich, 2013). The visual culture and physical spaces of public places have been quickly transformed over the past decade by camera phone apps (Hjorth & Hendry, 2015). Events and street art are determined by their 'Instagrammable' qualities. From taking a picture of a coffee as part of an everyday ritual to the sharing of a joyful moment between friends, camera phone apps like Instagram operate to capture, share and represent the mundane, intimate, ephemeral, tacit and phatic (Villi & Stocchetti, 2011). These images not only play with how place is experienced and mapped, but also how these cartographies are overlaid by co-presence across geographic, temporal, social and spatial contexts.

In this chapter we consider and contextualize the rise of mobile visuality, which is now understood as being synonymous with social media. We reflect upon how the rise of the camera phone through applification has led to different ways in which to overlay the relationship between place, image and sociality. Once defined as the network, we argue that the notion of emplaced visualities best conceptualizes contemporary visual social media. We then conclude with a counter-trend in the face of the abundance of over-sharing – the choice not to share images.

New networked and emplaced visualities

From celebrations to disasters, camera phones have been at hand as the bystander, eye-witness, disseminator and transmitter of these moments into networked visuality. While playing an unofficial role in everyday life, camera phones have seemingly colonized every experience. No experience is too banal or quotidian to photograph and share. In their everydayness they reflect and amplify the rhythm and movements across places, spaces and temporalities (Frohlich et al., 2002; Kindberg et al., 2005; Van House et al., 2005; Whittaker et al., 2010). Camera phone apps are unquestionably shaping how images, places and memories are mapped across art, user-created content and quotidian contexts.

As we noted above, camera phone practices shape, and are shaped by, various modes for conceptualizing place. As such, camera phone cultures provide particular ways in which to understand the role of cartography and co-presence as an overlay between media, visual culture and geography (Frohlich et al., 2002; Kindberg et al., 2005; Van House et al., 2005; Rubinstein & Sluis, 2008; van Dijck, 2008; Whittaker et al., 2010; Van House, 2011; Palmer, 2012; Zylinska, 2015). Camera phones are key players in the idea of representing place (for example, maps) as performative. Camera phone practices provide playful, ambient and reflective ways to remap places and spaces across co-present platforms, contexts and subjectivities. Genres such as the selfie have become an omnipresent barometer for contemporary networked global culture (Walker Rettberg, 2014; Senft & Baym, 2015) that represent new configurations between photography, digital culture and the aforementioned 'kinesthetic sociability' (Frosh, 2015). At the crossroads between the aesthetic and the social, camera phone practices can provide insight into contemporary digital media.

While camera phone images are shaped by the affordance of mobile technologies, they also play into broader photographic tropes and genres (Palmer, 2012; Zylinska, 2015). However, for Chris Chesher (2012), the iPhone 'universe of reference' disrupts the genealogy of mass amateur photography that was formed through the rise of the Kodak camera. Moreover, the creative capacities of mobile media are transforming how photography overlays the social with the aesthetic in ways that remediate as they define new visual phenomenon (van Dijck, 2007). José van Dijck (2007), in her detailed study of digital photography, highlighted the relationship between memory and remediation.

And yet, on the other hand, through their networked and nonetheless intimate capability, camera phones also depart in terms of their ability to transgress temporal and spatial distances and differences (Van House, 2011; Villi & Stocchetti, 2011). This transgression sees camera phone pictures as part of the acceleration of accumulative global images. A political crisis or uprising on one side of the world can be viewed and experienced almost instantaneously on the other side of the world (David, 2010). Networked images have the potential to impact, effect and affect in a manner unimagined by analog photography practice (Frohlich et al., 2002; Kindberg et al., 2005; Van House et al., 2005; Whittaker et al., 2010).

Expanding upon Kodak's advertising rhetoric of making moments 'memorable' events by photographing them, camera phones not only memorialize and accelerate the number of events shared between intimates, but also act as anonymous publics. Arguments about democratizing media and user-created content have been integral to the camera phone genealogy, helped in part by the likes of Nokia, which claims to have put more cameras in the hands of everyday users than in the whole history of photography (Palmer, 2012, 2014). According to some studies, of the world's population who have taken a photo, 90 per cent have done so only with their camera phone (Palmer, 2014). In millions of images taken, shared and forgotten daily, we could argue that now we photograph, following Kafka, in order to close our eyes and drive things out of our minds. After all, in the accelerated taking and sharing of images every day, who actually has the time to view all these images? The internet is full of haunted pictures, spectres unwatched and buried under the abundance of floating images.

Over the past decade we have witnessed a shift in visual sharing practices from first-generation 'networked visuality' to second-generation 'emplaced visuality'. While first-generation camera phone practices often required users to upload images to their computer and then Flickr, second-generation camera phone practices are characterized by the ease in which taking, editing and sharing is done on the move, whereby geo-tagging (linking a photograph to a physical location through GPS) is almost a default operation. Second-generation camera phone practices – as a practice embedded within the movements of the everyday through geo-tagging – are indicative of the creative and performative aspects of cartography described by Verhoeff (2012). With locative media, in the form of geo-tagging, creating different overlays between cartographies of the geographic, social, electronic and temporal, we need to conceptualize the role that camera phones take in the playful adaptation of maps and sense of place.

Instagram provides a fascinating study given that, only seven years after its launch, the application already has over 800 million active users who have shared nearly 20 billion photos from all over the globe. Once just a vehicle for dissemination, artists are now deploying what Nathan Jurgensen (2011) calls the 'nostalgia for the present' aesthetics of Instagram as an extension of their artistic expression. In Manovich and Hochman's Phototrails,[1] images posted to Instagram form the basis of a massive visualization (which we continue to explore in Chapter 8). Here, the idea of the city is transformed by different spatial and temporal representations of images taken by people across time and space. Such a project would have been impossible, and perhaps unthinkable, not much more than a decade ago.

As discussed further in Chapter 9, Instagram provides a compelling platform for studying the ways in which visual cultures are constructed, shared and curated. In Chapter 9, we reflect upon current research on the role of Instagram and selfies, which indicates that they are providing a critical space for self-reflection and also for politicizing the body; debates about the paradoxes between visibility and invisibility ensue (Olszanowski, 2014; Carah & Louw, 2015; Tiidenberg, 2015b; Kuntsman, 2017). Indeed, there is still much more work to be done, especially ethnographically, into understanding the meanings and motivations in collaboration and the taste discourses of hashtags (Highfield & Leaver, 2015).

Camera phone apps can be seen as part of broader shifts in the ways in which visuality, place and intimacy are entangled. Increasingly, camera phone practices are being overlaid with social and locative media in ways that change *how place and time contextualize the image*. Geo-tagging renders the image stuck within a spatial 'moment' as part of a sequence of everyday movements. This can be understood as a form of emplacement: temporal, spatial, emotional and geographic. Emplaced visuality puts a theory of movement at the centre of our understanding of contemporary media practice (Hjorth & Pink, 2014). Rather than movement being between nodes in the 'network', movement needs to be understood as central to the way people and images become emplaced. That is, movement across temporalities, spatialities and subjectivities.

Camera phone practices entangle the aesthetic with the sociotechnical, a process that is encoded by the representational in the form of 'networked image' (Rubinstein & Sluis, 2008) and non-representational in 'algorithmic photography' (Uricchio, 2011). Camera phones both extend and expand upon earlier photographic tropes (van Dijck, 2008; Palmer, 2014). In particular, it is their networked and intimate capacity that affords them the ability to transgress temporal and spatial distances and differences (Van House, 2011; Villi & Stocchetti, 2011). Camera phone photography reminds us that photography has always negotiated various forms of movement (Pink, 2011). Camera phone practices underwrite the phenomenon Christian Nold (2009) identifies as emotional cartography. They are representations of fleeting moments whereby the emotional and social are overlaid onto the geographic and spatial while being shared with co-present others.

While camera phone images are shaped by the affordance of mobile technologies, they also play into broader photographic tropes and genres. For example, there is a need to link contemporary camera phone sharing with the UK-based mass observation movement, which began to define the emergence of vernacular photography early in the 20th century. However, for Chris Chesher (2012), the iPhone 'universe of reference' disrupts the genealogy of mass amateur photography that was formed through the rise of the Kodak camera, while for Edgar Gómez Cruz and Eric Meyer (2012), iPhone photography represents a fifth stage in photography. The rise of social mobile media also challenges models for curating, incubation and collaboration. It creates new affordances for making as it remediates older practices (Berry & Schleser et al., 2014). In the next section, we draw on fieldwork conducted in Japan with Kana Ohashi and Yonnie Kim which explores the rise of a counter-trend – not sharing.

The non-shared image: Networked to emplaced visuality

As we have mentioned, many scholars, such as Villi & Stocchetti (2011), have argued that what defines mobile media visuality is its networked dimension (see also Ito, 2003; Petersen, 2008). And yet, despite the compulsion of the network to make sharing a function almost by default, some participants don't share some images. For some, the reason might be that they feel the image doesn't accurately reflect their online identity or might not be of enough interest to get 'likes'.

Japan has become famous for its high-school girl pager phenomenon (Fujimoto, 2005), in which practices like public photo booths (*Purikura* or 'print club') printing stickers from camera phone images have been pioneered (Ito et al., 2005). In 1999 Japanese company Kyocera launched the first inbuilt camera 'Visual Phone', which ensured that Japan would be seminal in the growth of mobile visuality. In the face of networked visuality, new forms of understanding the network as archive featured. As Rubenstein and Sluis note in relation to the first generation of networked images through sites like Flickr, 'within this avalanche of images, the practice of tagging one's photos acts as a strategy for preventing them from disappearing from view' (2008: 18).

And yet this link between sharing, the network and memory is not for all. Rather, for some, the intimacy with the image and its significance in terms of memories and context might make them not share. Beyond such phenomenon as *Kamera-josi* ('Camera girls' or young females who carry cameras and take a lot of photos) or *Moru* (meaning to embellish and manipulate self-images to look better), mobile visuality in its second iteration of camera apps seems to be more about emplacement (Hjorth & Pink, 2014).

For Pink, the emplacement of images can be understood as 'the production and consumption of images as happening in movement, and … [can be considered] as components of configurations of place' (2011: 4). Functions such as geo-tagging emplace the image in terms of geography – that is, a configuration that identifies a specific time and place. But there are many forms of emplacement that function to locate memories for the user. We argue that non-shared photography can be understood as a reflexive social practice that involves an intimacy and emplacement between the user and the image. As van Djick notes (2007), the role of digital photography is not just about the networked image. Rather, it is part of a toolkit for an individual's identity formation. Considering that personal choices of which images to share and not to share on social networks are made under clear strategies to manage one's visual presentation in cyberspace, the act of non-sharing does not mean the loss of the social, but rather it is a different reflexive mode of the social.

In the next three sections we discuss some of the findings from ethnographic fieldwork. Through the cases of Yui, Yuzuki and Hina below, we were able to clearly see how social perception and consciousness of others affect the reluctance to sharing images. At the same time, each case presents different contexts of the act of non-sharing: a feeling to keep one's own way, an anxiety for privacy and a will to maintain a good image in the social network.

Case of Yui

21-year-old female Yui hoped to work in an art-related position in the future. Her use of social media was prompted by the acquisition of a *sumaho* (a Japanese colloquial word for smartphone) when she entered a university in April 2014. Since then, the purpose of taking pictures changed from reviewing herself to sharing on social media. She used to share pictures of delicious foods on Twitter. However, she recently started to feel embarrassed about sharing something on Twitter, Facebook and Instagram, because she came to think that she didn't want to do something that everybody else does. This made her share something less frequently, but she still often used the mobile camera.

Case of Yuzuki

Having started to use iPhone five years ago, 24-year-old Yuzuki had been willingly sharing pictures on blog, Twitter, Instagram and Facebook. However, in order to concentrate on her studying, she stopped using social media and thus no longer shared pictures with others any more. She loved taking pictures of her travels, her fashion, haircut and daily experiences, but they were only for personal viewing (see Figure 7.1). She often reviewed those pictures, with the mobile phone operating like a mobile photo album. She said that if she shared pictures on social media, it bothered her how many 'likes' and friends' reactions she received on the post, which she thought of as a waste of time.

Figure 7.1   Yuzuki takes a lot of photos but they are only for her own reviewing

Case of Hina

As a trend lover, 24-year-old Hina usually shared 'stylish-like' pictures to Instagram. Around the time when she entered university, 'camera girls' (*Kamera-josi*) became popular and then she started to use her iPhone camera prolifically, along with photo-editing apps. Recently, in order to create a more distinctive image aesthetic, she even took pictures with an instant camera, 'Utsurundesu', whereby she printed, scanned and shared the images on social media – this mode was seen as popular among camera girls like her.

Hina took a lot of pictures so her *sumaho*'s data capacity was always almost full. She liked to take pictures of foods, cute stuff (*kawaii*) and selfies. Lately, she often used a photo-editing app SNOW, in which she could 'moru' (which literally means 'add' or 'serve', and means 'increase the cuteness' in this context) to make photos look better and cuter for uploading onto Instagram or LINE. Because it was important for Hina to look cute on social media, she never shared bad-looking or uncool images (see Figure 7.2). She referred to her friends commenting on the difference between the 'screen image' and 'who I really am'. This difference informed her reluctance to post and share. However, she saved even uncool images in her *sumaho* in order to share memories with close friends.

Figure 7.2   Hina likes to take cool lifestyle photos

Conclusion: Non-disclosure and sharing

As noted previously, movements towards practices that involve non-disclosure and non-sharing are emerging against the datafication of social media. And yet, for research-ers, this is a difficult topic to explore. How can you understand the motivations and images that are not shared? How do you recruit the participants and how do you develop sensitive methods to investigate?

In literature, non-sharing has been relatively overlooked in favour of focusing upon the networked function of mobile visuality. As algorithms and Big Data create anxieties around privacy, the option and right to not share will become more prevalent (boyd & Crawford, 2011). Moreover, with the rise in 'spontaneous' and ephemeral media like Snapchat, there is increasingly a need for researchers to think about mobile visuality beyond the archive. As we have suggested through fieldwork, non-sharing of mobile visuality is about different forms of intimacy, memory and emplacement. In turn, this requires us to develop new methods that understand this non-sharing practice as part of nuanced reading of everyday life.

The notion of emplaced visuality (Pink & Hjorth, 2012) can be viewed as an essential part of second-generation camera phone practices. Emplaced visuality sees movement – across temporalities, spatialities and subjectivities – as central to the practice. With camera phone images taken and shared on the run, we need to develop theories that understand this entanglement as part of the practice in the everyday. With the rise of camera phone apps, new forms of camera phone 'platformativity' (LaMarre, 2017) occur across identity work (Walker Rettberg, 2014; Wendt, 2014), performativity (Verhoeff, 2012) and its role in creative practice/art practice (Rieser, 2011; Palmer, 2014; Zylinska, 2015), in turn further amplifying the tensions and paradoxes between user creativity and normalizations around specific platform genres. For example, as Jurgenson (2011) notes in his essay on Instagram, particular tropes around analogue genres (i.e. polaroids) are romanticized and fetishized through Instagram filters.

And yet in these emplaced visuality practices, counter-tactics like non-sharing are being used to push against the over-sharing trend. From the instantaneous and ephemeral role of Snapchat to citizens who choose not to take and share images, the significance of the visual continues to dominate social media logic and vernacular. In the next chapter, we explore the shifting relationship between art and social media and how social media artists are creating space to rethink some of the paradoxes of related theory and practice.

Note

1. http://phototrails.net/

8

Mobile Media Art: The Art of the Social

Introduction

Cindy Sherman, a famous US photographer, released her new series of digital art on Instagram in August 2017. This was much more than an example of an artist using social media as a vehicle for publicity. In doing this, Sherman spearheaded the crucial role of social media – especially mobile media – in contemporary art practice. Sherman's use of Instagram as a gallery highlighted social media as a key context and platform for art production and exhibition. Unfazed by the complicated relationship between Instagram, artist and copyright, Sherman launched her new works by shifting her profile settings from private to public. Known for her analogue pre-social media 'selfies' (self-portraits) that are inspired by everything from Hollywood stars to grotesque monsters, Sherman continues to push our understandings of self-portraiture. The recent work by Sherman demonstrates mobile media's role as integral to contemporary art, both as a way of viewing art and as a subject of the art itself. Sherman showcased the selfie as art and at the same time has further problematized the complex relationship between art and mobile media art.

As we can understand from history, there is often a complex relationship between new technology and art. New technologies usher in new forms of art, which are often contested and also change the way that art is made. When photography was invented in the 19th century, some saw it as a replacement for painting, removing the need for painted portraits. Yet at the same time, the art world responded to photography in hundreds of different ways, becoming more abstract, or more hyper-real, demonstrating the modes of expression that an artist could access and share with audiences beyond what a device that simply captured light could achieve. At the same time, photography itself became a form of art, both a comment on the specificities of photography as a medium, and an exploration of the new forms of expression that the camera made possible – new visualities unlocked by high shutter speeds, or high magnification, for example.

More recently, mobile media and its attendant networked, ubiquitous online and social relations have become an important site for creative practice. In this chapter, we look at mobile media art and how its specificities have given rise to new forms of art, which are only made possible by and through the mobile device. This leads us to a more fundamental question, which we explore in this chapter: is it reasonable to subsume mobile art within the broader rubric of media arts, or is it emerging as a form of art in its own right? As we delve into the implications of this question in this chapter, we'll see how art challenges us to think about our social, political and cultural world, and to understand it through a different lens. Through the lens of mobile art, and the debate about its status within the art world, we reflect on the role of the mobile, and its role in the social in our modern world.

This chapter begins by outlining the question: 'Mobile art or mobile media art?' We define media art and quickly outline the basic territory of the debate before building on Hjorth's previous work in this area (this should assist with nailing down some definitions for readers who are less familiar with arts practice). We will discuss mobile art as a form and move from a discussion of mobile art as being more than locative media art, to exploring some of the features of mobile art that challenge the usefulness of identifying it simply as an instance of media art. Throughout we will use examples of artists and their works to illustrate and contextualize the points we are making.

Mobile art or mobile media art?

So, can mobile art be considered a form in and of itself, or is it better understood as a sub-category of a broader media arts practice? To engage with this question, it is useful first to define our terms. Media arts is a broad field of artistic practice and inquiry that has been an established and accepted mode of art practice since at least the 1960s. Media arts are distinguished from other art forms, such as painting, sculpture or photography, because media arts are often time-based. Examples include television, film and video works, but have increasingly come to incorporate computational and interactive art as computers have become ever more ubiquitous. The US National Endowment for the Arts (NEA) defines media arts as:

> all genres and forms that use electronic media, film and technology (analog and digital; old and new) as an artistic medium or a medium to broaden arts appreciation and awareness of any discipline. For example, this includes projects presented via film, television, radio, audio, video, the Internet, interactive and mobile technologies, video games, immersive and multi-platform storytelling, and satellite streaming.[1]

It's notable here that the NEA includes mobile technologies within the rubric of media arts. It demonstrates how mobile media art has been subsumed under the increasingly broad categorization of 'media art'. While this might be a sufficient operational definition for a funding body such as the NEA, it is not broadly useful for sustained discussion, given the breadth and complexity of the works within the *œuvre* of mobile media art. We might ask, for example, how supportable is this definition when we come to examine actual mobile art practice? As social mobile media becomes increasingly commonplace, it occupies a progressively complicated role in art practice, reception and production. While mobile media is often defined as quintessentially quotidian, as the NEA quote above demonstrates, within the art world it is often still classified – and rarefied – as media arts (Bishop, 2012a, 2012b).

Hjorth claimed that mobile art helps to reconceptualize the relationship between new media and art in innovative ways (Hjorth, 2016). In her article, she built upon earlier work by mobilities scholar Mimi Sheller (2014) and Adriana de Souza e Silva (2004), among others. Hjorth re-situated contemporary mobile art as a more diverse set of practices that were situational and process-driven, not simply the screening of digital art on portable devices. As Sheller points out:

> Mobile art has in fact expanded the spatial and social field in which art takes place by experimenting with the mobile interface as a bridge between digital and physical space, a hybrid mediation of human sensory perception, and technological connectivity. (2014: 376).

For Sheller, part of the problem with defining mobile art is the way in which it has been subsumed as a category of practice within media arts, itself situated within the even broader visual art discourses. This is further complicated as theorists have sometimes underestimated (or even dismissed) the role and importance of digital art in visual practice. A key example used by Sheller is what she sees as art critic and historian Claire Bishop's (2012a) dismissal of shifts in contemporary digital art that are impacting visual art practice more broadly.

According to Sheller, mobile art has the potential to expand the dimensions of art more broadly. Ignoring the potential of mobile art with respect to art practice more generally is a little like thinking about social media as something that 'computer-people' do, rather than as a substantial shift that is affecting many aspects of social and cultural life. Mobile art is not really just a form of practice for new media artists: the mobile has become a mode of art practice that provides new canvases, contexts and modes of engagement for a range of artists in many different fields.

Emphasizing mobile art's broad set of practices is its extensive diversity, in terms of form, subject and public profile. Artists such as Ai Weiwei (Twitter), Amy Sillman (iPhone) and Jonah Brucker-Cohen to Scott Snibbe (App art), Rafael Lozano Hemmer (locative media) and Man Bartlett ('Social Media Artist') have all been active in utilizing digital technologies under the banner of mobile art to erode the divisions between (new) media art and visual art. Some artists and collectives, such as Blast Theory and Proboscis, have engaged with locative media as the intersection between urban performance, transmedia storytelling (often involving augmented reality games [ARG]), play and mobile intervention.

While not focusing specifically on 'mobile art', collectives like MINA (Mobile Innovative Network Aoteroa; see Figure 8.1) have sought to explore the relationship between mobile media and creative practice as a way to reframe existing art practice, or to extend it in new ways made possible by the mobile device. For example, Marsha Berry and Max Schleser's edited volume details a range of new practices based around the smartphone, ranging across topics like photography, storytelling and mobile movie making (Berry & Schleser, 2014; see also Berry, 2017).

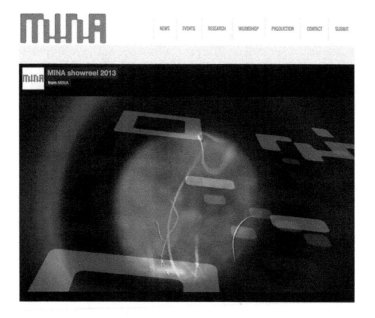

Figure 8.1   MINA brings together mobile media practitioners to reconceptualize creative practice

All these different artists and collectives bring together a complex interdisciplinary mix of artistic endeavour. Despite often coming from different disciplinary perspectives, their work interrogates the relationship between the aesthetic, kinaesthetic, social and spatial in ways that could expand the lens, compass and territory of art and mobile communication. To interrogate these ideas further, in the rest of this chapter we will look at four characteristics of mobile art as a way of organizing the discussion of the larger questions around the status of mobile art as a category of media arts. These characteristics are: everyday; mobile; networked, social and participatory; and critical and self-reflexive.

Everyday: First, mobile devices are increasingly mundane and everyday. It's simply not remarkable to see people engaging with their mobile devices. This everyday, ubiquitous element of mobile devices has implications for their use in mobile art on two levels. First, as they're always with us, mobile art can also become part of the everyday. Second, because they have become such a visible and quotidian element of modern society, it seems inevitable that artists reflecting on the modern world should engage with the mobile and its attendant social practices. We'll explore a number of artists who are doing just this below. Rather than examining the everyday nature of the mobile device (as we've discussed this in other chapters), you will see it emerging as a consistent theme in the sections below.

Mobility: Second, and most obviously, mobile art is mobile. The implications of this are important. Using geolocation services such as GPS, mobile devices can detect their location in the physical world and respond to this. This allows artists to integrate location awareness into their work. Since some of the best-known and earliest examples of mobile art were based around locative work, mobile art has sometimes been equated with locative practice, instead of seeing locative practices as just one element of mobile art. Hjorth (2016) has explored the role of mobile art as an often-overlooked area that has been historically sublimated under locative, hybrid, mixed reality or media arts. She argues that while having a long history through various genres, such as locative arts and vernacular art practices, mobile art is much broader than this, and so needs to be more robustly defined and taken more seriously by scholars.

Networked, social and participatory: Third, mobile devices are networked. That is, they are connected to each other through digital telecommunications infrastructure. This feature of the mobile device, alongside its mobility, is probably its most defining feature. Mobile art frequently engages with the social, either by reflecting on the implications of living in a networked always-on society, or, more practically, by integrating sociability directly into art practice through active participation.

Critical: Fourth, mobile art is critical; that is, it encourages us to reconsider and reframe the world around us, and by doing so raises questions that we might not otherwise have considered. Of course, good art does this too, but mobile art is in a unique position to engage with and address issues such as datafication, digital sociality and new visualities, which are born of the digital mobile device.

Together, these factors not only provide a framework for understanding the scope of mobile art (and, not unimportantly, provide a way to highlight some key works), but also emphasize that it is increasingly difficult to distinguish between digital and non-digital art practice, to define mobile art as a subcategory of media art, and as time goes on and our social lives become increasingly mobile, even brings into question whether mobile art isn't just art.

Mobile art: Beyond the locative

The fact that mobile devices are, as their name suggests, designed to be used untethered immediately implicates them with considerations of space and place. Mobile devices move with us through the world, and as we bring them along with us we also bring with them our attachments to networks. This provides us with a unique form of what Mimi Sheller (2014) refers to as mobile mediality. This doesn't exactly mean that mobile art is characterized by the device (although it may be) but, more than that, it is characterized as a way of thinking with and working through the world that is mobile-derived. For Sheller, an important element of this is that mobile art is engaged with both network and space (we'll pick up the discussion of networks more fully in the next section), and this mobile mediality leads to certain kinds of artistic practices that are quintessential to mobile art.

An immediate application of mobile mediality is locative media. As mentioned above, and discussed more fully in Chapter 6, locative media utilizes the mobile device's awareness of its location in space. This can be as simple as triggering a sound when someone moves within a fixed distance of a certain object or it may be a more complicated conversation between the artist, the device, the physical space and the user.

Compelling as locative media may be, its success is also a problem, as it has sometimes come to define mobile art practice. One of the reasons there has been a conflation of mobile art with media arts is due to its history in earlier exhibitions, such as *LA Replay* (2006), that have narrowly focused upon mobile media art only as locative media (de Souza e Silva, 2004; Hemment, 2006; Tuters & Varnelis, 2006; Benford & Giannachi, 2011). These earlier iterations sought to define mobile art in and around media or digital arts, but in doing so they highlighted some of the ways in which mobile art occupied an exciting area of possibility that promised to interrogate not just mobile communication but art practice more generally.

Media artists such as Rafael Lozano Hemmer (see Figure 8.2) were early adopters of mobile media and information and communications technology (ICTs) and helped to imagine the ways that mobile art could reside within the broader practice of visual arts. These early works tended to emphasize and engage with the time-based elements of the medium without reflecting upon many of the other dimensions of mobile art, which we discuss below. This succeeded inmaking mobile and new media art more visible, but didn't fully realize its many dimensions, and instead limited them to the category of media arts.

Figure 8.2 Rafael Lozano Hemmer, *Body Movies* (2001)

More recently, artists have begun reflecting more critically on mobile art, seeking to expand the field. Mimi Sheller, Jeremy Hight and Hana Iverson's *LA Re.Play* exhibition (2012) was one such exploration. In this exhibition, the curators sought to bring together works that, while still focusing on the importance of place, also embraced the social and quotidian. As Iverson said: 'This is public art, accessible in the context and sequence of our everyday lives. But it is invisible, ephemeral and magical.' [2]

The exhibition showed numerous examples of artists engaging in space as a social domain, utilizing the everydayness of the mobile device as a platform for enhancing and adjusting real-world spaces, and our experience within those spaces. Moving beyond the visual, Teri Rueb's *Elsewhere: Anderswo* (Figure 8.3) uses location-based audio to place the user/audience into different audial spaces:

> Sounds play automatically in response to their movements in the landscape. As they move through layer upon layer of responsive sound, 'little elsewheres' are grafted onto the landscape in the form of variously local and foreign, synchronous and asynchronous 'soundtracks'. (Sheller et al. 2016: 20)

Figure 8.3 Teri Rueb's *Elsewhere: Anderswo* (2009)

As Rueb's piece demonstrates, locative media quickly becomes about a relationship between artist, audience, place and technology, with each component contextualizing and anchoring the other. Physical locations become augmented and changed by the new visual or audial experiences provide by the technology, and can also change the user, who can be invited to move into and through the augmented space. In doing this, opportunities arise for participants to experience the spaces in new ways, with new eyes and ears. This is not simply media apart from the world, but an entanglement between people, technology and place. *Park Walk* by

Martha Ladly and Bruce Hinds (Figure 8.4) is indicative of the works in *LA Re.Play* and the role mobile art can play in performing, mapping and intervening in a sense of place.

Figure 8.4 *Park Walk* by Martha Ladly and Bruce Hinds in *LA Re.Play* (2012). (Image of the Park Walk Project, 2008. Copyright Martha Ladly, Bruce Hinds. Design: Nevena Niagolova)

Another example of spatial intervention can be seen in the 2012 augmented reality (AR) work of artist Nancy Baker Cahill, who engaged in direct dialogue with mobile media. Cahill's project was designed to be viewed in the context of the mobile device, whereby downloading an app enabled the viewer to load up the artworks and see them superimposed in the real world (as seen through the camera on the mobile device). They could occupy a room or dominate the skyline of a city. The juxtaposition of these works within different environments defines them as locative and mobile, but also raises important questions about the nature of the art. Is this new media art, public art, sculpture, painting, or something else altogether?

The diversity of works in *LA Re.Play* illustrates that mobile art cannot just be conflated with locative media. While locative media is a component of mobile art, there is much more variation within this genre. Further, works like *Park Walk* draw upon the audience's relationship with place to augment space and create a complex relationship between artist, work and place. Here, space is not just a canvas for the work; it's part of it. Reflecting this, in the exhibition summary mobile art was defined as more than just geo-located media. Instead, all the artworks explored different notions of place *and* sociality. While highlighting a diversity of practice, *LA Re.Play* also demonstrated the contested definitions constituting mobile media art.

Mobile arts and the social

As we explored the idea of mobility and place in the previous section, we also collided with another overlapping feature of mobile art – the social. From their earliest inception, one of the defining features of the mobile device (alongside its obvious mobility) was its fundamentally social function. As a mobile telephone, the device allowed us to connect with other people, no matter where we were, through both the traditional audio/voice modes of communication, and then, increasingly, through text. With the advent of mobile internet, smartphone technology and social media, the social dimensions of the mobile expanded greatly. This fundamental social element of the mobile device highlights another of its features beyond being another 'time-based' medium. Mobile art is increasingly reflecting and utilizing the social element of the mobile device.

As shown in the opening vignette of this chapter, Cindy Sherman's Instagram selfies highlight the way that art has always occupied a paradoxical relationship with respect to the everyday and social. This relationship extends from Duchamp's 'Fountain' in 1917, which challenged the relationship between art and the everyday by positioning a urinal in a gallery space, to the critical everyday artistic social interventions of the Situationist International (SI). In the 21st century the social has become more overt, with movements such as relational aesthetics (Bourriaud, 2002 [1998]) gaining currency – as typified by artists like Rikrit Tiravanija, in which the artwork is the social interaction that happens at an artist-staged event. Art practice in a post-relational aesthetics world has become increasingly preoccupied with the social as medium. For example, 'social practice' (Kester, 2011) is an artistic medium in which the focus of the art is the process of making the art rather than the final artwork itself. While artwork may, for example, see the production of a painting, the artwork is the production of that painting, and so being able to see the finished painting is not a way to experience the art. Indeed, in many instances social practice may not produce any final tangible artefact.

On the one hand, then, the social is an increasingly hot topic within the art world, while on the other hand social media itself is becoming increasingly implicated in the production of art. With the ubiquity of the mobile device, the always-at-hand social media, and more artists using social media apps on phones to create, edit and exhibit their work, mobile media art is becoming an important territory for artists exploring the relationship between the quotidian and art. Here mobile media are often implicated either inexplicitly or explicitly in art as a social/cultural encounter (Hjorth & Sharp, 2014: 128).

The diversity of mobile social media art is varied and often contradictory. For example, artist Richard Prince controversially appropriated people's Instagram pictures to exhibit and sell for US$100,000 at a gallery, highlighting the tenuous nature between individual intellectual property rights and social media. In Zach Gage's *best day ever* a Twitter bot posts an automatic post at 6.30am every day.[3] Jenny Holzer, known for her use of LED signage to present one-line textual provocations, had a fake Twitter account created by an impersonator. The account posts Holzer-like statements in capital letters, and has attracted more than 70,000 followers,[4] despite Holzer herself having nothing to do with the account. There are also many artists who conceptualize mobility for socially-driven art making, such as the project *pplkpr*[5] by Lauren McCarthy and Kyle McDonald. This collaboration developed an app to track, analyse and auto-manage social relationships. Using a smart watch to monitor the physical and emotional responses to the people around you, it enabled the user to 'optimize your social life accordingly'.

For Sheller et al. in their *LA Re.Play* mobile art exhibition, discussed above, the networked and social aspects of mobile art are key to their success. In, this exhibition, mobile media art encompassed:

> Playing upon the dynamic relations between physical place, digital space, and mobile access via smartphone, the mobile artworks highlighted in the exhibit and the panels adopt elements of location-based performance, mobile gaming, and mobile, networked activism to highlight the embodied performance of hybrid place and the social and collective politics of networked space. We explore art that incorporates cell phones, GPS and other mobile technology, revealing the complex social, political, technological and physiological effects of new mixed reality interactions. (Sheller et al. 2016: n.p.).

So, while the locative element played an important role in providing many of the works with spatiality, the networked elements of mobile artworks provided the important social facets that allowed the works to extend beyond an engagement with space alone. As an understanding of mobile art expands beyond the locative and into the social, the divide between what constitutes the digital and non-digital in art practice is now increasingly blurred.

Emphasizing this blur, a number of artists are increasingly using social and mobile media as part of participatory practice. This is a substantially important element of mobile art practice as it collides with a broader movement where the artist's aesthetic autonomy gives way to a practice that is perhaps better understood as collaboration between the artist and other participants. Through analysis of collaborative practice and moving outside the sanctuary of the gallery space (Jenkins, 2006; Kester, 2011), artists are increasingly embracing participatory practices. The key tool here is the networked, social mobile device.

There are numerous examples that illustrate the way that artists are using social and participatory techniques in their art via the mobile, either as a viewing frame where the viewer is participating through their engagement, or, more overtly, by becoming a collaborator in the production of the art itself. A great example of the multiplicity of the mobile device is Cardiff and Miller's *Alter Bahnhof Video Walk*, which was exhibited at the 2012 Venice Biennale. In this work, the viewer watches a recorded video on his or her mobile device while occupying the same physical space in which the video was originally filmed. The viewer moves around the space under the direction of the narrator in a form of digital wayfaring (Hjorth & Pink, 2014). While they do so, they experience two overlapping realities: the world as it is now, replete with the viewer's subjectivity; and, the world as it was then, when the video was recorded, complete with the audio of the artist and her subjectivity. Yet the art emerges in the interaction between the two subjectivities – it is never the same twice, as each play-through forming a unique, participatory and very much performative collaboration between artist and viewer (Figure 8.5).

Figure 8.5   An example of Cardiff and Miller's digital wayfaring work (2012)

In another project, this time located in Tokyo, artists engaged participants in a digital treasure hunt:

Participants will be given 15 minutes to take camera phone pictures of the sea creatures whose habitat is Tokyo. You must then distinguish between the real and imaginary, local and foreign objects and send ONLY the images of Tokyo-related sea creatures to the *keitai mizu* Twitter account (@keitaimizu) via camera phone apps like Instagram.[6]

In collaboration with the Boat People Association and the environmental art project *Spatial Dialogues*, and entitled *keitai mizu* (mobile water), the project sought to make audiences aware of the underwater cartographies hidden under a park. Here the gamification aspects of mobile apps can be deployed to enhance the audience's understanding of their environment through a hybrid reality of physical and digital wayfaring. Again, while the artists directed and created material for the event, the artwork itself was participatory, although this time motivated by playfulness and with an explicit gamic element (Figure 8.6).

@keitaimizu めだかの群れ。90年代
983 days ago via **jigtwi for Android**   ⊙ 115

@keitaimizu どじょう。90年代。
983 days ago via **jigtwi for Android**   ⊙ 124

Figure 8.6 Images from the *keitai mizu* mobile game – in the park and via Instagram

Larissa Hjorth's 2016 exhibition *The Art of Play*, at the Centre for Contemporary Photography on Melbourne, Australia, provides another example of the ways in which social media is used to support participatory art practice. Hjorth's work constructed a playful environment made up of wooden cubes, Lego building blocks, vinyl cloud stickers and grass cut-outs, referencing the constructively playful computer game *Minecraft*. Audiences were encouraged to engage with these items and construct their own worlds, which they could then photograph and share via Instagram. The shared images were printed and generatively exhibited on the wall, creating a participatory artwork (Figure 8.7).

Figure 8.7 CCP Gallery installation: *Minecraft* cubes filled Lego and *Minecraft* wall clouds (Photo: J. Forsyth)

During the exhibition period, the wall filled with the playful expressions and interventions of the audience-as-artist. Their images went up alongside the exhibited ethnographic images inside people's homes. The audience-as-artist images went from the sanctuary of the gallery space to social media and back to the gallery again – a journey that took on deploys Instagram and Facebook to comment on the politics (see Figure 8.8).

From these works, it becomes clear that the networked mobile device is a fundamentally social instrument that allows artists and their work to do much more than just be a platform for sharing of work. It presents an extremely effective site for the artist to engage with a larger discourse about art and the social, and the social and the everyday. Furthermore, mobile art represents an excellent site for participatory art practice, which, facilitated by the mobile and social media, can be seen in the work of a number of artists and collectives.

Figure 8.8   Social media images from audience-as-playmakers/artists

Critical mobile arts

A final key point about mobile art that helps distinguish it from other forms of art is the utility it provides for critiquing its own form. Most art is critical, in that it can challenge our beliefs and assumptions about the world around us. But mobile art, which as we have seen is fundamentally concerned with, and implicated in, the everyday and the social, is well situated towards building a critical perspective on mobile and social media.

Some artists have chosen to focus attention of sociality, modes of communication and the content of social media. For example, Anastasia Klose, who uses quotidian performance in her art, often deploys Instagram and Facebook to comment on the politics of social media in relation to art (Figure 8.9).

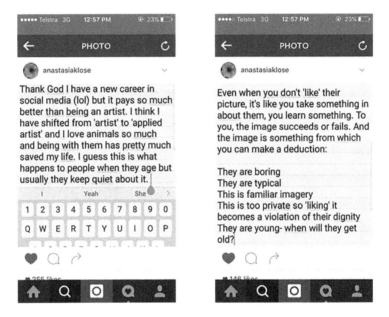

Figure 8.9 Anastasia Klose on Instagram comments on the politics of 'Like' and makes fun of social media careers

In Mann Bartlett's work, mobile media like Twitter become a social and political space to test the role of art. He toys with the collapse between the public and intimate – an adaptation of Lauren Berlant's notion of intimate publics (Hjorth et al., 2014). Hjorth et al. (2014: 2) note that as social, locative and mobile media render the intimate *public* and the public *intimate*, this is shaping – and being shaped by – the role of place, art practice and politics, which in turn provide new models for engagement, distribution and participation.

Ukrainian artist Nastya Ptichek draws upon symbology taken from social media para-linguistics such as *emojis* (picture characters) and emoticons (typographic characters) and uses them to reimagine and recast classic artworks. Ptichek reinvents and remedi-ates existing works through her paralinguistic interventions (Figures 8.10 and 8.11). These interventions are playful, sometimes irreverent and frequently humorous (assum-ing the viewer has at least a passing appreciation of modern mobile, computational or online cultures).

The long history of emoticons in media textual communication practice (Crystal, 2006) has been well documented. More recently, research into *emoji* has highlighted their significance as historical, social and cultural objects (Stark & Crawford, 2015). Their significance in human communication is also somewhat acknowledged by their inclu-sion in the Unicode standard, which defines the character codes for letters, characters and numbers on computer systems. The rise of *emojis* and other forms of ASCII-based non-standard variants, such as emoticons, highlights the role of digital media to create different affective affordances (Pavalanathan & Eisenstein, 2016).

Paralinguistic forms of communication continue to evolve and develop as the technologies – networks and devices – that support communication increase in capacity. Now we are beginning to see additional paralinguistic cues entering communication,

Figure 8.10   Nastya Ptichek

such as stickers. As Luke Stark and Kate Crawford (2015) note, LINE in Japan has introduced the 'next-level emoji' through their deployment of stickers. Facebook Messenger also has its own version of stickers, as does the Apple iPhone, and services such as Giphy provide additional paralinguistic elements such as short animated image-videos (Jiang et al., 2017). Ptichek's work suggests a more complex relationship in which paralinguistics can be understood as an emergent art form whose impact should not be underestimated.

Figure 8.11 Nastya Ptichek

As we introduced in Chapter 2 and discussed more substantially in Chapter 4, data politics has become an increasingly important consideration in the scholarship around social and mobile media. It's hardly surprising that artists are also engaging with data through the lens of mobile art as a space to comment on data politics in powerful ways. The role of the artist in critically reflecting on data is becoming increasingly valuable in a world where data plays an ever more important economic and political role in our lives, and yet frequently remains beyond mainstream critique. This is especially the case against the backdrop of the Quantified Self (QS), gamification and the increasingly 'playful' attitude of contemporary media (Sicart, 2014).

An important area of critical response is creative data visualization work using Big Data to investigate the socialities, intimacies and tensions that are reflected within them (Hochmann & Manovich, 2013). Lev Manovich, a well-known new media theorist and practitioner, has embraced Big Data with big visualizations. He and his collaborators combine art and computer science to produce visual images and interactive works that reveal patterns in data that might otherwise be hidden in complexity.

In one of his works, *Visual Earth*,[7] Manovich visualizes 270 million geo-tagged images posted on Twitter across the globe, and analyses the data collected to reveal patterns in the data, such as the negative correlation between the growth of image sharing on Twitter and economic development. In another collaborative project called *Phototrails* (2011), Manovich explores what he calls 'Big Visual Data' through millions of photographs shared at specific locations via Instagram (Figure 8.12). Manovich states that *Phototrails*

> is a research project that uses media visualization techniques (API) for exploring visual patterns, dynamics and structures in user generated photos. Using a sample of 2.3 million Instagram photos from 13 cities around the world, we show how temporal changes in the number of shared photos, their locations, and visual characteristics can uncover social, cultural and political insights about people's activity around the world.[8]

In *Phototrails*, Manovich and his team have used the collected data from millions of data points to produce visualizations that reveal patterns pointing to behaviours that are sometimes expected and sometimes surprising. Because of the flexibility of the data and approaches to visualization, it's possible to reconfigure images in different ways, revealing connections and relations between them that are not immediately visible. For example, Hochman and Manovich highlight that the key feature of geo-temporal tagging is that it 'suppresses temporal, vertical structures in favor of spatial connectivities' (2013: n.p.). In other words, it becomes possible to see relationships between place and space and image, which in turn yield new insights and questions about mobile image taking and sharing.

Some artists are using Big Data visualizations as a way to highlight experience that goes beyond the immediately mobile. The pervasiveness of modern data collection means that many everyday activities can be highlighted through thoughtful representation of collected data sets. Australian company Small Multiples, for example, describes itself as 'a

PHOTOTRAILS   ABOUT INSTAGRAM CITIES TECHNIQUES PUBLICATIONS EXHIBITION TEAM PRESS CONTACT

Figure 8.12 Manovich's *Phototrails*, Instagram Big Data visualization (2013)

multidisciplinary team of data specialists, designers and developers' who use data visualization as a tool that can reveal fascinating insights into the everyday. For example, their visualization of bus routes for Sydney's Star Casino reveal the deliberate relations between bus routes and non-English-speaking migrant communities in Sydney.[9]

Again, working with data, but this time on a more personal level, Regina Flores Mir and Hang Do Thi Duc aim to create a kind of mirror they call a 'data selfie'[10] that highlights the data that companies like Facebook collect, and which we share freely. Data selfie is an extension for the Chrome and Firefox browsers that tracks the interaction with Facebook and builds a profile of the individual from user clicks, likes and posts. By presenting this data back to the viewer, they highlight the way that apparently mundane Facebook interactions can begin to build a powerful snapshot of the individual.

Another intervention with the small data of the individual is seen in *Unfit Bits*. Reflecting on the Quantified Self and the uses and abuses of personal self-tracking data,

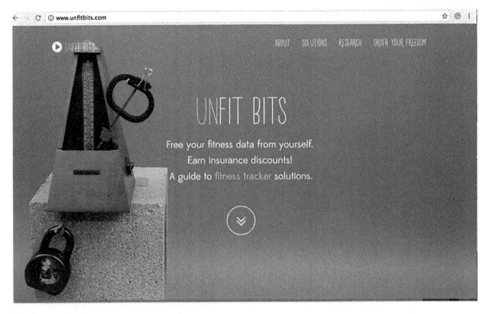

Figure 8.13   The playfully subversive *Unfit Bits* makes fun of the self-tracking phenomenon

the collective known as Unfit Bits takes a playful and humorous approach. Laced with irony, Unfit Bits encourages their audience to 'take the chip off the shoulder' and subvert health insurance companies by attaching tracking devices like FitBits to bicycles, drills and metronomes (Figure 8.13).

As we discussed in Chapter 4, interventions like *Unfit Bits* can be seen as part of a growing response to the colonization of everyday life by Big Data that is spearheaded by mobile artists. Other interventions, such as those by artists like Egor Tsvetkov, whose work we saw in Chapters 4 and 5, are critically reflecting on tracking and Big Data techniques, using those same techniques, with perhaps a darker and more subversive edge.

The examples explored in this section show only the smallest fragment of the ways that mobile art practice is critically exploring the consequences of a mobile social world. Across different methods, in each case artists utilize the specificities of the mobile data-entrenched world as a tool to reflect back on that world. Star Casino bus routes are made visible because of the ready availability of networked bus route data, which in turn becomes the 'paint' for exploration and exposition through data. The possibilities for mobile art to critique mobile and social media are endless.

More than a like: Conclusions on mobile art

In this chapter we've attempted to provide an overview of mobile art practice in order to show how mobile art is engaging with some of the more fundamental questions regarding the intersections between culture, society and mobile technology. We've argued that mobile art is doing much more than just providing a platform for the presentation and dissemination of art works. Instead, the ubiquity of the mobile and social media has become so entrenched in the everyday that it's now not uncommon for artists to engage with the mobile and the networked social, even if the artist doesn't identify as a media artist.

While mobile art may sometimes have been conflated with locative practice, we've seen that even locative mobile art engages with an entanglement between place and the social. Rueb's *Elsewhere: Anderswo* or Cardiff and Miller's *Alter Bahnhof Video Walk* both provide great examples of how mobile art interacts with space and place to understand it in different contexts.

Beyond this, mobile art's social element allows the artist to engage even more substantially with the viewer, bringing them into their world, or even making them partners in the production of collaborative participatory artworks, as we saw in Hjorth's *Art as Play* exhibition. The ease with which mobile art engages with the social is particularly cogent, as the social becomes a topic of increasing critical focus within the arts more broadly.

Finally, the potential for media art to provide a critical lens for the range of mobile and social media practices that configure so much of the world today highlights the role it can play in helping us come to terms with a social world that is constantly evolving through technologies and their uses. Whether it is through the whimsical interventions of works like *Data Selfie*, or the more hardheaded Big Data visualizations that Manovich and his collaborators are producing, mobile art (and art derived from mobile practices) provides us with insights into the social and mobile technologies and their implications.

Mobile art is an exciting and emerging field that raises questions and encourages us to participate in finding answers to those questions. It provides a place that is designed for experimentation within the messy space of the social and quotidian. While steeped in a history of new media practice, in many ways it transcends that history and invites us into conversations that are sometimes deemed difficult or challenging.

Notes

1. www.arts.gov/artistic-fields/media-arts
2. www.prweb.com/releases/2012/2/prweb9178552.htm

3. This work pays homage to conceptual works like On Kawara's *I GOT UP*, in which he stamped a postcard and sent it to his friends everyday from 1968 to 1979.
4. https://twitter.com/jennyholzer
5. http://pplkpr.com/
6. http://spatialdialogues.net/tokyo/keitaimizu/
7. http://visual-earth.net/
8. http://phototrails.info/
9. https://smallmultiples.com.au/projects/casino-bus-maps---the-cash-cow-suburbs/#
10. https://dataselfie.it

9

Museums & New Visualities

Introduction

A young girl leans back into the infamous picture of Ai Weiwei's middle-finger gesture photo of Tiananmen Square and mimics it as she takes an Instagram selfie. She hashtags it #aiweiwei #selfie. Within a few minutes many of her friends have liked the picture, along with strangers attracted by the hashtag. Elsewhere in another gallery, a mother takes an Instagram selfie of herself with her young baby to memorialize their first gallery visit together. In another city, three friends take an Instagram selfie while doing the peace fingers gesture against the backdrop of an Andy Warhol picture, so they can share the moment with co-present friends. In another museum, a curator takes an Instagram selfie with a famous artist who is installing their exhibition as a teaser-marketing ploy.

All of these vignettes involve Instagram selfies, and yet the motivations, context, aesthetics and meanings are distinctively different. They highlight some of the multiple ways in which Instagrams and selfies are infiltrating the museum and gallery context. Recognizing these changes in the way people engage with museums and galleries invites us to ask questions about how they are being reshaped and recalibrated in the age of social media. Examples of the kinds of questions range from how choices are made about what gets exhibited (i.e. 'Is it Instagrammable?'), to how curation works as a participatory, dynamic relation, and through to how education and outreach programming works when we involve communities more fully through social media.

In this chapter, we explore some of these questions through the way that social media – particularly visual forms like Instragram – are being integrated into the experience of visiting a museum. Underlying this is the observation that museums and galleries have changed significantly in recent years. While they still collect, preserve and show collections of artefacts, they have become increasingly proactive in engaging with communities. In part, this has been driven by changes in funding, with governments expecting to see evidence that investment in museums and galleries is translating to community benefit. This has in turn forced museums to become more outward-looking, and to think more about the experience of the visitor.

At the same time, people's experience of museums is changing due in no small part to mobile and social media technologies. Going to a museum or gallery with a smartphone is an opportunity to share an experience with co-present friends and family, allowing for a more personalized museum experience, and also opening up opportunities for museums and galleries to engage with visitors at a more personal level. Spurred by technology and policy, museums are now increasingly engaging with their visitors and encouraging them to participate in ways that were not possible in the past.

Some museums, for example, have already been experimenting with mobile media like augmented reality (AR) to create forms of emplacement that mediate place, image and history. With the coalescence of social, locative and mobile media in now commonplace smartphones, the intimate becomes *public* and the public the *intimate*. This process shapes, and is being shaped by, the role of place, art practice and politics, which in turn provide new models for engagement, distribution and participation (Hjorth et al., 2014).

This chapter builds on the ideas and concepts we explored in Chapter 7, 'Social Media Visualities', and expands that discussion to consider the specific role of Instagram and the selfie within the changing logic of the museum. As art museums and galleries become increasingly aggressive in their ways of engaging 'eyeballs', audiences and measuring cultural impact for funding bodies and philanthropy, media such as Instagram play a more complex and central role.

A key paradox that this chapter explores is the criticism that mobile devices often detract from an experience. This criticism is related to the perception of attentiveness; rather than being in the present, people are often criticized for focusing their attention on their phones rather than the world (or event, or exhibition, or gallery) around them. Yet despite this, one of the things that emerges from the discussion below is that instead of taking people away from the experience of the museum or gallery, devices may actually deepen the experience. They become a vehicle for a heightened, more personalized engagement while also bringing co-present people into the user's experience, thus extending the museum or gallery experience to people who may not even be able to visit. The paradox implicit here is that our devices can be seen both to distract from but also to enhance our experience of a time, place or event.

This chapter begins with a discussion of Instagram in the museum context. It then looks at how selfies are recalibrating contemporary visual cultures in ways that we are only now starting to comprehend. Far from mere vehicles for narcissism, selfies speak of complex overlays between sociality, identity and context and emerging aesthetics. We then turn to some insights from practitioners working in the field.

Setting the context

As Martin Rieser (2011) notes in *The Mobile Audiences: Media Art and Mobile Technologies*, mobile technologies are affording new types of audience engagement, art and narrative forms. Think about how iBeacon[1] (a virtual navigation app viewed through the mobile device) in the *Rijksacademie* in Amsterdam creates a particular mediation and context. As Nanna Verhoeff (2013) notes in her work on mobile devices as active curatorial tools in museums, social proprioception – that is, the embodied experience of movement as a social activity and way of knowing the world – and cartography are performative. This performative dimension is no more apparent than in the case of camera-phone practices in urban spaces where they meditate and re-present, reframe and play a powerful role in the experiencing, representation and performance of place as a cyclic visual culture.

And yet, few studies on camera phones have connected the potential citizenship and vernacular agency[2] around apps like Instagram (Kuntsman, 2017). There is a disconnect between the studies around identity work (Walker Rettberg, 2014; Wendt, 2014), creative practice/art practice (Rieser, 2011; Palmer, 2014; Zylinska, 2015) and its role in reconfiguring how we experience and represent place (Farman, 2011) and citizenship. Mobile media play a key role in emergent intimate publics, whereby binaries such as online/offline, public/private and work/personal are eschewed. Mobile media actively presence-bleed (Gregg, 2011) in ways that open up the hierarchies of arts institutions into new modes of art being in the world.

Increasingly, it is hard to visit an art gallery or museum and not have multiple mobile screens co-curating and sharing co-present images and interpretations via an extension of hashtag micronarratives. As scholars such as Kylie Budge and Adam Seuss (2018, n.p.) note, 'Instagram is changing the way we experience art, and that's a good thing'. As Budge and Seuss argue, far from a tool for narcissism, Instagram selfie culture is allowing audiences to become active makers in the curatorial shape of the exhibition context by adding their interpretations in creative ways. This can, in turn, lead to changing how other audiences perceive art. Having a healthy Instagram selfie culture around an institution is now a barometer of how 'engaging' and 'outreaching' it is. Social media metrics are now being used in annual reports as a measure of engagement:

> The modern day art gallery visitor engages in the emergent and mediated practice, of using a smart device to capture photographic images, and post them to social media networks such as Instagram. … Instagram facilitates users capturing images,

manipulating them with filters, adding comments and location tags. Followed by uploading to a profile that is viewable by the public or a selected group of users. Art exhibitions are in synergy with Instagram's model, offering a plethora of photographic opportunities. Art and Instagram intersect in a constructivist space, through dialogical processes where visitor meaning is constructed collectively through embodied and emplaced sharing. (Suess, 2017: 1)

As Suess notes in his thesis 'Art Gallery Visitors and Instagram', the role of Instagram in contemporary museum engagement cannot be underestimated. Using the increasingly common research practice of hashtag analysis (Highfield & Leaver, 2015), Suess studies the #qagoma to understand the ways in which Instagram images and texts are shared in everyday contexts. The researching of Instagram as a specific form of visual social media began with its evocation of the analogue aesthetics (Jurgenson, 2011; Hjorth & Pink, 2014) to become a dominant app that moves from genres such as friends, food, gadgets, captioned photos, pets, activities, selfies and fashion (Hu et al., 2014) to creative interventions (Olszanowski, 2014; Carah & Louw, 2015).

Instagram entangles the relationship between the digital and physical place in complex ways that emplace images in specific temporal and spatial relationships. As a shared image, it is a highly social form of visuality. And yet what does the Instagram image, in the context of the art museum, do to the ways in which art is experienced, engaged and remembered? Many galleries and museums today are making social media an important part of their strategic vision. And yet how can we understand the depths of engagement beyond or even in between hashtags, shares and likes? As Budge and Suess explain:

With 800 million users and growing, it was perhaps inevitable that Instagram would shake up the art world. The social photo platform has been accused by the media of fanning a narcissistic selfie culture. But in galleries, research is showing that the negative aspects are far outweighed by the positive. Instagram is changing the way we experience and share our visits to exhibitions, and how we perceive art. (2018: n.p.)

The role of mobile media mediation as a form of creativity in public spaces is starting to emerge (Quan-Haase & Martin, 2013; Hjorth et al., 2016) beyond the simplistic critiques of the mobile device interfering with the 'authentic' unmediated experience of the event (Chesher, 2012). Indeed, the notion that there is such a thing as an unmediated event precludes the fact that intimacy mediates everything – if not by technology, then by language, gestures and emotions and memories. The work of Lev Manovich's *Phototrails*, as discussed earlier, is indicative of the types of meanings Instagram can

Figure 9.1   NGV Triennale was very successful in its deployment of Instagram (Budge & Seuss, 2018)

speak in terms of place-making, memory and visual culture. And yet understanding the motivations and social dimensions of use is still in its infancy, as it is more nuanced than the hashtagged or Big Data visualizations (Hjorth & Burgess, 2014; Hu et al., 2014; Schwartz & Halegoua, 2014). As Hu et al. note: 'Having a deep understanding of Instagram is important because it will help us gain deep insights about social, cultural and environmental issues around people's activities (through the lens of their photos)' (2014: 595).

Indeed, the ways in which Instagram coalesces the social and aesthetic in unique ways has led researchers such as Hogan (2010) to ask whether we can distinguish between the performance of self and the relationality of the exhibition. This indivisibility is further magnified in the case of selfies, in which the shared and thus social portrait can take on multiple and contested meanings and interpretations (Wendt, 2014; Senft & Baym, 2015). As John (2013) argues, in the world of and on Instagram, we are sharing *fuzzy objects*. These objects are about relationality, about sharing, about the social (John, 2013). They are, as boyd (2011) pointed out earlier, about presence bleed in which sociality, aesthetics and lived experience become part of a shared digital story.

Instagram is often, in Western contexts, synonymous with contemporary visual culture. That is, it reflects the 'shared practices of a group, community, or society through which meanings are made out of the visual, aural, and textual world of representations' (Sturken & Cartwright, 2009: 3, cited in Rose, 2014). By partaking in visual cultures, Instagram, and especially through hashtagging, we see ways in which audiences can participate in the creative act of discovery and curiosity. Through Instagram, people can be enticed to go to galleries when they might not ordinarily go. They can become part of the curatorial practice through the entanglement of the digital presence with the physical (Consoli, 2014). As Budge and Burness argue:

> visitor engagement with museum objects on Instagram is informed by agency and authority on the part of the user, and a primary motivation to communicate shared experiences using photography. Findings include a significant focus on objects despite public concerns that social media use in museum spaces is leading to a decreased public engagement in this area. Implications stemming from the research include specific insights for museum practice and understandings that have a potential to impact communication, engagement, and contemporary cultural practices generally. (2018: 1)

As Suess notes, 'Instagram is a chronology of the everyday performance of life through image and text. Reflection encourages a deep and distinctive experience of the specific artworks, something gallery educators strive towards' (2017: 26). In other words, Instagram not only plays a key role in the curating, but also in the embedding of educational ideologies around outreach. For Suess, the reflective and creative dimension of Instagram provides users with conceptual, participatory and shared tools – the hallmarks of early Museum 2.0 discussions (Suess, 2017; see also Russo et al., 2008; Simon, 2010).

Thus, as an intrinsic part of visual culture, Instagram can provide ways for audiences to create and partake in digital intimate publics (Hjorth & Hendry, 2015). However, visual cultures are also about embodied action – especially through the act of the selfie. Through the lens of the selfie, the social proprioception of the visual is heightened.

Selfie contextualized: Embodied performativity of the present

As Grant Bollmer and Katherine Guiness (2017) argue in their study of the selfie as a phenomenon, discussion of the selfie as an extension of older, analogue practices, such as self-portraiture, neglects to engage with the complexity of the digital as an entanglement of the social, networked and affective. Instead, they point to the work of Paul Frosh, who defines the selfie as the 'embodied performativity of the present', where they are self-reflexive images making visible their 'own construction as an act and a production of mediation' (Frosh, 2015: 1621). As Brooke Wendt (2014) notes, selfies are not about narcissism as obsessive self-love, but about the numbness and misrecognition that trauma can bring with it. In her study, Wendt draws on McLuhan's discussion of narcissism as misrecognition or apperception. Selfies, in this light, are what Paul Frosh (2015) calls the 'gestural image' – that is, a combination of photographic theory and kinaesthetic sociality.

At the crossroads between the aesthetic and the social, camera-phone practices can provide insight into contemporary digital media. This phenomenon is magnified in the context of selfies as a barometer for changing relationships between media, memory and death (Walker Rettberg, 2014; Frosh, 2015; Senft & Baym, 2015). For Thumim (2017) and Kuntsman (2017), selfies are about politics and citizenship. They argue separately that the act of visualizing self-representation is an uneven process and highlights tacit normalities. The selfie can highlight that some bodies and faces are more normalized in mass media circulations than others. Take, for example, discussion in the recent Canadian Art blog about Art Selfies as Narcissistic (2018) in which Yayoi Kasama, as an 80-year-old Japanese woman embodied by her art, presents an alternative reading. In this way, inserting one's radicalized and sexualized body through the selfie becomes a political act in keeping with the work of Berlant's intimate publics (1998).

While the selfie might be one of the most all-pervasive forms of visual culture globally, it is far from even in its sociocultural dimensions. As one of the first locations to fully embrace camera phones, South Korea, the 'sel-ca' takes on particular characteristics that reflect both the micro and macro milieu. For example, the sel-ca in South Korea clearly speaks to the gender politics of the gaze. However, for feminist media scholar Dong-Hoo Lee, in one of the first studies in camera-phone practices in 2003, camera phones afforded Korean women with new forms of agency and creative expression (Lee, 2005). Moving behind the popular sel-ca taken by young pretty women, Lee explored how camera phones provided a vehicle for self-expression, creativity and empowerment for women who had previously felt such avenues were not available to them in the highly patriarchal Korean society. In interviews with hundreds of users across different age groups, Lee found that the camera phone provided not only a space for agency, but also a space for transition from amateur to professional photography.

The sel-ca in Korea has a strong history as part of young adults' coupledom (Hjorth, 2009). The camera phone has become a key player in the representation and maintenance of co-presence, with phones becoming intimate repositories for rituals. In particular, when heterosexual couples were initially 'getting together', the girlfriend would colonize the phone, both inside and outside. She would personalize the device with the characters and designs she liked. As the boyfriend carried around the phone, often on constant show, it would operate much like the engagement ring, signalling to others that he was 'engaged'. After all, what boy would do that feminized customization to his phone! In one scenario, a girlfriend had saved her eye as a screen saver on her boyfriend's phone (see Figure 9.2). Everywhere he went, his omnipresent girlfriend followed. Always-watching, always-reminding-him-to-behave. Sel-cas are not just important in the fostering of new intimacies and reiterating older rituals, but also in the memorialization of those departed. Camera-phone practices offer a lens onto the personal and cultural, the intimate and social. They magnify as they memorialize intimate publics. This paradoxical role of the selfie as a form of personal expression, citizenship and creativity enhances oscillation between agency and conformity, visibility and invisibility.

While the selfie has its origins in the emergence of first-generation camera phones in locations such as South Korea and Japan (Ito, 2003), its phenomenal rise can be attributed to good quality camera phones and second-generation networked visuality through mobile apps like Instagram (Grace, 2013). With the pervasiveness of digital

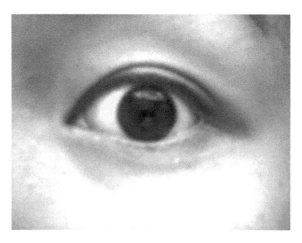

Figure 9.2   Girlfriend screensaver

photography and the affordances of smartphones, as Lasén and Gómez Cruz (2009: 213) note, 'people move within and between the public and the private, at times being in both simultaneously'.

As Katrin Tiidenberg (2015b) argues, selfies can be a political vehicle for pushing norms around femininity and gender performativity. Building on the work of Magda Olszanowski (2014), Jessa Lingel and danah boyd (2013), Tiidenberg (2014, 2015a) looks at NSFW (not safe for work, which mostly means sexually explicit) content on Tumblr.com to show how sharing selfies can be

> a practice of resisting body and hetero-normativity. Sharing and viewing selfies leads my participants to question the narrow standards of appearances, reject some consumerist aspects of visual economy that presume monetary gain from [the] exhibition of bodies, and thus (re)claim control over the aesthetic of bodies. (Tiidenberg, 2018: 63)

Tiidenberg (2018) conducted a discourse analysis of images of women over 40 and 50 years old. While noting that, from the outset, the dominant discourse is one of fashion and fitness, which align with post-feminist ideologies, a closer reading reveals subversion and critique. As Tiidenberg notes, 'taking, editing, posting, and interacting around selfies allowed my mature female participants to disconnect themselves from the discourses that have normalized the un-photographability of ageing female bodies' (2018: 61).

Selfies are not just political tools for inserting bodies not normally seen in traditional media. They are also embodied ways for being in the world. Through the selfie, one can emplace oneself in the world, using the social and networked visual culture as part of (and experienced emotionally and physically within) everyday life (Pink & Hjorth, 2012: 146). As noted elsewhere in the context of camera phones more generally, they ask us to consider and reflect upon our place in place – what we have called emplaced visuality. As argued elsewhere, 'the banality of the camera phone should not be understood only in terms of visual content of the images it produces, but also in its very use. It has become an embedded part of the ordinary, the routine, habitual and often-tacit practices in which we engage as we move through, sense and perceive environments' (Pink & Hjorth, 2012: 147).

With the rise of camera-phone apps like Instagram and genres like selfies, this has required a rethink in relation to earlier photographic genres, aesthetics and ideologies. While Instagram does invoke the aesthetics of the analogue – i.e. Polaroid (Palmer, 2012; Zylinska, 2015) – as a networked form of social visuality, it also departs from the earlier media.

The role of camera phones to highlight and challenge 'performances of power' and citizen agency are magnified during times of disasters and celebrations (Frosh, 2001).

For Paul Frosh, digital networked photography is not just a medium of visual communication; it also has the ability to render the performance of power visible (2001). Reflecting upon the role of digital photography in the aftermath of Princess Diana's death, Frosh 'explores the ways in which photographic performance at the public/ private boundary dramatizes power relations through forms of social transparency, voyeurism and memoralization' (2001: 43). This performativity dimension, in which 'affective witnessing' (Papalias, 2016) occurs, creates what LaMarre (2017) calls 'platformativity'. In the case of Instagram, it is an overlay between acts of personal expression and citizenship, while also partaking in the algorithmic consumer cultures (Abidin, 2016).

Visualizing engagement

In this section, we explore the ways in which curators and museum practitioners are positioning the role of visual social media in the museum. After interviewing ten curators and artists to gain a sense of the diversity of the debate, we will now focus upon one particular participant who, as a social media strategist, could provide the greatest of insights. We will call her 'Amy'. Amy is in her late twenties and has worked in the arts sector for nearly a decade in a variety of different contexts. When asked about whether the provocation 'Is it Instagrammable?' is ruling curatorial programmes, Amy says:

> In my experience, likes, Instagram-friendly content etc. is becoming more and more important to galleries and museums. I would say this is the case because board members, directors, general managers, members, visitors, sponsors etc. (i.e. the various stakeholders) are becoming more and more aware of a museum or gallery's social media presence. … However, I would also like to point out that despite an acute awareness of its presence on social media, the art space fails to accurately measure and report upon this 'presence'. One reason for this may be because the current funding environment of the Australian arts industry means small to medium sized galleries/art spaces etc. just do not have the resources to commit to accurately measuring and reporting their social media statistics/analytics. Also, the technology is still new to those in positions of power (i.e. directors, board members etc.) so there's a level of uncertainty and mistrust when someone starts mentioning likes/impressions/reach etc. … Consequently, because we're not measuring social media analytics properly/effectively, I don't think museums/galleries/art spaces can use these tools to comment accurately on their audience engagement. The art spaces I have been involved with recognize this shortcoming, and chose not to rely on likes or how Instagrammable they are when it comes to measuring their 'audience engagement'.

As Amy continues:

> I think social media is opening the gallery and museum not only to a wider audience but also to a greater level of engagement. Through social media you get to see other people's takes and responses to an exhibition (either in the form of their direct written comments provided on their personal social media platforms or via the images that people decide to take of and within an exhibition or gallery). ... I think social media can allow audiences to have a deeper experience outside of the typical 'come visit the gallery, read the wall text or catalogue, and hopefully be impacted or engaged'. Instead, *good* social media strategies allow for a deeper level of engagement with audiences.

Figure 9.3 Hans Ulrich Obrist's Instagram account (artists include Kathy Yaeji, Anne Carson, Ian Cheng, Ryan Gander & Gábor Domokos, Koo Jeong A and Damien Hirst)

Figure 9.4 #smARTmurals

As Amy says, there are multiple ways in which museums, galleries and artists use social media in creative ways not just to disseminate to audiences but also as an active tool in the living dimension that expands and extends an event across temporal, spatial and even social realms. As Amy concludes, galleries and museums need to take social media seriously. Key curators, such as Hans Ulrich Obrist, are seeing social media as an integral part of their curatorial practice, in which intimate publics are 24/7. Others will follow shortly.

As Budge and Suess (2018) note in their examination of Instagram use in Australian art museums like the Gallery of Modern Arts (Queensland), National Gallery of Victoria and Museum of Contemporary Art (New South Wales), incorporating Instagram as an integral tool for engagement and place-making is crucial:

> Instagram offers visitors authority and agency in sharing their experience. This connects audiences with museum content in a way that they can control and is meaningful to them. New research shows how this activity is also tied to place – the museum, and the city beyond it. Using Instagram in public spaces like museums and galleries is complex. It's tied to broader research that shows how social media use in public spaces is challenging a range of social norms. As researchers working in this

Figure 9.5 Nick Selenitsch, 'Life drawing in an age of Instagram' (2017)

emerging area, we see much value in curators and exhibition designers making use of Instagram to inform how they plan exhibitions. It could help build new audiences and strengthen connections with existing visitors. While removing all visitor photography restrictions is not possible, it is our view that visitor expectations and experiences have now changed. The future of cultural institutions needs to include Instagram. (2018, n.p.)

Conclusion

Increasingly, museums and galleries are incorporating social media as an embodied part of the experience of the event and place. Take, for example, the aforementioned Rijksacademy, or, more recently, activities such as the #smART Murals project in the UK, which sought to combine augmented reality (AR) to make audiences active producers and creators of the content as they were experiencing the art. Here the mobile device doesn't mediate or diminish the experience of the artwork but adds to the layers and textures. It becomes a creative cartographic performance (Verhoeff, 2013).

While current research on the role of Instagram and selfies indicates that they are providing a critical space for self-reflection, and also for politicizing the body, debates about the paradoxes between visibility and invisibility ensue (Olszanowski, 2014; Carah & Louw, 2015; Tiidenberg, 2015a; Kuntsman, 2017). Indeed, there is still much more work to be done, especially ethnographically, into understanding the meanings and motivations in collaboration with the taste discourses of hashtags. And like the spectres that haunt the selfie as merely being a vehicle for narcissism, we must be careful that these emergent visual cultures don't just create an ironic infinite regress. This infinite regress sees paradoxes around normalization and creative agency as dominant and subversive genres emerge around art institutions' social media discourses. As artist Nick Selenitsch demonstrates in 'Life drawing in an age of Instagram', in which he asked audiences to Instagram the picture of the model and then draw it from the Instagram, mediation is an intimate mediation of itself (Figure 9.5).

Notes

1. https://developer.apple.com/ibeacon/
2. We are using the term 'vernacular' in the sense of something that is domestic and functional. Vernacular agency refers to the ways we use media technologies in the everyday, rather than as specialists or experts. See, for example, Jean Burgess's thesis 'Vernacular Creativity and New Media' (2007).

PART 4

PRACTICES

10

Paralinguistics

Introduction

An employee sends her boss a smiley face in an email after a rewarding meeting. A 12-year-old son sends his mum an SMS smiley face via his iPhone to indicate he is on time for dinner. A grandmother clicks the smiley face on Facebook to respond to her grandchild's photo at the playground. A boyfriend sends his girlfriend a smiley face via WhatsApp to say he is thinking of her while at work. Once considered a niche practice, the role of paralinguistics – from *emojis* ('picture characters'), emoticons (typographic characters), stamps and stickers – in everyday social media vernacular has become a mainstream activity. And yet in this ubiquity, inequalities and differences around literacy and emotional labour play out, especially in terms of intergenerational usage.

The examples above all deploy a smiley to speak of very different relationships, feelings and dynamics. And yet as intergenerational and cross-cultural as paralinguistics have become, understanding their nuanced vernacular and playful creativity is yet to be fully realized. For some, paralinguistics highlight the corporate role of the platform, whereby specific platforms such as Facebook or LINE have their own specific paralinguistic personalization logic (Stark & Crawford, 2015). And yet for others, paralinguistics can be understood as providing playful forms of ambient co-presence and care-at-a-distance (Pink et al., 2018).

To help understand the work that is done by paralinguistics, it is useful to draw upon work in other fields. For example, as Arlie Hochschild (1983) noted in research around casual workers, emotional labour is the process of managing feelings and expressions to fulfil the emotional requirements of a job. More specifically, workers are expected to regulate their emotions during interactions with customers, co-workers and superiors. For Hochschild, emotional labour refers to the process by which workers are expected to manage their feelings in accordance with organizationally defined rules and guidelines.

In a similar way, emotional labour is heightened, evoked and tangled in the playful logic of paralinguistics. For Papacharissi (2014), drawing on Lauren Berlant's work on the rise of the intimate in public space (1998), alongside Williams' (1977) 'structures of feeling', emotional, affective labour operates constantly in what she conceptualizes as 'affective publics'. These affective publics are:

> Collaborative discourses generated through the logic of hashtags on Twitter may be understood as fostering tropes of belonging that evolve beyond the conventional mode of rational thought and deliberation. As affect mini-worlds, they invite a publicness that is politically sensitized yet generally dismissive of normatively defined political consciousness. (Papacharissi, 2014: 117)

Paralinguistics enact many of the paradoxes we have discussed in this book, including visibility and invisibility, disclosure and divulgence, user personalization and corporate platformativity. They highlight the often-tacit power relations that play out in social media discourses, especially around generational literacies.

This chapter draws from a longitudinal collaborative research project on social media in households in Tokyo to explore some of the issues surrounding play, emotional labour and intergenerational care-at-a-distance. A key point we make in this chapter is that we need to develop cultural and intergenerational understandings of paralinguistics as both localized and personalized practices of care-at-a-distance.

As explored in the previous chapters, social media is a space and practice that often oscillates and coalesces around paradoxical models of empowerment/exploitation, visibility/ invisibility, public/private, work/life, presence/co-presence. As Papacharissi (2014: 94) stresses, 'online technologies thrive on collapsing public and private boundaries'. In particular, mobile social media further 'bleeds' modes of presence (Gregg, 2011) and digital intimate public practices (Hjorth & Arnold, 2011). For Papacharissi, it is the emotional labour in and around social media practices that characterize affective publics, which potentially disrupt dominant political narratives as they make space for under represented viewpoints and experiences.

In this chapter we explore how the expansion of paralinguistics can be understood as part of broader social media practices that involve play, emotional labour and intergenerational care-at-a-distance. Through ethnographic fieldwork conducted in the context of intergenerational relationships in families in Japan and China, we consider the complex ways paralinguistics are used to maintain intimacy in the face of temporary or permanent distance.

The rise of *emoji* and other forms of ASCII-based non-standard variants such as emoticons is highlighting the role of digital media in creating affective affordances and, following Papacharissi, 'affective publics'. As Umashanthi Pavalanathan and Jacob Eisenstein (2016) identify, there is a competition for paralinguistic functions whereby the deployment of one paralinguistic function, such as *emojis*, will cancel the use of other ASCII-based conventions.

Paralinguistics in context

The long history of emoticons in media practice textual communication (Crystal, 2006) has been well-documented. More recently, research into *emoji* has highlighted their significance as historical, social and cultural objects (Stark & Crawford, 2015). The work of Kelly and Watts (2015) has identified how *emojis* can be deployed to maintain close ties. However, the power of paralinguistics beyond autonomy in various platformativity tropes has been overlooked. In this chapter we argue for cultural and intergenerational understandings of paralinguistics as both localized and personalized practices of care-at-a-distance. We further argue that understanding the emotional and affective labour around *emojis* can provide insight into the intergenerational dimensions of care-at-a-distance. We conclude by recommending further research into *emoji* as a global phenomenon.

Contemporary digital media practice has been defined as playful (Sicart, 2014). This is epitomized by the playfulness of the paralinguistics – *emojis* (picture characters), emoticons (typographic characters), stamps and stickers. The emoticon was developed to represent mood or the emotion in the absence of being able to see visual expression in text-based communications (Park et al., 2014: 14). The use of paralinguistics has become an increasingly popular and playful way of personalizing digital media communications. In Asian countries such as Japan, the historical trajectories towards *emoji* use are tied to the role of the cute (*kawaii*) in existing subcultural practices. The birth of the *emoji*, initially in Japan, can be linked to the history of *kawaii* – 'kitten' writing pioneered by high school girls as part of the mobile pager revolution in the 1990s (Hjorth, 2003a; Okada, 2005).

Kawaii cultures were born in response to a few key Japanese phenomena. First, Japan's particular premature adulthood, whereby children are expected to cram school work most nights to pass an exam at age 10. In this academic preoccupation, there is little time for free play (Kinsella, 1995). Second, the *kawaii* became a tool for subversive gender and subcultural play (Kinsella, 1995; Hjorth, 2003a, 2003b, 2005). The rise of online technologies saw the further development of *kawaii* cultures through ASCII paralinguistics, especially by high school girls who creolized *hiragana* (Japanese alphabet) with ASCII in what has now been called the high school pager revolution (Fujimoto, 2005; Ito et al., 2005; Hjorth, 2009). Third, there is a long history of deploying the *kawaii* to make friendly or 'warm' the coldest of new technologies (Hjorth, 2003a).

Drawing on these *kawaii* genealogies, the *emoji* was invented by Shigetaka Kurita in 1999 when designing the mobile internet platform NTT DoCoMo's i-mode. The i-mode has been defined as the precursor to smartphones in that it allowed Japan to leap frog into mobile internet (as opposed to wireless internet) at the turn of the century, when most were still accessing the internet from the computer. I-mode was not just a special phone (hardware), but also a gated version of the internet with DoCoMo approved services – much like the ways in which mobile apps act as gatekeepers for how we experience online technologies. Parallels can be made with Apple in the West in terms of not just pioneering the hardware, but also in controlling software (for example, iTunes approvals). Part of i-mode's success was its ability to converge subcultural and mainstream personalization techniques, which pre-empt the 'app' platform phenomenon.

The historical context in Japan offers a useful starting point for considering how such personalization practices have come about, and suggests that we would likewise find similar but different visible forms of (cute) customization in other cultures (Hjorth, 2009). It is not our objective to take up that question here as much research has been done on the history of *kawaii* personalization. Instead, we seek to explore preliminary research into how mapping the transnationalism of digital paralinguistics can be understood as part of the emotional labour of care-at-a-distance for families. We have found that with the pervasive (albeit uneven) uptake of mobile social media in the Asia-Pacific region, localized forms of cute character culture have become prevalent across cultures, and now comprise the maintenance of intergenerational relationships.

In ethnographic cross-cultural fieldwork conducted in Tokyo and Shanghai through the ARC project *Locating the Mobile*, the project interviewers focused on tensions between adult children and their parents, where the interviewers saw some of the ways in which generations are challenging norms around notions of media literacy, co-present intimacy and affective playbour. Once deployed in the context of players' modding of computer games, Julian Kücklich's (2005) notion of playbour (play and labour) has become ubiquitous in contemporary media. *Emojis*, we argue, can be seen as an extension of 'playbour' – that is, involving emotional, creative and social labour in and around their playfulness. In turn, *emojis* identify a fundamental paradox underscoring digital labour – it is both a *playground* and a *factory* (Scholz, 2012).

Emojis, stamps and the politics of affective labour

As Stark and Crawford (2015) note, LINE in Japan has introduced the 'next-level emoji' (Byford, 2014) through their deployment of stickers. Other platforms, such as Facebook Messenger also have their own platform-based version of stickers. As Stark and Crawford observe: 'Stickers, crucially, are proprietary to each platform that sells them.' They argue that 'stickers represent an attempt on the part of social media platforms – seemingly successful in the short run – to re-commodify the affective labour which, at least in part, had been lost with the standardization of *emoji* into Unicode' (Stark & Crawford, 2015: 8). They explain how:

> Individual users will be able to express themselves within preselected bands of racial, emotional, or otherwise idiosyncratic diversity – but at a new financial cost. Established platforms such as Facebook have sought to include stickers, *emoji*, and emotional signifiers in their user experience design, to compete with platforms like LINE and with an eye toward the further commoditization and monetization of social affect. Facebook's sticker strategy, part of what the company terms 'compassion research', appears to involve using stickers as inducements for users to engage more frequently with its in platform messaging apps. (Stark & Crawford, 2015: 8)

According to Stark and Crawford, *emojis*, like the original smiley, can be understood as expressions of 'cruel optimism'. Affect theorist Lauren Berlant (2011: 2) defines this state as an affective zone in which 'the object/scene that ignites a sense of possibility actually makes it impossible to attain the expansive transformation for which a person or a people risks striving'. However, the ambiguities of *emojis* and stickers in and across work contexts like emails and social media can confuse and be viewed as part of broader problematic affective labour practices. In the case of families dealing with distance, paralanguages like *emojis* can provide a sense of playful warmth that alludes to a feeling of intimacy – an important way to maintain a feeling of emotional closeness when physical distance is at work. This care-at-a-distance work is a form of emotional labour that maintains many intergenerational relationships (Wilding, 2006).

Drawing from fieldwork conducted in Tokyo and Shanghai with families coping with intergenerational geographic distance and mobility, in this chapter we suggest that paralinguistics, like *emojis* and stickers, provide complex ways in which humanizing and affective vernacular can be deployed as part of care-at-a-distance. We first turn to examples from the everyday practices of research participants in Japan – home to some of the first cute customization, especially around *keitai* mobile-phone cultures (Hjorth, 2003b). We then turn to examples from Shanghai to conclude with a set of insights about the paradoxes around *emojis* and stickers as affective labour and care-at-a-distance. In each location we provide two examples of young adults deploying *emojis* and stickers to maintain intimacy and co-presence with family members living elsewhere.

Tokyo, Japan

Given that *emojis* were born in Japan it seems fitting that we start with our Japanese families. The role of the *keitai* in Japanese culture for building and maintaining various forms of intimacies is well documented over the past 20 years from the aforementioned launch of NTT DoCoMo i-mode in 1999. In addition to modes such as banking, entertainment-oriented services such as 'game', 'chaku-uta' (downloadable ringtones made up of the melodies of songs), *decomail* (decoration email) were introduced and became widely used. *Decomail* service enhanced emails using different templates, images, colour and fonts, andattained wide popularity, especially among young female users. In sum, it afforded a creolizing of paralinguistic styles.

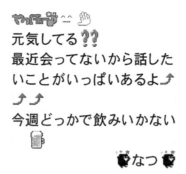

やっほーッ ⌒⌒ 🖐
元気してる⁇
最近会ってないから話した
いことがいっぱいあるよ♪
♪ ♪
今週どっかで飲みいかない
🍺
🐗なつ🐗

Figure 10.1   *decomail* (NTT DoCoMo, 1999)

Decomail can be understood as a form of *emoji* that functions to decorate messages without using explicit words and phrases. It is more than a simple smiley exchange in that each character has a more specific and detailed context. Currently, most *keitai* users have become *sumaho* (smartphone) users. While they have a new set of applications and configurations, their basic needs – being in perpetual contact with friends and family members while at a distance – remain the same. Given that most of the Japanese users were familiar with *decomail* and similar *emoji*-like expressions on screens, it seems quite natural that they use stamps frequently on LINE or on other messenger services (see Figure 10.2). Stamps are customized and colourful illustrative icons. Often friends and family will choose particular stamp characters to use between each other.

In the next section we discuss two participants from the Japanese fieldwork. While ten families were interviewed over a three-year period, we have chosen these participants because of the ways in which they epitomize the diversity of familial use.

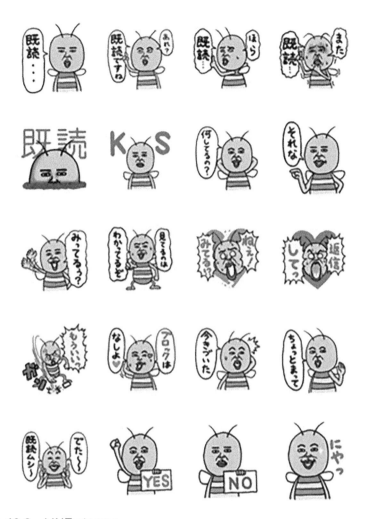

Figure 10.2 LINE stamps

Haruna

Haruna, a 22-year-old undergraduate student, lived alone near her university campus. Her mother and father lived together in her hometown in the western part of Japan. Her elder sister was married and had a child. For Haruna, 'family' meant her mother (57 years old), father (59 years old) and elder sister (28 years old). She used LINE, Twitter, Facebook, Instagram and Swarm on a daily basis. Her favourite place to use social media was on the sofa in her room.

She used LINE and Facebook with her mother and elder sister, but not with her father. She often chatted with her mother on LINE. The conversation was peppered with stamps.

Sometimes it was *only* stamps. At first, Haruna's mother didn't know how to use stamps, but Haruna taught her how to use them over time. Sometimes her mother sent strange stamps or incomprehensible stamps that Haruna couldn't quite understand, as much as she tried. Haruna saw them as a powerful way to create a sense of feeling close and intimate with her mother when they were physically apart.

Figure 10.3 Haruna exchanged messages and stamps with her mother on LINE

Haruko

Haruko was a 22-year-old undergraduate student who lived with her parents. Her family consisted of her parents and a younger brother who studied abroad. From 2013, communication with her family shifted to LINE. Haruko created three groups on LINE for communicating with her family members: an 'official' group of family, a group of family members who live together (excluding her brother), and a group of just her mother and herself. In the official group, they told one another what was going on in their lives. As Haruko told us:

> For sharing information with family, Facebook is not convenient. LINE is very useful in sending messages, pictures, videos, etc. When our family members' life styles started to change, we became LINE users. LINE's design is very nice. It feels

like we are talking. It's not like email. When my brother graduated from a college abroad, he sent us a warm message and pictures on LINE for telling his graduation and appreciation to the family. At that time, I was also away from Japan for studying and my father was also on a business trip. All the family members were in different places. It was very moving to see my brother's message on LINE. I also sent them a message from abroad. It was very warm moment. I was really relieved.

In the group of family members who lived together (which excluded her brother), they arranged mundane and daily things, for example, to discuss what to eat for dinner. In the chat group consisting of just Haruko and her mother, they 'care' and did 'kin-work' (di Leonardo, 1987; Baldassar, 2017). Paralinguistics, we suggest, provide a space to explore emotions in ways that traditional forms of language in media platforms cannot. Entangled within vernacular, mundane digital media practices of care (see Lynch & McLaughlin, 1995; Yeates, 2004), our insights into the uses of and feelings that are generated through paralinguistics build on research around how family members 'do family' at a distance through everyday activities that extend beyond the home, including through digital media (Morgan, 1997; Wajcman et al., 2008; Madianou, 2016, 2017). Haruko elaborates:

After my brother and I grew up, my parents spend more time together. I always worry about them and if they are nice to each other – they are so different and they often have a fight. When they were travelling to Hokkaido, my father sent pictures with their smile to the official group of family. But my mother sent me a message to the group of us to show me that she was tired and bored. So I sent a message for asking her if she is ok. I often send my mother stamps, too.

She sent stamps to her mother, especially when she wanted to tell her 'thank you' or send encouragement. However, she didn't do this kind of communication with her father. For Haruko, frequent stamp exchange was a highly gendered activity. Haruko viewed stamps as partly functional – they can abbreviate a longer text or illustrate a complex emotion. However, it is more than economical; it is about embedding emotion and intimacy. It is a feature that paralinguistics do well in the face of traditional forms of mediated communication.

Shanghai, China

While LINE dominates Japan, instant messaging services QQ and WeChat prevails in mainland China. The company Tencent owns both QQ and WeChat. QQ can be understood as the precursor of WeChat and still features in regional areas where internet access is poor. Launched at the beginning of 2011, WeChat has become the most popular social media among family members across the whole of Chinese society. According to Tencent's 2016 interim report, WeChat's monthly active users has exceeded 0.761 billion (Tencent, 2016).

あの短時間にお弁当きれい
に詰めてくれて、ありがと
う！感動した笑 ごちそさま
ー

15:58

15:58

Figure 10.4 Haruko sent a message and stamp to thank her mother on LINE

From its launch, WeChat had two kinds of default emotional icons: the old emotional icons derived from QQ and a system similar to Japanese *emojis*. However, like LINE in Japan, WeChat was quick to make its own proprietary system in the form of stickers. In July 2015, WeChat initially launched its popular stars' stickers like 'Hello' and 'I miss you', which were created by popular Chinese celebrities invited by WeChat. They were charged 6 RMB for each set. One month later, WeChat opened its sticker platform for all designers to contribute their work. Although most of the designs were free, many users would pay different amounts, like 5 or 10 RMB, for special designs. WeChat also encourages users to upload their customized (bought) stickers. Custom stickers have been gaining much popularity among young WeChat users. Popular customized stickers change along with online hot topics, playing a parallel role to a meme. By using interesting stickers, dialogues on WeChat become not only textual but also visual, which makes communication on WeChat more playful.

At the same time, *emojis* are also used on one of China's oldest social media, QQ. According to the *China Emoji Usage Report* (Tencent, 2014), more than 90 per cent of all 0.8 billion QQ users have employed *emojis* when chatting, with a total *emoji* usage over 533.8 billion. The study also found that young users deploy *emojis* more often: *jiu ling hou* (those born in the 1990s) use *emojis* around 25.2 times a week, more than twice of the usage frequency of those *qi ling hou* (born in the 1970s) at 11.5 times a week.

In the next section we discuss two examples from the China fieldwork in which we see the dominance of WeChat stickers and *emojis* to help maintain constant contact between grown children and their parents. Unlike the Japanese fieldwork in which half of the grown adults still lived with their parents (or nearby), in China the phenomenon of moving away to study at university has seen the rise of paralinguistic intergenerational literacies.

Biyu

Biyu was a graduate student in Shanghai. She left her hometown of Sichuan at the age of 18. Biyu started to use WeChat when she was a sophomore. Two years later, she downloaded the app WeChat for her mother when she was at home during the summer vacation from university. Biyu told her mother that it was free to chat and make calls on WeChat and taught her how to write or read a message step by step. Biyu said, 'I taught mom how to use WeChat. I felt that I was giving back a little of all that mom did for me when I was little.'

Biyu deployed WeChat to keep her parents in constant contact and to diarize her activities so her parents could vicariously keep abreast of her experiences throughout her busy university life. Every time she won a competition or hung out with friends, she would repost the photo to her family group. On most occasions her parents would reply with a smiling face sticker after a short period of time. She said, 'Now, my parents also start to share their life with me, like their hiking photo on the last weekend.' Biyu enjoyed watching her mother learn to playfully experiment with paraliguistics to communicate her everyday feelings. Biyu said: 'My parents like to use the thumb-up and smiling emotional icons most. ... They also use some other stickers as positive responses to show love and care.'

In Figures 10.5 and 10.6 we see a typical exchange between Biyu and her parents. In Figure 10.5 on the left, Biyu showed her parents the lunch she made for herself; her mother replied with a thumb up to express encouragement. In Figure 10.6 on the right, Biyu shared

Figures 10.5 and 10.6   Screenshots of Biyu's talk with her parents

her travel photos, to which her father sent a sticker of an older cartoon character touching the head of a smaller one while saying 'lovely'. Biyu saw this as an expression of her father's love to his daughter. Here we see a play between the genders intergenerationally in China – a practice not found in the Japanese fieldwork.

Chen

Chen was the oldest sister of four siblings. Chen's family had six members: her mother, her father and her three brothers. Her parents and her second younger brother still lived in her hometown in Hebei Province (Northern China). Her oldest brother was working in Henan Province (Middle China), her youngest brother was studying in Qinhuangdao (Northeastern China), and Chen herself was studying in Shanghai. She had two family groups on WeChat: a larger one including all family members and relatives, and a smaller one which only includes the four siblings and their aunt, who was added into the group later. In the family groups, Chen said that they usually shared family videos or important information, such as when she was going back home. In the smaller group, the siblings shared what they could to help each other as well as mundane details they didn't want to bother their parents with.

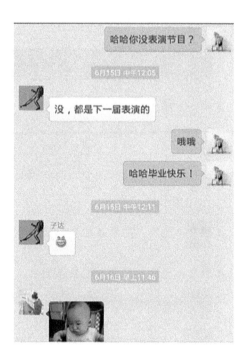

Figures 10.7 and 10.8 Screenshots of Chen's family WeChat groups

In terms of *emojis* and stickers, Chen said stickers such as 'good bye' and 'good night' became the most frequently used daily greetings. Chen observed that each member of her family uses different *emojis* or stickers to represent their feelings and experience. Here paralinguistics is deployed like a cross between an avatar and a symbol of emotion. In Figures 10.7 and 10.8 we can see a typical family exchange. In Figure 10.7 on the left (the smaller group for young people), her cousin uses her idol's sticker to express 'love you'. Chen replies with a cute bear clapping its hands. In Figure 10.8 on the right , Chen asks for details about her younger brother's graduation and sends him a 'happy graduation' message. Her brother replies with a smiling icon. Later, her sister-in-law shares a photo of her nephew. Across the different modes of paralinguistic exchange, intimacy and closeness is being reinforced.

Conclusion: Emotions at a distance

As Lee et al. (2016: 5) argue, in addition to expressing emotion, stickers also serve strategic and functional purposes. Strategic uses include benign participation in conversations even when the individual feels they have nothing to say, showing distinctiveness and humour from others, and to reveal true emotional intentions. Functional uses include substitution for text and as social greetings to overcome lulls after saying 'sorry' or goodbye' (Lee et al., 2016). In China, *emoji* and sticker usage on WeChat and QQ facilitate family communication, especially for those families whose members live apart because of domestic migration. For young adults who don't live with their parents, the *emojis* and stickers are deployed to maintain intimacy and co-presence with family members living elsewhere.

In this chapter we see the power of *emoji* in what Stark and Crawford (2015: 1) describe as 'conduits for affective labor in the social networks of informational capitalism'. Different generations, cultures and labour settings are all deploying the *emoji* with numerous affective and creative practices. As Stark and Crawford note, *emojis* help to creatively manage 'everyday biopolitics'. They argue:

> The patterns of use for emoji over time between friends and partners can become abstract and cryptic, or can degenerate to become pro forma: just plain basic. In the best case, there is a unique personal subtext to that exchange of a rainbow or the love-heart smile, many layers of unspoken meaning that would be difficult for intelligence analysts or machine-learning algorithm to parse. Nonetheless, this complexity has not stopped institutions from making the attempt, and commercializing emoji sociality in other ways. (Stark & Crawford, 2015: 6)

In this chapter we have drawn on ethnographic research in Tokyo and Shanghai to consider the affective power of *emojis* as an intergenerational lynchpin that helps to create a sense of emotion, affect and care-at-a-distance. Through the case studies, we can see the role of paralinguistics in the maintenance of intimacy intergenerationally, especially when distance is an issue. As we saw in the case of Japan and China, young adults teach their parents to use paralinguistic methods when they move away from home as a way to keep in constant contact. In Japan, the usage between mothers and daughters dominates.

This chapter has taken the first steps towards understanding the phenomenon of paralinguistics as part of mundane intimate vernacular. We conclude by proposing that since *emojis* appear to be here to stay, at least for the immediate future, the role that they play in the everyday mundane and affective lives needs further ethnographic investigation. This is important since such a research agenda seeks to reveal not simply how and why *emojis* are important in the affective lives of families, but also suggests how such intergenerational relationships are bound up in the problematic global political economies of digital media, technology and labour that are inseparable from this context. We need to account for the emotional and affective labour associated with paralinguistics as part of broader negotiations of familial care-at-a-distance. Moreover, returning to the introduction, we need more analysis of the literacies around paralinguistics as part of the growing 'affective publics' and their vernacular practices.

11

Social Media & Mixed Reality

Introduction

With Facebook investing billions into virtual reality (VR) (through their Oculus headset) in recent years, the relationship between mixed reality (MR) and social media has become more apparent. Apple and Facebook are committing to mobile augmented reality (AR) as the next mainstream application, with estimates of one billion users and a business value of US$60 billion by 2020 (Merel, 2018). As Tim Merel notes, the divergence between ubiquitous mobile AR and stand-alone AR is growing as mobile technology ushers in new audiences and modes of accessibility. According to Merel, 'AR (mobile AR, smartglasses) could approach three and a half billion installed base and $85 billion to $90 billion revenue within five years' (2018: n.p.). However, with this mainstreaming of mixed reality comes the reoccurring theme of equality. As social media convergences with hybrid reality, paradoxes around empowerment and exploitation and privacy and surveillance will prevail.

As VR moves towards 'social VR' and 'social AR', we need to put these debates into context, theoretically and historically (de Souza e Silva & Hjorth, 2009). This chapter situates mixed reality like AR and VR within the history of urban play movements, and then focuses on what we can learn from the paradoxes surrounding the rise and fall of *Pokémon GO*. As was highlighted in the global phenomenon of *Pokémon GO* of 2016, in which AR went mainstream, hybrid reality has the ability to reinforce inequality (especially in terms of the racialized body; see Salen, 2017) as well as creating new forms of sociality that can transcend corporeal inequalities.

In this chapter we explore the role of social media games in the form of hybrid reality. In order to do so, we first begin with a discussion of *Pokémon GO*, which epitomized the mainstreaming of hybrid reality gaming. We then contextualize the *Pokémon GO* phenomenon in terms of longer locative media art experimentation, and then locate this tradition in terms of older forms of mobile play linked to the 19th-century mobility discourses.

Pokémon GO

Within the first weeks of its launch in July 2016, millions of people across several countries downloaded the *Pokémon GO* app onto their iOS and Android devices. They entered an augmented reality, wandered their neighbourhoods and public spaces in search of *Pokémon* and *PokéStops*, competing with other players at virtual *Pokémon* gyms. In this location-based hybrid reality, users are required to move through physical space as they tag, collect, trade and battle for digital artefacts and player achievements. Effectively, they access a game microworld through their smartphone, via the digital overlay of game objects and virtual locations across the actual environment.

Through this augmented layering of the digital onto place, banal and familiar surroundings are transformed to become significant game locations. A *Pokémon* can be found and caught in one's own bathroom, a gym or *PokéStop* might be situated at the local library, café or graveyard. The popularity of *Pokémon GO*, which was touted as the first ever *really* successful location-based game, has already been the subject of much criticism and celebration. The unprecedented success of *Pokémon GO* in the first months of its release provides urban media researchers with an opportunity to explore and document the experience of *en masse* location-based mobile gameplay. It is clear that the game, including its uptake, is situated within historical, social and cultural contexts. It brings together decades of mobile media use, locative arts, gaming practices and Japanese culture.

For some, *Pokémon GO* is a positive experience; the gameplay evokes twenty-something nostalgia (Surman, 2009; McCrea, 2017), encouraging physical exercise, facilitating 'genuine human-to-human interaction' (Wawro, 2016: n.p.) and effectively enhancing our sense of wellbeing and belonging (Vella et al., 2017). Yet, as with mobile media and mobile games more generally, *Pokémon GO* can be flexibly deployed by users as a way to facilitate social interaction, or as a 'shield' to avoid engagement with others in public spaces.

For others, the game forces us to reflect on the ongoing gendered, racial, socio-economic, age-based and bodily inequities of urban mobility that affect many of us on a daily basis (Isbister, 2016). Jordan Frith (2017) explores the 'commercial potential of augmented reality', and how *Pokémon GO* can be used by businesses to attract foot traffic through the placement of 'lures', revealing how digital 'objects' can influence our movement and behaviour in the physical world. As we enact the pedestrian labour of location-based gaming, and interweave digital and physical information, the 'spatial legibility' of urban space – or the way urban environments appear as coherent and recognizable patterns – is transformed (Frith, 2013). Yet, as Miguel Sicart (2017) warns, while *Pokémon GO* may open up new possibilities for design and play in augmented reality, we should be wary of the potential for corporate appropriation of public spaces enabled by the game.

Pokémon GO is manifestly ambient, as the game becomes diffused through our daily routines, pedestrian movement and interaction with the familiar strangers populating our neighbourhoods and urban spaces. As we have suggested, in a very fundamental way the mobile interface changes what we pay attention to, and the modalities and duration of that attentiveness. This is clearly evidenced by the wide-scale integration of casual mobile games such as *Candy Crush* and *Angry Birds* into our daily lives (Keogh & Richardson, 2017). Yet even more significantly and poignantly, our involvement with location-based hybrid reality games such as *Pokémon GO* require us to adopt an 'as-if' structure of experience, moving through the environment 'as if' it was game terrain or an urban playground. That is, *Pokémon GO* is not just a casual mobile game. While we might play it in the midst of other daily activities, it also explicitly intervenes with and modifies those activities and relations.

As some media theorists have suggested, there is evidence that games such as *Pokémon GO* may act as catalyst for large-scale changes in people's 'destination choice' or 'trip distribution' (Colley et al., 2017). In other words, such games have the potential to incentivize 'people to do something they rarely do: substantially change where they choose to go' (Colley et al., 2017: 8). Although it is just a game, *Pokémon GO* reveals how our experience of public space is mediated by networked connectivity and is increasingly 'transformed through collisions of the digital and the urban' (Iveson, 2016: n.p.).

As media become more mobile and playful, and games embed geolocative data, our everyday experience of place is interwoven with playful virtual environments. Familiar neighbourhoods and urban environments are transformed into ludic spaces. Lammes (2016) has explored the way location-based games (such as *RunZombieRun* and others) effectively turn maps into 'navigational interfaces and gameboards', a description that can equally be applied to *Pokémon GO*. With developments in mobile technologies and the growth of collaborative platforms, making and sharing maps has taken on new playful, ambient and co-present dimensions.

Yet we are also reminded of the inherently *spatial* and *mobile* nature of popular culture and media more generally, and how popular cultural forms have always been part of our everyday geographies (Horton, 2012: 11–12). In bringing together childhood and play studies with human geography, for example, Horton documents how his young research participants integrated *Pokémon GO* play into the structure of their mundane spatial practices and daily space-time routines, effectively remaking their homes, local shops and neighbourhoods as part of the *Pokémon* universe (Horton, 2012).

In the context of location-based AR games, it is important to highlight the uneven ways players come to the game space and how gameplay is interwoven with our own culture and location. That is, certain bodies have more latitude to deviate from normalized practices, while some, as Katie Salen (2017) argues, don't. Salen turns to the potential disempowerment and marginalization that affects players of augmented reality games and mobile location-based apps such as *Pokémon GO*. That is, *Pokémon GO* requires users to explore their (sub)urban environment, a form of gameplay that is underscored by issues of racial inequity and the relative freedom people have to move playfully through their neighbourhoods and cities.

Salen asks, what can *Pokémon GO* teach us about mobility, accessibility, race and privilege? It is clearly more dangerous for some bodies to be in some places at certain times, and there is undoubtedly a hierarchy of risk at work that acts upon our bodies differently, depending on our age, gender, ethnicity or social milieu. In their study of the racial and ethnic bias of *Pokémon GO*, Colley et al. (2017) examine how the game's data and code, which 'augments' reality, often 'reinforces preexisting power structures' and 'geographic contours of advantage and disadvantage', as *PokéStops* and game resources are distributed more densely in wealthier areas with predominantly white non-minority populations.

On the one hand, *Pokémon GO* highlights the powerful role of the playful in contemporary media and consolidates decades of urban and hybrid reality gaming and place-making experimentation. On the other hand, we might argue that *Pokémon GO* players are narrowly goal-oriented, driven to collect and compete for virtual items as they engage in what is essentially a gamified activity. That is, *Pokémon GO* could be seen as a simplified reduction of a popular but fairly complex trading game that was originally targeted at preteens.

In addition to the paradoxes around inequality in digital and offline worlds, *Pokémon GO* highlighted the hybrid and contextual nature of mobile play as it transforms the urban environment into a ludic or playful space. In the next section, we discuss the tradition from which *Pokémon GO* emerged.

Location-based mobile games: Transforming urban environments into playspaces

Over the past decade we have seen a proliferation of location-based games and playful apps that invite us to upload and share our personal and local content in-the-moment. In this way, we enact a hybrid, layered and multifaceted experience of place, presence and communication.

Location-based services typically provide situational information about the urban environment via online databases and media libraries, such that informational changes on the mobile screen change both our navigation and experience of physical space. In this way, 'being online' becomes enfolded inside present contexts and activities, as we find our way through the city, search for a good place to eat, drive to a friend's house for the first time, or tag our location on location-based apps such as *Foursquare*. Location-based mobile gaming is a particularly robust example of this emergent hybrid experience.

Historically, location-based games – referred to as urban games, big games, pervasive games and mixed reality games – emerged out of avant-garde new media art, and involved creative experimentation with new media interfaces, platforms and networks. In the 1970s and 1980s, the New Games Movement, currently experiencing a revival, sought to popularize cooperative and creative urban play, and deliberately challenged and disrupted the mundane and familiar by transforming public spaces into playful places. Yet although location-based social games were once considered experimental, they have now become mainstreamed and commodified, and part of the more general cultural shift towards gamification, where game techniques are embedded into non-game activities. For example, the playful app-based service *Foursquare* (with a purported 30 million users) invites users to share first-hand recommendations of 'the best places to go' and integrates the tagging of places visited into friend-networks. It offers consumer rewards for the most prolific taggers.

Against this turn towards gamification and commodification, creators of urban and community games, such as the UK new media group Blast Theory, continue to deliberately 'hack' public space, inviting players to experience a de-familiarization of their everyday perceptions of the urban environment. In this way, location-aware and hybrid reality mobile games can transform urban spaces into participatory gameworlds. This potential can be seen in 'sandbox' games that encourage an emergent mode of play that often embeds player-centred design and relies on community feedback and content contribution. New York game designer Frank Lantz, who has been involved in such pivotal projects as *Pac-Manhattan*, argues that big urban games will play a significant role in the future of gaming. Big games are, for Lantz, 'large-scale, real-world games that occupy urban streets and other public spaces and combine the richness, complexity, and procedural depth of digital media with physical activity and face-to-face social interaction' (2006: n.p.).

In his analysis of *Geocaching*, Jason Farman (2009) describes the mixed or augmented realities of pervasive location-based games where bodies, networks and material space converge. Played in over 200 countries, *Geocaching* is a treasure hunt game requiring game players to hide 'geocache containers' marked with GPS data in public places. Players then 'use their mobile devices (from GPS receivers to iPhones) to track down the container, sign the log, and leave tradable and trackable items in the cache' (Farman, 2009: 1). In such games, we must seamlessly combine and accommodate both the *immediate* and *mediated* experience of the world.

In an early incarnation of location-based gaming, the game *Mogi*, launched in 2003, represented the city of Tokyo as both a map on players' mobile phones and on the web. The latter provided computer players with an expanded view of the gamespace overlaying the city, along with both the geographic and gameworld location of all players. Mobile and computer players both accessed different views of the gamespace, and collaborated to collect virtual objects and creatures at various locations throughout the city. It is this collaboration that worked to 'construct' the hybrid space. Licoppe and Inada (2006: 52) described players of the game *Mogi* as 'hybrid beings' who are able to 'smoothly integrate the embodied lived experience of the body and the mediated perception of oneself and of the environment'.

Location-based mobile games generate hybrid experiences of place and presence, requiring the player to integrate their own situated and embodied perception of the world with dynamic GPS-enabled information, embedded within an augmented and networked game reality. As Farman (2011: 108) notes, 'this is one of the characteristics of mobile technologies, which have effectively transformed our experience of presence and absence into perpetual co-presence'. Indeed, we would suggest that mobile media users experience different kinds of presence: co-located presence (while in the same physical space as others), telepresence (while talking on the phone), absent presence (viewing blog or Facebook posts), distributed presence (online multiplayer gaming) and ambient presence (the perpetual sense of others in the network) (Okabe & Ito, 2005; Hjorth & Richardson, 2014). In this way, location-based mobile games and applications can be said to add a complex *dimensionality* to place and space.

The consequence of this is that we need to rethink the spatial and place-based experience of being-in-public, as we increasingly integrate online information about our immediate environment into the patterns of urban life and pedestrian movement. Gordon and de Souza e Silva (2011) have argued that such hybrid practices generate what they term 'net-local public space', which describes a paradoxical sense of simultaneous immediate proximity and distance. Net-local public space includes those engaging in location-based activities with mobile devices, those (both co-present and online) participating in this network activity and those non-participants who are co-located in the urban setting.

For Pellegrino (2010), hybridity is the key word that describes this 'co-constructed dimension of participation' in contemporary media culture. De Souza e Silva (2006) and Pellegrino (2010: 99) use the term 'hybridity' to refer to the way in which our experience of presence and participation have been transformed in contemporary life, 'through multiple forms of proximity, both physical and virtual'. We used to clearly differentiate between the actual and the virtual and the online and offline, but now these dichotomies have collapsed, such that our attention and sense of presence has become ambient and dispersed.

Casual gaming in public: The mobilization of private space

Genealogically, we can trace the roots of mobile play to the late 19th century. As Parikka and Suominen (2006) identify, the various situational contexts of modernization at that time – including industrialization, transportation and urbanization – enabled particular forms of mobility and movement. These processes entangled changing notions of leisure, spectatorship and the rise of personalization and individualization. From playing cards to portable chess and the stereoscope, games were part of the Victorian mediascape, which emphasized mechanization, consumption and mobility.

For Parikka and Suominen (2006), the mobile phone re-enacts a 'third place' between public and private space. It is a new form of an old habitual practice already common in the 19th century:

[W]hat is new in this division of space and creation of a place of one's own? Instead of seeing this solely as a trend of digital mobile culture, we argue that this is more a phenomenon that took off with the creation of modern urban space and the new paradigms of media consumption. ... [T]he pattern of mobile entertainment usage as the creation of a private sphere was already part of the railway culture of the nineteenth century – even if people consumed such media content as newspapers and books instead of digital entertainment. (Parikka & Suominen, 2006, n.p.)

This mediated closing-off is perhaps more common with the ubiquity of mobile interfaces, prompting Groening (2010: 1340) to comment that a society of 'portable personal electronics is a society in which private space is as physically mobile as the populace and privacy itself is radically mobile'. For Hjorth (2013), the mobile phone is frequently used as a micro-mobile home or metaphoric caravan, allowing us to carry private space in our pockets and activate it when needed.

Mobile games also exemplify and extend Raymond Williams' (1975) notion of mobile privatization. Williams coined the term in the 1970s to highlight the deep contradictions around domestic television, which traversed and provided access to the public domain but made users feel more 'at home'. Mobile privatization has been heightened with the rise of mobile media, which has seen a further tethering to notions of the home (that is, the containment of familiar content and services, and the provision of familial connectivity that is enabled by the mobile device), while also setting the user 'free' to roam (Morley, 2003).

Domestication approaches to technology acknowledge the blurring distinctions between work and leisure with mobile media (Ling & Haddon, 2003). One way of understanding this entanglement between work and leisure in terms of contemporary mobile media is through Sicart's notion of 'playfulness' (2014). Many of the affordances of mobile media apps draw on users' playful engagement with media, and frequently employ gamification strategies, as in the case of productivity, self-monitoring and fitness apps that reward the user with game-like digital objects such as badges, icons and virtual currency.

Wilmott et al. (2017) argue that GPS-enabled smart watches and smart bands encourage us to redefine our quotidian environments as playful laborious playgrounds, where leisure activities are redefined in terms of work and quantifiable data. This blurring of work and leisure practices by mobile media has been highlighted by many cultural scholars (Wajcman, 1991; Gregg, 2011) and is also encapsulated by Julian Kücklich's (2005) term 'playbour', which describes how various player practices (such as modding, remixing, sharing and liking) produce social, creative and cultural capital. In these terms, mobile media can be mutually characterized by both ambient play and soft labour (Hjorth, 2017).

Mobile media practices are often characterized by paradoxes. They allow us to roam physically but also oblige us to be constantly on-call. Yet despite this tethering, our use of mobile screens is quite different from the dedicated attentiveness we give to other screens, such as television, cinema and even home computers. We often 'turn towards' them momentarily and for minutes at a time, checking for messages, social media posts or a missed call, playing a level of *Kick the Buddy* while waiting for the bus. Mobile-phone engagement is characterized by interruption, and sporadic or split attention between other activities.

This has been recognized by mobile-phone game developers, who have labelled the mobile player a 'casual gamer'. Casual mobile games are typically interruptible, allowing play to become intertwined with everyday routines and the existing patterns of daily life. Within the game literature, casual games are often described in terms of their properties; that is, they are designed for casual use, are easy to learn (such as simple puzzle, card and word games), offer quick rewards and consist of levels of short duration. Thus, casual gaming is often understood as a mode of engagement that requires relatively low-level skills and only sporadic attention up to a threshold of around five minutes. When researchers ask their participants to describe their mobile game play, they often pass it off as an incidental distraction, a peripheral and unimportant activity. Some are even embarrassed to admit they play such trivial games.

Yet the pejorative term 'casual' actually disguises the substantial investments made by some casual gamers, and oversimplifies an increasingly diverse and rapidly developing mode of gameplay (Taylor, 2012). As Mia Consalvo (2012: 184) notes, smartphones and mobile touchscreens have put mobile gaming platforms 'in the hands of millions of people who would never consider themselves gamers'.

Like being 'online', games have become normalized, embedded in the many other navigational, informational, productivity and social media apps within our mobile mediascape, all of which change the way we move through and experience the urban environment. It is this normalization of mobile games, together with their mode of perpetual availability, which renders mobile play ambient, as it increasingly infiltrates our habitudes and routines.

It has been argued that portable music devices such as the Walkman, iPod, mp3 player and mobile phone provide us with a kind of 'auditory privatization' of urban space, transforming how we behave in public (Helyer, 2007). As Michael Bull (2005: 169) has commented: 'Mediated isolation itself becomes a form of control over spaces of urban culture in which we withdraw into a world small enough to control.' For Amparo Lásen (2017), mobile listening also can be understood as a form of public engagement with urban spaces, which has a long history of portable media, including the transistor radio, boom boxes (Schloss & Boyer, 2014), personal stereos (Bull, 2000) and the boom car (Bull, 2007).

Yet while music players provide discrete sound bubbles or 'sonorous envelopes' that allow us to shut out the bustling noise of urban life, the mobile phone is also a communicative and networked device. It is unpredictable and disruptive, puncturing the soundscape as users pepper urban space with their own 'noises' of familiarity and intimacy, eruptions of personal ringtones, bleeps and one-sided conversations. Nevertheless, a number of studies have found that much like listening to music, mobile-phone use and casual gaming are often used as a proxy 'do not disturb' sign when we are alone in public. This kind of behaviour is now one that we all recognize, a mode of media distraction similar to book- or newspaper-reading on public transport, an indicator of privacy well understood by those around us.

When gameplay is mobile and situated in public places, the particular way we engage with the game is determined by the motility and mobility of the pedestrian body, taking place in the interstices of productive and goal-oriented activity. We play casual mobile games while waiting – for a friend, at a bus stop, or for a journey to end – and use our mobile devices as a means of managing the bodily agitation of impatience, aloneness and boredom in public, enabling a mobilization of personal entertainment while 'being-with-others' (Hjorth & Richardson, 2010). In this way, the mobile device becomes co-opted into the labour of waiting, filling and suturing the 'dead' or 'fractured' times and spaces that are part of everyday urban life (Bissell, 2007).

Here, the activity of casual gaming enacts a particular kind of 'face-work' in Goffman's sense – the deliberate posture we present to the public – yet at the same time it permits an 'environmental knowing', or a peripheral awareness of our surroundings in readiness for the busy-ness of life to resume (Goffman, 1972). This transient and non-dedicated attentiveness to the small screen – you can 'switch off' but not 'totally' – allows us to remain alert to the 'arrival' which marks the end of waiting, yet we are also able to cooperate in a kind of tacit social agreement of non-interaction among strangers. For many, this kind of engagement with the mobile screen provides safe seclusion from unwelcome interaction in potentially risky situations of co-present waiting, while still remaining 'open' or attentive to the proximity of that risk.

As discussed, mobile location-based gaming enacts and enables a quite different experience of space and place in urban environments, opening up a *hybrid space* that merges physical location and online networks, transforming urban spaces into ambient and collaborative playgrounds.

Conclusion

In this chapter we have conceptually sketched the burgeoning and dynamic field of mobile gaming in the context of broader cultural and historical trends. As a way of capturing the various worlds of mobile play – domestic, casual and urban – we have brought together two modalities of media practice: ambient play and digital wayfaring. As we have argued, mobile games extend and transform earlier patterns of media use that saw the increasing mobilization of private space. As a casual form of gaming, they have become infused into our daily routines and habitudes. Finally, we traced the emergence of augmented or hybrid reality gaming, culminating in the mainstream popularity of *Pokémon GO*. In each of these instances of mobile gaming, we can see the coalescence of ambient play – the diffusion of gameplay across temporal and spatial dimensions of everyday life, and digital wayfaring – the movement of digital information into our experience of place and our movement through the environment.

12

Social Media & Death

Introduction

They say the future is death.

Figure 12.1   Sendai Airport after 3/11[1]

In mid-afternoon on 11 March 2011 one of the largest earthquakes ever measured occurred deep under the sea, off the Eastern coast of Japan's main island Honshu. The earthquake, sometimes referred to as 3/11, created an enormous tsunami that devastated parts of the Eastern Honshu coast, killing more than 15,000 people and causing a nuclear reactor incident in Fukushima. Earthquakes and tsunami are an omnipresent danger for Japan, and have featured in Japanese culture for centuries, as captured by Hokusai's *The Great Wave off Kanagawa*.

This time, however, the latest technologies captured the event as camera phones and security footage began flooding social media with images, sounds and video of the event as it unfolded. Suddenly everyone could be there via their devices as webcams and mobile footage replayed on media streaming sites. Posts on social media showed water pouring over sea walls, picking up cars as though they were children's toys. We witnessed people sitting in their lounge rooms as sea water knocked down doors and walls and engulfed homes and businesses.

In the days and weeks that followed, social media continued to show recovery efforts, repair work, and the aftermath on lives and livelihoods. And alongside this was the discussion, not only from the people who were there and their immediate friends and family, but also from a much wider co-present planet. Social media took an event that in past decades may have been perceived as a remote disaster happening somewhere else and turned it into something that affected people across the world on a personal level.

This significant event provides us with insights into the way that social media is changing how we experience loss and death. In this chapter, we look at how social media mediates loss and death, and remediates the rituals surrounding death, raising important questions about how death is represented online. We are seeing older interactions between technology and death (such as the role of the camera in memorial practices) being renewed through social media practices, for example, funeral selfies (Meese et al., 2015). At the same time, social media opens up new avenues for experiencing death and loss, from accessing Facebook tribute pages during public disasters to the lingering digital traces on a smartphone of someone who has died (Graham et al., 2013; Lingel, 2013; Refslund Christensen & Gotved, 2014; Gibbs et al.; Gibson, 2015).

This chapter begins by looking at how social and mobile media are redefining our relationship with death. We then look at ways in which the intimacy of mobile and social media becomes a means for people to become more deeply connected with death, loss and grieving in everyday lives. Finally, we turn to consider the digital afterlife; the implications of digital data persisting beyond the life of its owner and the challenges this poses for researchers.

A key paradox that underlies this chapter is the tension between the intimate and the public. We see this in the way that grief is, on the one hand, a deeply personal thing, with each person experiencing it in different ways. And yet, on the other hand, grief and mourning are also something that we see experienced in very public ways, especially during large-scale tragedies and disasters. As we have seen throughout this book, social media encompasses this paradox: intimacy is fundamental to understanding the way that publics are formed and maintained online (Papacharassi, 2014). When it comes to grief and mourning, then, the public intimacy of social media is seeing the rituals of grief being mediated and re-mediated through digital devices.

Death and digital media

Social and mobile media are having a substantial impact on the way we think about and deal with death, loss and grief. As we have seen throughout this book, our relationship with social media and the mobile devices we use to access social media and the array of other attendant media technologies can often be best characterized through understanding a series of intimate relationships. Often these relationships are considered with respect to the living, but increasingly we need to consider the implications of the intimacy associated with social and mobile media, and how we use these to relate to death and loss.

At least since the Victorian era, death has often been described as a taboo subject. However, as John Troyer, director of the Centre for Death and Society (University of Bath), argues, death isn't taboo (Troyer, 2017). As he notes, there is a deep paradox in the way death is managed and experienced in contemporary culture. He argues:

> Contrary to the popular wisdom that it's a taboo subject, we love discussing death. Dead bodies fascinate us and some of our favourite television shows have been about death and forensic pathology. … But since the mid-to-late 19th century when the Victorians celebrated death and funerals with much theatricality – so the argument goes – we've repressed death to the point of it being hidden. Even worse, death has become so distant that it terrifies first-world humans and the best we can do is learn to manage an overpowering sense of dread. (Troyer, 2014: n.p.)

Now digital data allow for new ways to think about, configure and contextualize death (Gotved, 2014; Baumer et al., 2015). As we have seen throughout this book, social media has changed many facets of offline and online practice, sometimes creating new experiences, and at other times recasting older experiences through a digital lens. Much of the literature around the way that digital media has changed our relationship with death has focused upon online memorials (de Vries & Rutherford, 2004) and other forms of grieving online (Veale, 2003). Researchers are now beginning to delve deeper and are looking at the way engagement with death online is complicated due to the way that our online and offline lives have become entangled through social and mobile media, and thus necessarily also rituals and processes around death, dying and after-death (Graham et al., 2013). Where Victorian rituals of death (Walter et al., 2011) once compartmentalized death to the grave, and psychological models have constructed grief as something that one can 'get over'

(Rosenblatt, 1996), the everydayness of digital media sees that 'death and (after-) death are, once again, becoming more public and everyday' (Graham et al., 2013: 136).

A key function of the mobile device here is the way that it not only mediates death, but also remediates and 'mediatizes' death (Refslund Christensen & Govted, 2014: 1). So, for example, when a celebrity dies, their death is mediatized as it is reported and represented in various news feeds and status updates as text, images and video. Mobile devices also remediate death, by re-presenting these images in new contexts. The digital networked image is a remediation of a photograph, and may be remediated still further within another medium, like an instant-messaging app, for example.

Death is also becoming mediatized, changed by the way it exists as a thing that happens in the media (in contrast to the actual event itself). Much of our everyday contact with death is not an experience of the actual death itself, but an experience of the media arte-facts of that death (especially in the case of large tragedies or celebrity deaths). Of course, death is also mediated, remediated and mediatized by other media forms, such as televi-sion and print, but the affordances of mobile and social media is heightened, providing continuity with older technologies while also remediating rituals around death and grief.

Hoskins (2011: 270) has pointed to what he calls a 'post-scarcity memorial media boom', in which the ubiquity of networked mobile devices and social media, combined with the ease with which images and video can be created and circulated, has led to a greater emphasis on the memorialization of events. Through digital networked technol-ogies, these events are circulated, bringing mourning into the everyday 'with little or no delay' (Gibson, 2015: 339), and can persist through time, rather than fading, as memories tend to do, in what Gibson refers to as 'a regenerative media archive' (2015: 339).

Mobile and social media bring together a series of unique affordances that not only contextualize death within the everyday, but does so in more immediate and personal ways. Our devices don't just mediate death and its attendant rituals, but also remediate and mediatize, allowing for the emergence of different interactions between individuals, intimate publics, peri-mortem and post-mortem rituals. The next section picks up on the importance of this intimate dimension to social and mobile media.

Loss, social media and affect

On 16 April 2014 the ferry *MV Sewol* was en route from Incheon to Jeju in South Korea, carrying 476 people, many of them second-grade high school students. At 8.49am the ferry made a sharp turn and began to sink. Over the following few hours the ferry sunk, taking the lives of over 250 school children. Students on board the *Sewol* were in contact with their families during the event via their mobile devices. Mobile phones captured and relayed images and video of terrified passengers, and documented the failed procedures and lack of training that was in part responsible for the tragedy. The images, video and texts connected people to the tragedy as it unfolded, and also in the days and weeks after the tragedy where the replayed event was witnessed in thousands of ways by millions of people around the globe, and consolidated a worldwide public outcry.

The *Sewol* disaster was immediate, personal and still affects us years later. The selfies-as-eulogies, which were captured by passengers and spread across the world via social media, demonstrate the emergent ways in which mobile media practices are recalibrating the relationship between peri- and post-mortem modes of representation and witnessing.

The *Sewol* disaster and the 3/11 tsunami in Japan, discussed at the beginning of this chapter, are two examples of the multiple ways in which mobile and social media are transforming how we experience, share and represent events of emotional significance in our lives during disasters. Increasingly, mobile and social media are not just a way of recording, annotating and disseminating elements of an event, they also play a role in amplifying the affect of an event.

In both examples, specific kinds of knowing and knowledge are constructed – what Reading (2009a) refers to as 'memory capital', a concept that is linked to Pierre Bourdieu's (1984 [1979]) conception of cultural and social capital. These knowledges afford certain kinds of intimate connections within the publics that form around and beyond the event. People are effectively brought together by a common sense of grief, mediated by technology. There has been substantial work in memory studies around digital media (Volkmer, 2006; van Dijck, 2007; Richardson & Hessey, 2009; Ernst, 2012; Hoskins, 2011; Hand, 2013), but here we want to consider how mobile media (Reading, 2009a, 2009b), and social media more specifically, differs from other media contexts in the ways that memory is shaped.

Social media differs in a number of ways, but most notably the intimacy and embodied characteristics of social and mobile media engages us in an event in a more personal, affective way. Through being able to see and participate co-presently in these events (even if at a distance) via social media, we become witnesses to the event. Penelope Papailias (2016) has referred to this as 'affective witnessing'. Witnessing, in this context, refers to the act not just of seeing images or video of events related to death, but of a personal affective involvement in those events, even if we were not personally involved in them.

Papailias (2016) points to the way that online social media allow people to participate in the event, to relate it back to themselves. Papailias uses the example of an online memorial to a bus tragedy that took place in Greece. This online memorial, originally a website, was remediated as a YouTube video, which again changed the way people related to it. Papailias's case study shows how in some ways social media functions like a memorial to a person or event, providing a space that focuses memory and attention. Yet social media also stores and records; people don't just access and watch YouTube videos (to draw upon Papailias's case study, for example), but may also interact by leaving comments.

For Papailias, the database (a searchable repository of information, including social media) possesses a viral quality, because the social media depictions and remediation of an event, such as a tragedy, become representations of that event, allowing people to participate in the event and become part of it. Comments on a YouTube video are not separate from the video; commenting, responding to comments and reading comments become part of the YouTube experience, taking it beyond a remediation of television and into something else.

This idea of virality that Papailias uses is a term that 'captures the temporality, spatiality, materiality, and mimeticism of these formations [the online memorials], as well as their frequent pathologization' (Papailias, 2016: 1). Others adopt similar terms, for example Hoskins (2011: 270) refers to memorials as 'being a contagion of the past'. This idea of virality and contagion refers to the way that the immediacy and intimacy of social media can spread the impact of an event through space and time. This intimate and immediate 'affect' of mobile media means that the witnessing affect is more embodied. The impact of Japan's 3/11 upon the world is inextricably linked with the horror-laden mobile-phone footage of the tsunami wave engulfing cars and houses as if they were toys. This footage had a significant *affect* and *effect* that differed from traditional media depictions of the event, and persists well beyond the event, continuing to haunt YouTube recommendations and playlists today.

Drawing from Deleuze and Guattari's (1987) concept of the machinic assemblage, Papailias (2016) talks of a procedural assemblage of mourning and witnessing. Rather than a divide between the mourner and those that witness, affective viral media shapes new types of witnesses–mourner interpellations. This is at the heart of what she calls 'affective witnessing' (Papailias, 2016). In this process, Papailias signals to Judith Butler's (2004, 2009) work on the unevenness of mournable bodies in media – the way that some bodies are more affective and grievable than others. In this work, we need to understand the uneven landscape not only of cultural intimacy but also as digital intimate publics.

Among these considerations, it is important to remember that mobile and social media are not single media, but involve multiple platforms and affordances that allow us to consider the role of media. We should avoid focusing too much on a single platform but instead recognize that social media is frequently experienced and deployed as what Madianou and Miller (2012) would call 'polymedia'. In other words, we should be wary of the limitations of any analysis that seeks to understand the relationship between loss, an individual or group, and any single platform. Although sometimes masquerading in the literature as the quintessential online memorial, a Facebook memorial is frequently just part of a larger array of digital responses to a death or tragic event. Furthermore, we need to always remember that no single platform holds a monopoly. As we have seen consistently throughout this book, Facebook is not even the most significant social network in many countries.

Framing and contextualizing particular forms of intimacy and loss enables an argument in which the bringing together of the mobile visuality and mobile memories is informed by 'mobile-emotive' processes – the adaptation of culturally-specific, affect-laden rituals in, and around, mobile media practices. Understanding how loss is framed by and through mobile media, as argued in *Haunting Hands: Mobile Media Practices and Loss*

(Cumiskey & Hjorth, 2017), can be described as 'Ghosts in the mobile' – a phenomenon whereby the mobile device can become haunted, digitally and materially, and contribute to the building of an occulture not readily recognized or acknowledged.

The digital afterlife

In the past when a loved one passed away, those left behind continue to have duties to the deceased. Material possessions are sorted, sold or gifted, and traces of the deceased, such as photos or the most personal possessions, are stored as memorial keepsakes. Today, as we have seen across earlier chapters, it is hard not to leave a digital footprint. Many people have at least one social media profile, and as we increasingly use technologies like wearables to track our behaviour, and even as our consumption moves from physical media, to broadcast and live streaming media, we accrue a digital presence, replete with digital possessions and us-shaped data patterns in the digital firmament. What happens to these digital possessions and traces that defined a person in life? What are the issues we need to consider in the digital afterlife?

Graham et al. (2013) have argued new media are changing our relationship with life and death. They are enabling new modes for life to be 'extended, prolonged and ultimately transformed through the new circulations, repetitions, and recontextualizations on the Internet and other platforms' (Graham et al., 2013: 133). Digital data allow new ways in which to construct one's life, death and after-death (Bennett & Bennett, 2000; Veale, 2003; de Vries & Rutherford, 2004; Jones, 2004; Stanyek & Piekut, 2010; Bollmer, 2013). As we have seen already in this chapter, this is especially the case with mobile media as a witness, repository, disseminator and magnifier of events. However, we are also seeing the development of novel ways to engage with death at a personal level through social media, with new genres such as 'selfies at funeral' signalling emergent relations between intimacy, mobile media, etiquette and affect (Gibbs et al., 2015; Meese et al., 2015).

Through its assemblage of intimate and yet public textures, mobile media makes us reconsider the relationship between death and afterlife, especially with the digital afterlife and posthumous performativity, which is still relatively underexplored (Stanyek & Piekut, 2010). As Refslund Christensen and Gotved (2014: 1) observe, 'media are materialities that allow us to communicate with the dead or about the dead over the gaps between the world of the living and whatever spatial and temporal sphere the dead may reside without being absorbed into these gaps ourselves'. These materialities potentially includes a vast range of digital possessions and derived data, ranging from social media accounts to music collections, from collected data such as exercise and other QS data to all manner of things which are now stored on the cloud. These media materialities provide often significantly intimate connections with the deceased, and raise important questions about what is to be done with this data, and who should make decisions about that data on behalf of the dead. We are now witnessing the emergence of digital afterlife roles, such as 'stewarding' (or managing online media of a posthumous loved one), that involves often invisible and yet symbolic practices not often acknowledged in the visual labour of social media (Brubaker, 2016).

For social media companies, the spectre of death has significant operational, legal and algorithmic implications. With social media feeds weaving in and out of lives, the dead and death becomes an integral part of the algorithms (Leaver, 2013; Gibbs et al., 2015). As Tama Leaver considers:

> The death of a social media user provides a moment of rupture which highlights the significant value of the media traces a user leaves behind. More to the point, the value of these media becomes most evident to those left behind precisely because that individual can no longer be social. While beginning to address the issue of posthumous user data, Google and Facebook both have very blunt tools; Google might offer executors access while Facebook provides the option of locking a deceased user's account as a memorial or removing it altogether. Neither of these responses do justice to the value that these media traces hold for the living, but emerging digital legacy management tools are increasingly providing a richer set of options for digital executors. While the differences between material and digital assets provoke an array of legal, spiritual and moral issues, digital traces nevertheless clearly hold significant and demonstrable value. (2013: n.p.)

Given the intertwining of life, death and digital data, the politics of networks and image ownership quickly becomes a key factor when thinking about death and social media. As Bollmer (2013, 2015) has eloquently noted, we do not fully understand the implications of digital data when the owner or subject dies. In 'Fragile Storage, Digital Futures' (2015), Bollmer considers the paradoxes around 'the specific material conditions required to preserve and maintain digital storage, which is too often imagined as both ephemeral and everlasting'. For Bollmer, there is a need to reconcile approaches in media archaeology (the archaeological analysis of material culture and the digital humanities) in order to fully understand the complex dynamic proposed by digital futures.

Bollmer's work speaks to the rise in what has been defined by Facebook as compassion research. Led by scholars such as Brubaker, the research seeks to explore how stewards navigate this new and changing landscape where rules and etiquette are often tacit and suffocated by the numbness of grief. Research into the relationships between death, grief and social media will increase in importance for other researchers, too, as our interactions with death and grief via social media provides valuable insights into life, death and afterlife processes (Brubaker et al., 2014).

It will be increasingly important for researchers to engage with death and grief online, not only to understand the complexity of social media, but also as the divide between social media and everyday life blurs, to understand how death and grief are dealt with in our increasingly networked digital lives. For researchers, the role of dealing with this difficult data means thinking through the methods and politics of the digital. For example, what does it mean to do digital ethnography when the subject is dead? How does this challenge the reflexivity and power relations?

Facebook is one company that has most visibly engaged with some of these issues, but many digital industries have faced the need to understand and develop an ethics for research integrity in, and around, our treatment of images and other data of the dead. Researchers have a substantial role to play in helping us understand the role of data and its haunting capacity. There are an enormous number of questions that we are only beginning to ask in this respect. It is up to researchers to set the standards for how we treat, contextualize and understand the 'data of the dead'.

For some, establishing stewards as people who can step in as advocates for the dead is one solution. However, this requires someone to be contacted, for people to be available and willing to be stewards. What happens to data on accounts that are forgotten? Does the researcher have a responsibility to contact family members of the deceased before they use their data? What are the sensitivities surrounding this? Is it, in fact, the role of the researcher to act as advocate on behalf of the dead and their loved ones?

Let us return to Papailias's (2016) powerful 'affective witnessing' notion that we discussed in the previous section of this chapter. It is becoming important for researchers to understand the uneven landscape of not only affective witnessing and cultural intimacy, but also the role of the research in this circulation culture. What types of responsibilities should researchers take on board in terms of their research giving back to the community? And so how do we, as researchers, reconcile the affective witnessing of the deceased with the life of those loved ones? What are the politics and ethics of intimacy when dealing with mobile intimacy? What methods should we be recalibrating? What are we missing? As death online is informing more and more complex cartographies and genres, we need to ensure that, as researchers, we have robust methods as well as an understanding of its impact upon the families of the deceased.

Increasingly, new etiquette and practices are emerging in and around mobile media grief. From selfies at funerals (Meese et al., 2015) to industries around digital legacy and memorialization (Nansen et al., 2014), the role of mobile media is playing a key role in the transformation of boundaries and limits. Understanding the relationship between social media and grief will require researchers who are sensitive to the affordances of social and mobile media. They will need to appreciate the intimate relationship we have with our devices and social media, but will also need to think beyond the immediacy of the technology, and look into how social and mobile media persist in time and continue to influence longer-term ongoing processes of grief and grieving.

The Western idea that the funeral marks the end of the death and grieving process needs to be more fully interrogated in a world where images and the deceased haunt our devices, and may even speak to us through archived posts and automated reminders. Here longitudinal research could help us to understand how this persistence affects the bereavement process long after someone has died.

Conclusion

In this chapter we have looked at death, grief and the complex and not always well understood relationship they have with social media. A key point we have made throughout the chapter is that social and mobile media are changing the way we deal with death and grief. This happens in a variety of ways, but is mostly related to two key factors: the way that social media can remediate older rituals such as memorialization and grieving; and the way that mobile and social media are intimate media that can affect us in ways that earlier media technologies could not.

Grief is not something that is strictly defined by a series of universal rules. Like mobile media, it is informed by communal rules that change from culture to culture and even from individual to individual. Grief is inextricably interwoven with the social, as it is with the cultural, and much like social media, is constituted through the complex networks within intimate publics. As Cumiskey and Hjorth (2017: 10) put it: 'The experience of mourning, while at times a private experience, is one that is unique to the individual; and as such it becomes an experience that is constituted through reflection, individualized through the interpretations of events, and understood in conversation with others.'

Mobile and social media can provide us with insights into how we communicate, share, memorialize and understand loss. Our relationship with death may be changing as our devices make death more a part of everyday life. Mobile and social media entangle the online and offline worlds through the various technologies that capture, remediate and transmit conversations and memories, and in doing this also become entangled in processes of grief and death. While opening up new possibilities, social media can also confound grief and rituals around death. For example, mobile devices do not integrate neatly into funereal traditions (Haverinen, 2014; Nansen et al., 2014).

Life and death are all happening in the palm of our hand. To speak of the life of social media is to also engage with its death. The death of our loved ones remains alive in feeds. The death of a stranger becomes strangely intimate. In this mobile and yet intimate world, both the material and digital play out and affect in ways that we are only starting to comprehend. Indeed, as John Troyer (2017) notes, if there will eventually be more dead users than live ones on Facebook, the relationality between life and death will undoubtedly take on more significance and we will need tools to navigate the paradoxes of death becoming personal and everyday at the same time as it becomes part of our datafied cultures.

Note

1.   Image source: Ministry of Land, Infrastructure, Transport and Tourism (MLIT) (Japan)

13

Conclusion

It seems fitting that we begin this conclusion with a case study that embodies the paradoxes of social media today – that is, something that encapsulates the very texture and affect of social media as it becomes increasingly visual, intimate and mobile. Let us begin with Pon and Bon or Bonpon511. Indicative of what Crystal Abidin (2016) calls 'influencers', Japanese couple Tsuyoshi and Tomi Seki, both in their 60s, sum up the new spirit of Instagram.

Each day the creatively dressed couple document their attire via an iPhone and upload and share on Instagram. Each day their 720,000 followers gain inspiration from the childhood sweethearts' clothing style. So much so that Japanese department store Isetan Mitsukoshi has commissioned their own clothing range and they have published two books. Much of their wardrobe comes from affordable shops, such as Uniqlo. Pon and Bon are on a mission: they hope their visibility on social media will inspire other older couples that have retired to begin a 'second life' – which is the title of one of their books as opposed to the virtual reality platform of the same name.

Many are looking towards Japan, with one of the biggest ageing populations, to see how they will manage the care and infrastructures required. And, as we saw in Chapter 6, social media will progressively be part of those processes as the demographics and subsequent social media usage change. Social media will, as we suggested in previous chapters, be used by families for intergenerational care-at-a-distance and 'friendly surveillance'. And as increasingly ageing populations age and die on social media, how we relate and reflect upon life, death and afterlife will change (Cumiskey & Hjorth, 2017). As we noted in the previous chapter, social media platforms like Facebook and LINE will, in the next couple of decades, start to have more dead users than living users. Our feeds will increasingly be filled with images of deceased loved ones. Their data will become part of a contested ethical terrain with platforms 'owning' the information.

Indeed, far from just a medium for beautiful and young people, Instagram, like its audiences, are diversifying. Audiences are getting older and alternative, non-normative modes of body and performativity are being celebrated (Olszanowski, 2014; Tiidenberg, 2014, 2015a; Carah & Louw, 2015). As we argued in the first edition of *Understanding Social Media* (2013), as social media becomes more mobile, it also becomes a space for different modes of intimacy in often public spaces and contexts (Hinton & Hjorth, 2013: 3). As social media becomes more mobile, more visual, and more about the politics and practices of intimacy, it further instils key paradoxes around visibility/invisibility, empowerment/exploitation, the personal/corporate, the public/private, privacy/datafication. In practice, social media is often eschewing these paradoxes in ways that seem ambiguous, to say the least. And yet, it is in this grey area of practice where we are reminded that notions such as intimacy have always been mediated and often within public contexts (Berlant, 1998; Hjorth & Arnold, 2013).

From the example of Pon and Bon to its use in museums for audience engagement, Instagram does make for a compelling case towards understanding the past, present and future of social media. It is inherently shaped by the intimate and visual nature of the mobile device. It is also shaping the trajectory of social media discourse in curious ways (Hjorth & Hendry, 2015). The statistics are compelling: 95 million photos and videos are shared on Instagram per day. Over 40 billion photos and videos have been shared on the Instagram platform since its inception. With just over 800 million active monthly users, 500 million of these users are active daily (Dumas et al., 2017).

As noted in Chapter 7 on mobile visuality, Instagram is often, in Western contexts, synonymous with contemporary visual culture. That is, it reflects 'shared practices of a group, community, or society through which meanings are made out of the visual, aural, and textual world of representations' (Sturken & Cartwright, 2009: 3, cited in Rose, 2014). Instagram is creating new avenues for self-expression and activism for non-conformist body types (Olszanowski, 2014) as well as providing ways in which to document, archive and share stories about the places and events in our everyday lives. It is an important tool for emplacing visuality as we move through our lives in ways that are both digital and material (Hjorth & Pink, 2014). Instagram entangles the relationship between the digital and physical place in complex ways that emplace images in specific temporal and spatial ways. As a shared image, it is a highly social form of visuality. It is also indicative of contemporary digital intimate publics in which public and private, visibility and invisibility take various forms. And so, in this Conclusion, we see some emerging fields for the future of social media research.

First, as the users age and die, the 'life' of social media will also be about different understandings of death and afterlife, especially in terms of the haunting of data and what social repercussions are at stake. What are the ethics of platforms such as Facebook to reappropriate the lives of their dead users and how will this impact their loved ones?

As we explored in Chapter 12, as mobile media becomes increasingly synonymous with social media, they progressively become vessels for the ways in which death and dying manifest ambiently in our everyday lives. Affect becomes a key rubric in the rhythms and textures of social media. In particular, the highly visual nature of social mobile media creates unique forms of intimacy, embodiment and what Papailias (2016) calls 'affective witnessing'. With the increased circulation of images during and after significant events, this creates affective witnessing, a blurring between distinctions of the mourner and the witness.

For Papacharissi (2014), affect is core to understanding the texture and impact of social media in our lives. She coins the term 'affective publics' to describe the second generation of networked cultures as they move in and out of mobile devices and material realities. It is the intimacy and yet publicness of mobile media that plays into processes of continuity and discontinuity, mediation and remediation, life and death (Cumiskey & Hjorth, 2017).

The paradoxes of social media can be seen as part of broader, remediated tensions around the role of media in communication. The history of mobile communication and the ongoing development of general-purpose gateways between web browsers and mobile applications is illustrative of this phenomenon, which has been defined by paradoxical and sometimes contradictory aspects from the outset (Arnold, 2003). Rather, in the field of mobile and social media, tensions bleeding between public and private have long haunted debates on social capital and perceptions of its decline (Katz & Aakhus, 2002; Cumiskey & Hjorth, 2017; Serrano Telleria, 2017). However, as mobile devices become vehicles for complex data trails and datafication, in which personal information is given over to corporate platforms (van Dijck, 2017), they entangle our lives and deaths in even more multifaceted ways across various platforms, modes of telepresence and representations. These cadences will shape social media lives and deaths to come.

Second, as social media becomes more mobile and intimate (Hinton & Hjorth, 2013) in both its texture and terrain, the types of visuality that emerge start to diverge from norms, as discussed in Chapter 7. As the influencers Bon and Pon demonstrate, age performativity is being reinvented. And age isn't the only norm being circumvented. The work of Olszanowski (2014) and Tiidenberg (2015b) are illustrative of the new ways in which feminists and activists are using visual culture like Instagram to question the politics of normalization, ensuring different body types, shapes and ideologies are shared and therefore included within contemporary discourse.

Indeed, some, such as Leaver et al. (forthcoming), argue that the burgeoning dominance of visual culture apps such as Instagram in social media is only set to grow. As Leaver and Highfield (2016) note, Instagram creates and curates particular affordances of and for intimacy. They argue: 'Unlike other social media platforms, grief on Instagram is found to be more about personal expressions of loss rather than affording spaces of collective commemoration' (Leaver & Highfield, 2016: 33). The particular aesthetics and affordances of Instagram are about its own 'platform vernacular' (Gibbs et al., 2015).

Third, the politics and practices of datafication are going to continue to imbue social media with core paradoxes around privacy, 'platformativity' and corporate control. As discussed in Chapters 4 and 5, datafication and algorithmic cultures are now commonplace – that is, where data penetrate, invade and analyse our daily lives – and causing anxiety when potentially inaccurate statistical data are captured. These tensions and the paradoxes of power/powerless, tactic/strategy and identity/anonymity are highlighted through the lens of artists 'playfully resisting' through creative projects that scrutinize the normaliza-tion ('bell-curving') of QS and datafication usage at a broader and everyday socio-political level. For some, self-tracking and QS allow for a better sense of the body – a deeper proprioception. But for others, the emphasis on numbers and quantification goes against real understanding of practice as something that is story-based and nuanced and can't be summed up by numbers (Lupton, 2016b; Humphreys, 2018).

Fourth, as a response to the commodity-making of datafication, creative interventions can be found to comment on and disrupt dominant norms. We see that in Chapter 7 and Chapter 8, where artists explore the limits of platformativity and platform vernacular. Creative practitioners are using social media in their social practice to reflect upon con-temporary popular culture and politics, as can be seen in Cindy Sherman's selfie 'moment' via Instagram. Mobile art provides new insights into social media usage (including selfie subjectivities) and reinforces that artists have always engaged in the paradoxes of the everyday and the social. Social media as art medium further complicates these paradoxes.

Fifth, social media is transforming how public spaces, such as the museum, engage publics. Social media infiltration in museums and gallery structures is changing the logic of public spaces and pushing a curation of intimate publics, generating new ways of expe-riencing art that is further emphasizing the paradoxical role of intimacy within the public realms. That is, we are seeing the intimate becoming public while the public becomes intimate. As an example, Instagram selfie culture can be deployed to enhance the art expe-rience for the viewer, and at the same time changes the role of the curator, as the audience actively shapes the exhibition. The selfie can also be understood as embodied performance of the present, as cultural acts and as ways of being in the world. This social media entan-glement between public and the intimate not adds textuality to the artworks themselves which opens debates about the paradox of visibility and invisibility. However, when we consider that social media is also used to measure not only engagement but also impact, a feedback loop appears, forming an ironic infinite regress in which social media curates and creates art in a space that is increasingly blurred between the public and the intimate. More ethnographic work is needed to thicken these arguments.

Sixth, as platforms burgeon, other vernaculars are growing, such as paralinguistics. Intergenerational and cross-cultural forms of media literacy shape these practices. In Chapter 10 we explored the rise of visuality in terms of paralinguistics and examined the many paradoxes outlined in this book, such as visibility and invisibility, disclosure and divulgence, user personalization and corporate platformativity. As paralinguistic forms are now considered mainstream activity, there also remains the paradox of inequalities and differences, especially in terms of intergenerational communication. These observations were underpinned and drew on the *Locating the Mobile* project, ethnographic fieldwork to augment our understandings of some of the issues around paralinguistic practice.

Seventh, the role of hybrid and augmented reality will constantly move in and out of focus in everyday social media practices. The fact that Facebook purchased Oculus is indicative of the movement towards technologies such as social virtual reality (VR). In Chapter 11 we explored some of the relevant paradoxes through the *Pokémon GO* example in order to consider the ongoing debate that has plagued the internet from the onset – do these hybrid realities reinforce inequalities or create new socialities and possibilities?

In this concluding chapter we ask the reader to consider some of these social media futures and reflect upon how current practices may or may not inform these prospects. Just as Bon and Pon illustrate how social media might be used as a tool for creatively ageing well, the future of social media will inevitably face issues about ageing and dying. While much of the earlier work in the field focused on social media *lives*, increasingly our practices and questions will reflect upon social media *death* and *afterlives*.

References

Abend, P., & Fuchs, M. (2016). Introduction. *Digital Culture & Society*, *2*(1), 5–22. doi: 10.14361/dcs-2016-0102

Abidin, C. (2016). Visibility labour: Engaging with influencers' fashion brands and #OOTD advertorial campaigns on Instagram. *Media International Australia*, *161*(1), 86–100. doi: 10.1177/1329878X16665177

Albrechtslund, A. (2008). Online social networking as participatory surveillance. *First Monday*, *13*(3). Retrieved from http://firstmonday.org/ojs/index.php/fm/index

Albury, K., & Byron, K. (2016). Safe on my phone? Same-sex attracted young people's negotiations of intimacy, visibility, and risk on digital hook-up apps. *Social Media & Society*, *2*(4). doi:10.1177/2056305116672887

Alharbi, M., Straiton, N., & Gallagher, R. (2017). Harnessing the potential of wearable activity trackers for heart failure self-care. *Current Heart Failure Reports*, *14*(1), 23–29. doi: 10.1007/s11897-017-0318-z

Andrejevic, M. (2006). The discipline of watching: Detection, risk, and lateral surveillance. *Critical Studies in Media Communication*, *23*(5), 391–407. doi: 10.1080/0739 3180601046147

Andrejevic, M. (2011). Social network exploitation. In Z. Papacharissi (Ed.), *A Networked Self* (pp. 82–101). New York: Routledge.

Andrejevic, M. (2013). *Infoglut: How Too Much Information is Changing the Way We Think and Know*. New York: Routledge.

Arnold, M. (2003). On the phenomenology of technology: The "Janus-faces" of mobile phones. *Information and Organization*, *13*(4), 231–256.

Baddeley, B., Sornalingam, S., & Cooper, M. (2016). Sitting is the new smoking: Where do we stand? *British Journal of General Practice*, *66*(646), 258. doi: 10.3399/ bjgp16X685009

Baldassar, L. (2017). Transformations in transnational aging: A century of caring among Italians in Australia. In P. Aziz Dossa & C. Coe (Eds.), *Transnational Aging and Reconfigurations of Kin Work* (pp. 120–138). New Brunswick, NJ: Rutgers University Press.

Baldassar, L., Nedelcu, M., Merla, L., & Wilding, R. (2016). ICT-based co-presence in transnational families and communities: Challenging the premise of face-to-face proximity in sustaining relationships. *Global Networks*, *16*(2), 133–144. doi: 10.1111/glob.12108

Banks, J., & Humphreys, S. (2008). The labour of user co-creators. *Convergence*, *14*(4), 401–418. doi: 10.1177/1354856508094660

Barlow, J. P. (1996). A Cyberspace Independence Declaration. Retrieved from http://w2.eff.org/Censorship/Internet_censorship_bills/barlow_0296.declaration.

Barta, K., & Neff, G. (2016). Technologies for sharing: Lessons from Quantified Self about the political economy of platforms. *Information, Communication & Society*, *19*(4), 518–531. doi: 10.1080/1369118X.2015.1118520

Baumer, E. P. S., Ames, M. G., Burrell, J., Brubaker, J. R., & Dourish, P. (2015). Why study technology nonuse? *First Monday*, *20*(11). Retrieved from http://firstmonday.org/ojs/index.php/fm/article/view/6310/5137

Baym, N. (1998). The emergence of online community. In S. Jones (Ed.), *CyberSociety 2.0: Revisiting Computer-Mediated Communication and Community* (pp. 35–68). Thousand Oaks, CA: Sage.

Bellacasa Puig de la, M. (2017). *Matters of Care: Speculative Ethics in More than Human Worlds*. Minneapolis, MN: University of Minnesota Press.

Benford, S., & Giannachi, G. (2011). *Performing Mixed Reality*. Cambridge, MA: MIT Press.

Beniger, J. R. (1986). *The Control Revolution: Technological and Economic Origins of the Information Society*. Cambridge, MA: Harvard University Press.

Bennett, G., & Bennett, K. M. (2000). The presence of the dead: An empirical study. *Mortality*, *5*(2), 139–157. doi: 10.1080/13576270050076795

Berlant, L. (1998). Intimacy: A special issue. *Critical Inquiry*, *24*(2), 281–288.

Berlant, L (2008). *The Female Complaint: The Unfinished Business of Sentimentality in American Culture*. Durham, NC: Duke University Press.

Berlant, L. (2011). *Cruel Optimism*. Durham, NC: Duke University Press.

Berry, D. (2011). *The Philosophy of Software: Code and Mediation in the Digital Age*. London: Palgrave Macmillan.

Berry, D. (2012). *Understanding Digital Humanities*. London: Palgrave Macmillan.

Berry, M. (2017). *Creating with Mobile Media*. London: Palgrave Macmillan.

Berry, M., & Schleser, M. (Eds.). (2014). *Mobile Media Making in an Age of Smartphones*. New York: Palgrave Macmillan.

Bishop, C. (2012a). Digital divide: Contemporary art and new media. *Artforum*, September. Retrieved from http://artforum.com/talkback/id=70724.

Bishop, C. (2012b). *Artificial Hells: Participatory Art and the Politics of Spectatorship*. London: Verso.

Bissell, D. (2007). Animating suspension: Waiting for mobilities. *Mobilities*, *2*(2): 277–298. doi: 10.1080/17450100701381581

Blackwell, C., Birnholtz, J., & Abbott, C. (2014). Co-situation and impression formation using Grindr, a location-aware gay dating app. *New Media & Society*, *17*(7), 1117–1136. doi: 10.1177/1461444814521595

Blas, Z. (2017). Contra-Internet. Retrieved from www.zachblas.info/

Blas, Z., & Gaboury, J. (2016). Biometrics and opacity: A conversation. *Camera Obscura: Feminism, Culture, and Media Studies, 31*(2 (92)), 155–165. doi: 10.1215/02705346-3592510

Böhme, G. (1993). Atmosphere as the fundamental concept of a new aesthetics. *Thesis Eleven, 36*, 113–126. doi: 10.1177/072551369303600107

Bollmer, G. (2013). Millions now living will never die: Cultural anxieties about the afterlife of information. *The Information Society, 29*(3), 142–151. doi: 10.1080/01972243.2013.777297

Bollmer, G. (2015). Fragile storage, archival futures. *Journal of Contemporary Archaeology, 2*(1), 66–72. doi: 10.1558/jca.v2i1.27078

Bollmer, G., & Guiness, K. (2017). Phenomenology for the selfie. *Cultural Politics, 13*(2), 156–176. doi: 10.1215/17432197-4129113

Boris, E., & Salazar Parreñas, R. (Eds.). (2010). *Intimate Labors: Cultures, Technologies, and the Politics of Care*. Stanford, CA: Stanford University Press.

Bourdieu, P. (1984 [1979]). *Distinctions*. Cambridge, MA: Harvard University Press.

Bourriaud, N. (2002 [1998]). *Relational Aesthetics*. Translated by S. Pleasance & F. Woods with M. Copeland. Dijon: Les presses du reel. First published in French 1998, by same publisher as *Esthétique relationnelle*.

boyd, d. (2011). Social network sites as networked publics: Affordances, dynamics, and implications. In Z. Papacharissi (Ed.), *A Networked Self: Identity, Community and Culture on Social Network Sites*. New York: Routledge, 39–58.

boyd, d. (2012). The politics of 'real names'. *Communications of the ACM, 55*(8), 29–31. doi: 10.1145/2240236.2240247

boyd, d., & Crawford, K. (2011). Six provocations for Big Data. In *A Decade in Internet Time: Symposium on the Dynamics of the Internet and Society*, September. Retrieved from https://papers.ssrn.com/sol3/pape's.cfm?abstract_id=1926431

boyd, d., & Crawford, K. (2012). Critical questions for Big Data: Provocations for a cultural, technological, and scholarly phenomenon. *Information, Communication & Society, 5*, 662–679. doi: 10.1080/1369118X.2012.678878

boyd, d., & Marwick, A. E. (2011). Social privacy in networked publics: Teens' attitudes, practices, and strategies. Retrieved from http://papers.ssrn.com/sol3/papers.cfm?abstract_id=1925128

Brandt, T., Bendler, J., & Neumann, D. (2017). Social media analytics and value creation in urban smart tourism ecosystems. *Information & Management, 54*(6), 703–713. doi: 10.1016/j.im.2017.01.004

Brighenti, A. (2010). *Visibility in Social Theory and Social Research*. London: Palgrave Macmillan.

Brinson, N. H., & Rutherford, D. N. (2016). Quantified Self and personal health privacy policy limitations (SSRN Scholarly Paper No. ID 2757453). Rochester, NY: Social Science Research Network. Retrieved from https://papers.ssrn.com/abstract=2757453

Browne, S., & Blas, Z. (2017). Beyond the internet and all control diagrams. *The New Inquiry*, 25 January. Retrieved from https://thenewinquiry.com/beyond-the-internet-and-all-control-diagrams/

Brubaker, J. R. (2016, June 13). Stewarding someone else's self: A study of stewardship experiences of post-mortem profiles on Facebook. Paper presented at the International Communication Association Annual Conference, Fukuoka, Japan.

Brubaker, J. R., Ananny, M., & Crawford, K. (2014). Departing glances: A socio-technical account of 'leaving' Grindr. *New Media & Society*, *18*(3), 373–390. doi: 10.1177/1461444814542311

Brubaker, J. R., Dombrowski, L., Gilbert, A., Kusumakaulika, N., & Hayes, G. R. (2014). Stewarding a legacy: Responsibilities and relationships in the management of post-mortem data. *Proceedings of CHI 2014*. Toronto, Canada, 26 April–1 May.

Bruns, A. (2005). Some exploratory notes on produsers and produsage. *Snurblog*, 3 November. Retrieved from http://snurb.info/index.php?q=node/329.

Bruns, A., Moon, B., Münch, F., & Sadkowsky, T. (2017). The Australian twittersphere in 2016: Mapping the follower/followee network. *Social Media Society*, *3*(4). doi: 10.1177/2056305117748162

Budge, K., & Burness, A. (2018). Museum objects and Instagram: Agency and communication in digital engagement. *Continuum*, *32*(2). doi: 10.1080/10304312.2017.1337079

Budge, K., & Suess, A. (2018). Instagram is changing the way we experience art, and that's a good thing. *The Conversation*, 1 February. Retrieved from https://theconversation.com/instagram-is-changing-the-way-we-experience-art-and-thats-a-good-thing-90232

Bull, M. (2000). *Sounding Out the City: Personal Stereos and the Management of Everyday Life*. Oxford: Berg.

Bull, M. (2005). The intimate sounds of urban experience: An auditory epistemology of everyday mobility. In K. Nyíri (Ed.), *A Sense of Place: The Global and the Local in Mobile Communication* (pp. 169–178). Vienna: Passagen.

Bull, M. (2007). *Sound Moves: iPod Culture and Urban Experience*. London: Routledge.

Burgess, J. (2007) Vernacular Creativity and New Media (PhD thesis). Queensland University of Technology: Creative Industries Faculty. Retrieved from https://eprints.qut.edu.au/16378/

Burgess, J., & Bruns, A. (2012). Twitter Archives and the challenges of 'Big Social Data' for media and communication research. *M/C Journal*, *15*(5). Retrieved from http://journal.media-culture.org.au/index.php/mcjournal/article/view/561Driscoll

Burgess, J., & Bruns, A. (2015). Easy data, hard data: The politics and pragmatics of Twitter research after the computational turn. In G. Langlois, J. Redden & G. Elmer (Eds.), *Compromised Data: From Social Media to Big Data* (pp. 93–111). London: Bloomsbury.

Burgess, J., Bruns, A., & Hjorth, L. (2013). Emerging methods for digital media research: An introduction. *Journal of Broadcasting & Electronic Media*, *57*(1), 1–3. doi: 10.1080/08838151.2012.761706

Burgess, J., Marwick, A., & Poell, T. (2018). *The Sage Handbook of Social Media*. London: Sage.

Burroughs, B. (2017). YouTube kids: The app economy and mobile parenting. *Social Media & Society*, *3*(2). doi: 10.1177/2056305117707189

Butler, J. (2004). *Precarious Life: The Powers of Mourning and Violence*. New York: Verso.

Butler, J. (2009). *Frames of War: When Is Life Grievable*. London: Verso.

Byford, S. (2014). Line's bears and bunnies are coming for America. *The Verge*, 7 August. Retrieved from www.theverge.com/2014/8/7/5977195/chat-app-line-is-coming-for-america

Calvo, R. A., & Peters, D. (2013). The irony and re-interpretation of our Quantified Self. In *Proceedings of the 25th Australian Computer–Human Interaction Conference: Augmentation, Application, Innovation, Collaboration* (pp. 367–370). New York: ACM. doi: 10.1145/2541016.2541070

Carah, N., & Louw, E. (2015). *Media and Society: Production, Content & Participation*. London: Sage.

Carr, C. T., & Hayes, R. A. (2015). Social media: Defining, developing, and divining. *Atlantic Journal of Communication*, *23*, 46–65. doi: 10.1080/15456870.2015.972282

Castells, M. (2001). *The Internet Galaxy: Reflections on the Internet, Business, and Society*. New York: Oxford University Press.

Castells, M. (2010). *The Power of Identity* (2nd ed.). Malden, MA: Wiley-Blackwell.

Cheney-Lippold, J. (2011). A new algorithmic identity. *Theory, Culture & Society*, *28*(6), 164–181. doi: 10.1177/0263276411424420

Cheon, E., Jarrahi, M. H., & Su, N. M. (2016). Technology isn't always the best: The intersection of health tracking technologies and information practices of digital natives. In *2016 IEEE International Conference on Healthcare Informatics (ICHI)* (pp. 207–215). Chicago: CPS. doi: 10.1109/ICHI.2016.30

Chesher, C. (2012). Between image and information: The iPhone camera in the history of photography. In L. Hjorth, J. Burgess & I. Richardson (Eds.), *Studying Mobile Media: Cultural Technologies, Mobile Communication, and the iPhone* (pp. 98–117). New York: Routledge.

Christovich, M. M. (2016). Why should we care what Fitbit shares—A proposed statutory solution to protect sensitive personal fitness information. *Hastings Communications and Entertainment Law Journal*, *38*, 91–116. Retrieved from http://heinonline.org/HOL/P?h=hein.journals/hascom38&i=105

Chughtai, H., & Myers, M. D. (2014). A ludic perspective on everyday practices: Evidence from ethnographic fieldwork. Paper presented at AMCIS2014: 20th Americas Conference on Information Systems, United States, 7–9 August.

Chun, W. (2006). *Control and Freedom: Power and Paranoia in the Age of Fiber Optics*. Cambridge, MA: MIT Press.

Cincotta, K., Ashford, K., & Michael, K. (2011). The new privacy predators. *Women's Health*, November. Retrieved from www.womenshealth.com.au/

Clark, L. S. (2012). *The Parent App: Understanding Families in the Digital Age*. Oxford: Oxford University Press.

Clarke, R. (2000, 24 February). *Information wants to be free...* Retrieved from www.rogerclarke.com/II/IWtbF.html

Colley, A. J., Thebault-Spieker, A. Y., Lin, D., Degraen, B., Fischman, J., Hakkila, K., Nisi, V., Nunes, N. J., Wenig, N., Wenig, D., Hecht, B., & Schoning, J. (2017). The geography of Pokémon GO: Beneficial and problematic effects on places and movement. Paper presented at the *CHI 2017*, 6–11 May, Denver, CO, USA.

Consalvo, M. (2012). Slingshot to victory: Games, play and the iPhone. In P. Snickars & P. Vonderau (Eds.), *Moving Data: The iPhone and the Future of Media* (pp. 184–194). New York: Columbia University Press.

Consoli, G. (2014). The emergence of the modern mind: An evolutionary perspective on aesthetic experience. *The Journal of Aesthetics and Art Criticism*, *72*(1): 37–55. doi: 10.1111/jaac.12059

Costello, L. L., Wallace, R., & McDermott, M. (2017). Netnography: Range of practices, misperceptions, and missed opportunities. *International Journal of Qualitative Methods*, *16*(1), 1–12. doi: 10.1177/1609406917700647

Crawford, K., Lingel, J., & Karppi, T. (2015). Our metrics, ourselves: A hundred years of self-tracking from the weight scale to the wrist wearable device. *European Journal of Cultural Studies*, *18*(4–5), 479–496. doi: 10.1177/1367549415584857

Crystal, D. (2006). *Language and the Internet* (2nd ed.). Cambridge: Cambridge University Press.

Cumiskey, K., & Hjorth, L. (2017). *Haunting Hands: Mobile Media Practices and Loss*. New York: Oxford University Press.

Dahlberg, L. (2001). The Internet and democratic discourse: Exploring the prospects of online deliberative forums extending the public sphere. *Information, Communication & Society*, *4*(4), 615–633. doi: 10.1080/13691180110097030

David, G. (2010). Camera phone images, videos and live streaming: A contemporary visual trend. *Visual Studies*, *25*(1), 89–98. doi: 10.1080/14725861003607017

Davidson, J. (2016). Plenary address – A year of living 'dangerously': Reflections on risk, trust, trauma and change. *Emotion, Space and Society*, *18*, 28–34. doi: 10.1016/j.emospa.2016.01.002

de Certeau, M. (1984). *The Practice of Everyday Life*. Berkeley, CA: University of California Press.

de Lange, M. (2015). The playful city: Using play and games to foster citizen participation. In A. Skaržauskiene (Ed.), *Social Technologies and Collective Intelligence* (pp. 426–434). Vilnius: Mykolas Romeris University.

de Souza e Silva, A. (2004). Art by telephone: From static to mobile interfaces. *Leonardo Electronic Almanac*, *12*(10). Retrieved from www.leoalmanac.org/leonardo-electronic-almanac-volume-12-no-10-october-2004/

de Souza e Silva, A. (2006). From cyber to hybrid: Mobile technologies as interfaces of hybrid spaces. *Space and Culture, 9*(3), 261–278. doi: 10.1177/1206331206289022

de Souza e Silva, A., & Frith, J. (2012). *Mobile Interfaces in Public Spaces: Locational Privacy, Control, and Urban Sociability.* New York: Routledge.

de Souza e Silva, A., & Hjorth, L. (2009). Urban spaces as playful spaces: A historical approach to mobile urban games. *Simulation and Gaming, 40*(5), 602–625. doi: 10.1177/1046878109333723

de Vries, B., & Rutherford, J. (2004). Memorializing loved ones on the world wide web. *Omega: Journal of Death and Dying, 49*(1), 5–26. doi: 10.2190/DR46-RU57-UY6P-NEWM

Deleuze, G. and Guattari, F. (1987). *A Thousand Plateaus: Capitalism and Schizophrenia.* New York: Continuum.

Delwiche, A. (2018). The rise and fall of the BBS scene (1977–1995). In J. Burgess, A. Marwick & T. Poell (Eds.), *The Sage Handbook of Social Media* (pp. 35–52). London: Sage.

Deterding, S., Dixon, D., Khlaed R., & Nacke, L. (2011). From game design elements to gamefulness: Defining 'gamification'. In *Mindtrek 11: Proceedings of the 15th International Academic Mindtrek Conference* (pp. 9–15). New York: ACM.

Deuze, M. (2012). *Media Life.* Cambridge: Polity Press.

di Leonardo, M. (1987). The female world of cards and holidays: Women, families, and the work of kinship. *Signs: Journal of Women in Culture and Society, 12*(Spring), 440–453. doi: 10.1086/494338?journalCode=signs

DiNucci, D. (1999). Fragmented future. *Print, 53*(4).

Dobson, A. S., Robards, B., & Carah, N. (Eds.). (2018). *Digital Intimate Publics and Social Media.* Basingstoke: Palgrave Macmillan.

Dodge, M., Kitchen, R., & Perkins, C. R. (2009). *Rethinking Maps.* Abingdon: Routledge.

Dourish, P., & Anderson, K. (2006). Collective information practice. *Human–Computer Interaction, 21*(3), 319–342. doi: 10.1207/s15327051hci2103_2

Duguay, S. (2016). Lesbian, gay, bisexual, trans, and queer visibility through selfies: Comparing platform mediators across Ruby Rose's Instagram and Vine presence. *Social Media & Society, 2*(2). doi: 10.1177/2056305116641975

Dumas, T., Maxwell-Smith, M., Davis, J. P., & Giulietti, P. A. (2017). Lying or longing for likes? Narcissism, peer belonging, loneliness and normative versus deceptive like-seeking on Instagram in emerging adulthood. *Computers in Human Behavior, 71*, 1–10. doi: 10.1016/j.chb.2017.01.037.

Elmer-Dewitt, P. (1993, December 6). First Nation in Cyberspace. *TIME International* No. 49.

Ernst, W. (2012). *Digital Memory and the Archive.* Minneapolis, MN: University of Minnesota Press.

Facebook (2015, 30 January). *Terms of Service*. Retrieved from www.facebook.com/terms.php

Farman, J. (2009). Locative life: Geocaching, mobile gaming, and embodiment. In *Proceedings of the Digital Arts and Culture Conference—After Media: Embodiment and Context*. University of California, Irvine, CA, 12–15 December.

Farman, J. (2010). Mapping the digital empire: Google earth and the process of postmodern cartography. *New Media & Society*, *12*(6), 869–888. doi: 10.1177/1461444809350900

Farman, J. (2011). *Mobile Interface Theory: Embodied Space and Locative Media*. New York: Routledge.

Farman, J. (2014a). Creative misuse as resistance: Surveillance, mobile technologies, and locative games. *Surveillance & Society*, *12*(3), 377–388.

Farman, J. (2014b). Site specificity, pervasive computing, and the reading interface. In J. Farman (Ed.), *The Mobile Story* (pp. 3–16). New York: Routledge.

Fitchard, K. (2012). By 2016, 70M families will keep tabs on each other with GPS. *Gigaom*, 4 September. Retrieved from https://gigaom.com/2012/09/04/by-2016-70m-families-will-keep-tabs-on-each-other-with-gps/

Flanagan, M. (2009). *Critical Play*. Cambridge, MA: MIT Press.

Fortunati, L. (2002). The mobile phone: Towards new categories and social relations. *Information, Communication & Society*, *5*(4), 513–528. doi: 10.1080/13691180208538803

Frissen, V., Lammes, S., de Lange, M., de Mul, J., & Raessens, J. (2015). *Playful Identities: The Ludification of Digital Media Cultures*. Amsterdam: Amsterdam University Press.

Frith, J. (2013). Turning life into a game: Foursquare, gamification, and personal mobility. *Mobile Media and Communication*, *1*(2), 248–262

Frith, J. (2017). The digital 'lure': Small businesses and Pokémon GO. *Mobile Media & Communication*, *5*(1), 51–54. doi: 10.1177/2050157916677861

Frohlich, D., Kuchinsky, A., Pering, C., Don, A., & Ariss, S. (2002). Requirements for photoware. In *CSCW '02: Proceedings of the 2002 ACM conference on Computer Supported Cooperative Work* (pp. 166–175). New York: ACM Press.

Frosh, P. (2001). The public eye and the citizen-voyeur: Photography as a performance of power. *Social Semiotics*, *11*(1), 43–59. doi: 10.1080/10350330123316

Frosh, P. (2015). The gestural image: The selfie, photography theory, and kinesthetic sociability. *International Journal of Communication*, *9*(1), 1607–1628. Retrieved from http://ijoc.org/index.php/ijoc/article/view/3146

Fuchs, C. (2014). *Social Media: A Critical Introduction*. London: Sage.

Fuchs, C. (2017). *Social Media: A Critical Introduction* (2nd ed.). London: Sage.

Fuchs, M., Brain, T., Mattu, S., & Abend, P. (2016). I think it worked because Mercury was in the house of Jupiter! *Digital Culture & Society*, *2*(1), 185–194. doi: 10.14361/dcs-2016-0115

Fujimoto, K. (2005). The third stage paradigm. In M. Ito, M. Matsuda & D. Okabe (Eds.), *Personal, Portable, Pedestrian: Mobile Phones in Japanese Life*. Cambridge, MA: MIT Press.

Garland, D. (2001). *The Culture of Control: Crime and Social Order in Contemporary Society*. Chicago: University of Chicago Press.

Gaunt, K., Nacsa, J., & Penz, M. (2014). Baby lucent: Pitfalls of applying Quantified Self to baby products. In *CHI '14 Extended Abstracts on Human Factors in Computing Systems* (pp. 263–268). New York: ACM. doi: 10.1145/2559206.2580937

Gazzard, A. (2011). Location, location, location: Collecting space and place in mobile media. *Convergence: The International Journal of Research into New Media Technologies*, *17*(4), 405–417. doi: 10.1177/1354856511414344

Gerges, M. (2018). So what if selfies are narcissistic? *Canadian Art*. 1 March. Retrieved from https://canadianart.ca/features/so-what-if-art-selfies-are-narcissistic/

Gibbs, M., Meese, J., Arnold, M., Nansen, B., & Carter, M. (2015). #Funeral and Instagram: Death, social media, and platform vernacular. *Information, Communication & Society*, *18*(3), 255–268. doi: 10.1080/1369118X.2014.987152

Gibson, M. (2015). Automatic and automated mourning: Messengers of death and messages from the dead. *Continuum*, *29*(3), 339–353. doi: 10.1080/10304312.2015.1025369

Giddens, A. (1992). *The Transformation of Intimacy: Sexuality, Love and Eroticism in Modern Societies*. Stanford, CA: Stanford University Press.

Gillespie, T. (2010). The politics of 'platforms'. *New Media & Society*, *12*(3), 347–363. doi: 10.1177/1461444809342738

Gilmore, J. N. (2016). Everywear: The quantified self and wearable fitness technologies. *New Media & Society*, *18*(11), 2524–2539. doi: 10.1177/1461444815588768

Goffman, E. (1972). *Relations in Public: Microstudies of the Public Order*. Harmondsworth: Penguin Books.

Goggin, G. (2011). Ubiquitous apps: Politics of openness in global mobile cultures. *Digital Creativity*, *22*(3), 148–159. doi: 10.1080/14626268.2011.603733

Goggin, G. (2014). Facebook's mobile career. *New Media & Society*, *16*(7), 1068–1086. doi: 10.1177/1461444814543996

Goggin, G., & McLelland, M. (Eds.). (2017). *The Routledge Companion to Global Internet Histories*. New York: Routledge.

Goldsmith, B. (2014). The smartphone app economy and app ecosystems. In G. Goggin & L. Hjorth (Eds.), *The Routledge Companion to Mobile Media*. New York: Routledge.

Gómez Cruz, E., & Meyer, E. (2012). Creation and control in the photographic process: iPhones and the emerging fifth moment of photography. *Photographies*, *5*(2), 203–221. doi: 10.1080/17540763.2012.702123

Gordon, E., & de Souza e Silva, A. (2011). *Net Locality*. London: Wiley-Blackwell.

Gotved, S. (2014). Research review: Death online – alive and kicking! *Thanatos*, *3*(1), 112–180. Retrieved from https://thanatosjournal.files.wordpress.com/2012/12/gotved_deathonline2.pdf

Grace, H. (2013). iPhone girl: Assembly, assemblages and affect in the life of an image. In C. Berry, J. Harbord & R. Moore (Eds.), *Public Space, Media Space* (pp. 135–161). London: Palgrave Macmillan.

Graham, C., Gibbs, M., & Aceti, L. (2013). Introduction to the special issue on the death, afterlife, and immortality of bodies and data. *The Information Society, 29*(3), 133–141. doi: 10.1080/01972243.2013.777296.

Gray, M. L. (2009). Negotiating identities/queering desires: Coming out online and the remediation of the coming-out story. *Journal of Computer-Mediated Communication, 14*(4), 1162–1189. doi:10.1111/j.1083-6101.2009.01485.x

Gregg, M. (2011). *Work's Intimacy*. Cambridge: Polity Press.

Groening, S. (2010). From 'a box in the theater of the world' to 'the world as your living room': Cellular phones, television and mobile privatization. *New Media & Society, 12*(8), 1331–1347. doi: 10.1177/1461444810362094

Gye, L. (2007). Picture this: The impact of mobile camera phones on personal photographic practices. *Continuum, 21*(2), 279–288. doi: 10.1080/10304310701269107

Hand, M. (2013). *Ubiquitous Photography*. New York: John Wiley & Sons.

Hartley, J. (2018). Pushing back: Social media as an evolutionary phenomenon. In J. Burgess, A. Marwick & T. Poell (Eds.), *The SAGE Handbook of Social Media* (pp. 38–72). London: Sage.

Haverinen, A. (2014). Death and mourning rituals in online environments. PhD Dissertation. University of Turku, Helsinki, Finland.

Haythornthwaite, C., & Wellman, B. (1998). Work, friendship, and media use for information exchange in a networked organization. *Journal of the Association for Information Science and Technology, 49*(12), 1101–1114. doi: 10.1002/(SICI)1097-4571(1998)49%3A12<1101%3A%3AAID-ASI6>3.0.CO%3B2-Z

Helyer, N. (2007). The sonic commons: Embrace or retreat? *Scan Journal of Media Arts Culture, 4*(3). Retrieved from http://scan.net.au/scan/index.php

Hemment, D. (Ed.). (2006). LEA Locative media (special issue). *Leonardo, 14*(3). Retrieved from http://leoalmanac.org/journal/vol_14/lea_v14_n03-04/guested.asp.

Hendry, N. (2017). Social media bodies: Revealing the entanglement of sexual well-being, mental health, and social media in education. In M. Rasmussen & L. Allen (Eds.), *The Palgrave Handbook of Sexuality Education* (pp. 509–526). Basingstoke: Palgrave Macmillan. doi: 10.1057/978-1-137-40033-8.

Herzfeld, M. (1997). *Cultural Intimacy: Social Poetics in the Nation State*. New York: Routledge.

Hesse-Biber, S. and Griffin, A. (2013). Internet-mediated technologies and mixed methods research: problems and prospects. *Journal of Mixed Methods Research, 7*(1), 43–61.

Highfield, T., & Leaver, T. (2015). A methodology for mapping Instagram hashtags. *First Monday, 20*(1). Retrieved from http://firstmonday.org/ojs/index.php/fm/index

Highmore, B. (Ed.). (2002). *The Everyday Life Reader*. London: Routledge.

Hine, C. (2000). *Virtual Ethnography*. London: Sage.

Hinton, S., & Hjorth, L. (2013). *Understanding Social Media*. London: Sage.

Hjorth, L. (2003a). Kawaii@keitai. In N. Gottlieb & M. McLelland (Eds.), *Japanese Cybercultures* (pp. 50–59). New York: Routledge.

Hjorth, L. (2003b). Pop and ma. In F. Martin, A. Yue & C. Berry (Eds.), *Mobile Cultures* (pp. 158–179). Durham, NC: Duke University Press.

Hjorth, L. (2005). Odours of mobility: Mobile phones and Japanese cute culture in the Asia-Pacific. *Journal of Intercultural Studies, 26*(1–2), 39–55. doi: 10.1080/07525686050074003

Hjorth, L. (2007). Snapshots of almost contact. *Continuum, 21*(2), 227–238. doi: 10.1080/10304310701278140

Hjorth, L. (2009). *Mobile Media in the Asia-Pacific: Gender and the Art of Being Mobile*. London: Routledge.

Hjorth, L. (2013). Frames of discontent: Social media, mobile intimacy and the boundaries of media practice. In J. Macgregor Wise & H. Koskela (Eds.), *New Visualities, New Technologies: The New Ecstasy of Communication* (pp. 99–118). New York: Ashgate.

Hjorth, L. (2016). Mobile art: Rethinking intersections between art, user created content (UCC) and the quotidian. *Mobile Media & Communication, 4*(2), 168–185. doi: 10.1177/2050157915619210

Hjorth, L. (2017). Ambient and soft play: Play, labour and the digital in everyday life. *European Journal of Cultural Studies, 21*(1), 3–12. doi: 10.1177/1367549417705606

Hjorth, L., & Arnold, M. (2011). The personal and the political: Social networking in Manila. *International Journal of Learning and Media, 3*(1), 29–39. doi: 10.1162/IJLM_a_00059

Hjorth, L., & Arnold, M. (2013). *Online@Asia-Pacific*. London: Routledge.

Hjorth, L., & Burgess, J. (2014). Intimate banalities: The emotional currency of shared camera phone images during the Queensland flood disaster. In G. Goggin & L. Hjorth (Eds.), *The Routledge Companion to Mobile Media* (pp. 499–513). New York: Routledge.

Hjorth, L., & Hendry, N. (2015). A snapshot of social media: Camera phone practices. *Social Media Society, 1*(1). doi: 10.1177/2056305115580478

Hjorth, L., King, N., & Kataoka, M. (2014). Intimate publics: The place of art and media cultures in the Asia-Pacific region. In L. Hjorth, N. King & M. Kataoka (Eds.), *Art in the Asia-Pacific: Intimate Publics* (pp. 1–22). New York: Routledge.

Hjorth, L., & Lim, S. S. (2012). Mobile intimacy in an age of affective mobile media. *Feminist Media Studies, 12*(4), 477–484. doi: 10.1080/14680777.2012.741860

Hjorth, L., & Pink, S. (2014). New visualities and the digital wayfarer: Reconceptualizing camera phone photography and locative media. *Mobile Media and Communication, 2*(1), 40–57. doi: 10.1177/2050157913505257

Hjorth, L., Pink, S., & Horst, H. (2018). Being at home with privacy: Privacy and mundane intimacy through same-sex locative media practices. *International Journal of Communication, 12*, 1209–1227. Retrieved from http://ijoc.org/index.php/ijoc

Hjorth, L., Pink, S., Sharp, K., & Williams, L. (2016). *Screen Ecologies: Art, Media, and the Environment in the Asia-Pacific Region*. Cambridge, MA: MIT Press.

Hjorth, L., & Richardson, I. (2010). Playing the waiting game: Casual mobile gaming. In H. Greif, L. Hjorth, A. Lasén & C. Lobet-Maris (Eds.), *Cultures of Participation: Media Practices, Politics and Literacy* (pp. 111–125). Berlin: Peter Lang.

Hjorth, L., & Richardson, I. (2014). *Gaming in Social, Locative and Mobile Media*. Basingstoke: Palgrave.

Hjorth, L., & Richardson, I. (2017). Pokémon GO: Mobile media play, place-making, and the digital wayfarer. *Mobile Media & Communication*, *5*(1), 3–14. doi: 10.1177/20 50157916680015

Hjorth, L., & Richardson, I. (2019). *Ambient Play*. Cambridge, MA: MIT Press.

Hjorth, L., & Sharp, K. (2014). The art of ethnography: The aesthetics or ethics of participation? *Visual Studies Journal*, *29*(2), 128–135. doi: 10.1080/1472586X.2014.887261

Hochman, N., & Manovich, L. (2013). Zooming into an Instagram city: Reading the local through social media. *First Monday*, July. Retrieved from http://firstmonday.org/ojs/index.php/fm/article/view/4711/3698

Hochschild, A. R. (1979). Emotion work, feeling rules, and social structure. *American Journal of Sociology*, *85*(3), 551–575.

Hochschild, A. R. (1983). *The Managed Heart: Commercialization of Human Feeling*. Berkeley, CA: University of California Press.

Hogan, B. (2010). The presentation of self in the age of social media: Distinguishing performances and exhibitions online. *Bulletin of Science, Technology & Society*, *30*(6), 377–386. doi: 10.1177/0270467610385893

Hope, A. (2016). Biopower and school surveillance technologies 2.0. *British Journal of Sociology of Education*, *37*(7), 885–904. doi: 10.1080/01425692.2014.1001060

Horst, H. A. (2006). The blessings and burdens of communication: Cell phones in Jamaican transnational social fields. *Global Networks*, *6*(2), 143–159. doi: 10.1111/j.1471-0374.2006.00138.x

Horton, J. (2012). 'Got my shoes, got my Pokémon': Everyday geographies of children's popular culture. *Geoforum*, *43*(1), 4–13. doi: 10.1016/j.geoforum.2011.07.005

Hoskins, A. (2011). Media, memory, metaphor: Remembering and the connective turn. *Parallax*, *17*(4), 19–31. doi: 10.1080/13534645.2011.605573

Hu, Y., Manikonda, L., & Kambhampati, S. (2014). What we Instagram: A first analysis of Instagram photo content and user types. *Proceedings of the Eighth International AAAI Conference on Weblogs and Social Media* (pp. 595–598). Michigan, USA, 1–4 June.

Huizinga, J. (1955). *Homo Ludens: A Study of the Play Element in Culture*. Boston, MA: Beacon Press.

Hughes, M. (2015). How to Adapt Your Recruitment and HR Strategy to Wearable Technology. *ITProPortal*, 3 August 2015. Retrieved from http://www.itproportal.com/2015/08/03/how-to-adapt-your-recruitment-and-hr-strategy-to-wearable-technology/

Humphreys, L. (2007). Mobile social networks and spatial practice: A case study of dodgeball. *Journal of Computer Mediated Communication, 13*(1), 341–360. doi: 10.1111/j.1083-6101.2007.00399.x

Humphreys, L. (2013). Mobile social networks and surveillance: Users' perspectives. In A. Jansson & M. Christensen (Eds.), *Media, Surveillance, and Identity: A Social Perspective* (pp. 109–126). New York: Peter Lang.

Humphreys, L. (2018). *The Qualified Self: Social Media and the Cataloguing of Everyday Life*. Cambridge, MA: MIT Press.

Isbister, K. (2016). Why Pokémon GO became an instant phenomenon. *The Conversation*, 16 July. Retrieved from http://theconversation.com/why-pokemon-go-became-an-instant-phenomenon-62412

Ito, M. (2003). Mobiles and the appropriation of place. *Receiver*, 8. Retrieved from www.academia.edu/2717464/Mobiles_and_the_appropriation_of_place

Ito, M., Matsuda, M., & Okabe, D. (Eds.). (2005). *Personal, Portable, Pedestrian: Mobile Phones in Japanese Life*. Cambridge, MA: MIT Press.

Iveson, K. (2016). Pokémon GO and public space. *Cities and Citizenship Blog*. Retrieved from http://citiesandcitizenship.blogspot.com.au/2016/08/pokemon-go-and-public-space.html

Jacobsson, K. (2016). *Urban Grassroots Movements in Central and Eastern Europe*. New York: Routledge.

Jamieson, L. (2011). Intimacy as a concept: Explaining social change in the context of globalisation or another form of ethnocentricism? *Sociological Research Online, 16*(4). Retrieved from www.socresonline.org.uk/16/4/15.html> 10.5153/sro.2497

Jansson, A. (2015). Interveillance: A new culture of recognition and mediatization. *Media and Communication, 3*(3), 81–90. doi: 10.17645/mac.v3i3.305

Jenkins, H. (2006). *Convergence Culture: Where Old and New Media Collide*. New York: New York University Press.

Jiang, J., Brubaker, J., & Fiesler, C. (2017). Understanding diverse interpretations of animated GIFs. Paper presented at the *Proceedings of the 2017 CHI Conference Extended Abstracts on Human Factors in Computing Systems*, Denver, CO, 6–11 May.

John, N. (2013). Sharing and Web 2.0: The emergence of a keyword. *New Media & Society, 15*(2), 167–182. doi: 10.1177/1461444812450684

John, N. A. (2016). *The Age of Sharing*. Cambridge: Polity Press.

Joinson, A. N. (2008). 'Looking at', 'looking up' or 'keeping up with' people? Motives and uses of Facebook. In *CHI '08 Proceedings of the SIGCHI Conference on Human Factors in Computing Systems* (pp. 1027–1036). New York: ACM Press. doi: 10.1145/1357054.1357213

Jones, Steve (2004). 404 not found: The internet and the afterlife. *Omega: Journal of Death and Dying, 49*(1), 83–88. doi: 10.2190/8UUF-GLEG-X6T5-UNJM

Jordan, S. A., & Lindner, C. (2016). *Cities Interrupted: Visual Culture and Urban Space*. London: Bloomsbury Academic.

Jurgenson, Nathan (2011). Cyborgology. *The Society Pages*, 14 May. Retrieved from https://thesocietypages.org/cyborgology/2011/05/14/the-faux-vintage-photo-full-essay-parts-i-ii-and-iii/

Kaplan, A., & Haenlein, M. (2010). Users of the world, unite! The challenges and opportunities of Social Media. *Business Horizons, 53*(1), 59–68. doi: 10.1016/j.bushor.2009.09.003

Katz, J. E. and Aakhus, M. (2002). Perpetual Contact: mobile communication, private talk, public performance. Cambridge MA: Cambridge University Press.

Keating, P., & Cambrosio, A. (2003). *Biomedical Platforms: Realigning the Normal and the Pathological in Late-Twentieth Century Medicine.* Cambridge, MA: MIT Press.

Kelly, R., & Watts, L. (2015). Characterising the inventive appropriation of emoji as relationally meaningful in mediated close personal relationships. Paper presented at Experiences of Technology Appropriation: Unanticipated Users, Usage, Circumstances, and Design, Oslo, Norway.

Kendall, L. (2002). *Hanging Out in the Virtual Pub: Masculinities and Relationships Online.* Berkeley, CA: University of California Press.

Keogh, B., & Richardson, I. (2017). Waiting to play: The labour of background games. *European Journal of Cultural Studies, 21*(1), 13–25. doi: 10.1177/1367549417705603

Kerr, A. (2006). *The Business and Culture of Digital Games.* London: Sage.

Kester, G. (2011). *The One and the Many: Contemporary Collaborative Art in a Global Context.* Durham, NC: Duke University Press.

Kindberg, T., Spasojevic, M., Fleck, R., & Sellen, A. (2005). The ubiquitous camera: An in-depth study of camera phone use. *IEEE Pervasive Computing, 4*(2), 42–50. doi: 10.1109/MPRV.2005.42

Kinsella, S. (1995). Cuties in Japan. In L. Skov & B. Moeran (Eds.), *Women, Media, and Consumption in Japan* (pp. 220–254). Richmond: Curzon Press.

Koskinen, I. (2007). Managing banality in mobile multimedia. In R. Pertierra (Ed.), *The Social Construction and Usage of Communication Technologies.* Singapore: Singapore University Press.

Kozinets, R. (2002). The field behind the screen: Using netnography for marketing research in online communications. *Journal of Marketing Research, 39*(1), 61–72.

Kücklich, J. (2005). Modders and the games industry. *Fibreculture Journal, 5.* Retrieved from http://five.fibreculturejournal.org/fcj-025-precarious-playbour-modders-and-the-digital-games-industry/.

Kuntsman, A. (2017). *Selfie Citizenship.* Cham: Palgrave Macmillan.

LaMarre, T. (2017). Platformativity: Media studies, area studies. *Asiascape: Digital Asia, 4*(3), 1–31.

Lamberton, C. T., & Stephen, A. (2016). A thematic exploration of digital, social media, and mobile marketing: Research evolution from 2000 to 2015 and an agenda for future inquiry. *Journal of Marketing, 80*(6), 146–172. doi: 10.1509/jm.15.0415

Lammes, S. (2016). Digital mapping interfaces: From immutable mobiles to mutable images. *New Media & Society, 19*(7), 1019–1033. doi: 10.1177/1461444815625920

Lampe, C., Ellison, N., & Steinfeld, C. (2006). A Face(book) in the crowd: Social searching vs. social browsing. In *Proceedings of 2006 Anniversary Conference on Computer-Supported Cooperative Work* (pp. 167–170). New York: ACM Press.

Lantz, F. (2006). Big games and the porous border between the real and the mediated. *Receiver, 16*. Retrieved from www.receiver.vodafone.com/16/articles/index07.html

Lasén, A. (2004). Affective technologies. *Receiver, 11*. Retrieved from www.scribd.com/doc/142953400/Lasen-Amparo-2004-Affective-technologies#scribd

Lasén, A. (2017). Disruptive ambient music: Mobile phone music listening as portable urbanism. *European Journal of Cultural Studies, 21*(1), 96–110. doi:10.1177/1367549417705607

Lasén, A., & Gómez-Cruz, E. (2009). Digital photography and picture sharing: Redefining the public/private divide. *Knowledge, Technology & Policy, 22*(3), 205–215. doi: 10.1007/s12130-009-9086-8

Lawson, S., Kirman, B., Linehan, C., Feltwell, T., & Hopkins, L. (2015). Problematising upstream technology through speculative design: The case of quantified cats and dogs. In *Proceedings of the 33rd Annual ACM Conference on Human Factors in Computing Systems* (pp. 2663–2672). New York: ACM Press. doi: 10.1145/2702123.2702260

Leaver, T. (2013). The social media contradiction: Data mining and digital death. *M/C Journal, 16*(2). Retrieved from http://journal.media-culture.org.au/index.php/mcjournal/article/view/625

Leaver, T. (2017). Intimate surveillance: Normalizing parental monitoring and mediation of infants online. *Social Media Society, 3*(2), 1–10. doi: 10.1177/2056305117707192

Leaver, T., & Highfield, T. (2016). Visualising the ends of identity: Pre-birth and post-death on Instagram. *Information, Communication & Society, 21*(1), 30–45. doi: 10.1080/1369118X.2016.1259343

Leaver, T., Highfield, T., & Abidin, C. (forthcoming, 2019). *Instagram: Visual Social Media Cultures*. Cambridge: Polity Press.

Lee, D. H. (2005). Women's creation of camera phone culture. *Fibreculture Journal, 6*. Retrieved from https://doaj.org/article/24e1f0ac3a50467492b750f1fda203a7

Lee, J. Y., Hong, N., Kim, S., Oh, J., & Lee, J. (2016). Smiley face: Why we use emoticon stickers in mobile messaging. In *Proceedings of the 18th International Conference on Human–Computer Interaction with Mobile Devices and Services Adjunct* (pp. 760–766). New York: ACM Press.

Lee, M., & Lee, M. R. (2015). Beyond the wearable hype. *IT Professional, 17*(5), 59–61. doi: 10.1109/MITP.2015.78

Leorke, D. (2012). Rebranding the platform: The limitations of 'platform studies'. *Digital Culture and Education*, Retrieved from www.digitalcultureandeducation.com/uncategorized/dce1073_leorke_2012_html/

Leys, R. (2011). "The turn to affect: a critique". *Critical Enquiry, 37*(3), 434–472. doi: 10.1086/659353

Licoppe, C., & Inada, Y. (2006). Emergent uses of a multiplayer location-aware mobile game: The interactional consequences of mediated encounters. *Mobilities, 1*(1), 39–61. doi: 10.1080/17450100500489221

Ling, R., & Haddon, L. (2003). Mobile telephony, mobility, and the coordination of everyday life. In J. E. Katz (Ed.), *Machines that Become Us: The Social Context of Personal Communication Technology* (pp. 245–265). New Brunswick, NJ: Transaction.

Lingel, J. (2013). The digital remains: Social media and practices of online grief. *The Information Society: An International Journal, 29*(3), 190–195. doi: 10.1080/01972243.2013.777311

Lingel, J., & boyd, d. (2013). 'Keep it secret, keep it safe': Information poverty, information norms, and stigma. *Journal of the American Society for Information Science and Technology, 64*(5), 981–991. doi: 10.1002/asi.22800

Little, K. (2016, 15 June). Fitness trackers belong in the 'junk drawer': CrossFit CEO. Retrieved from www.cnbc.com/2016/06/15/fitness-trackers-belong-in-the-junk-drawer-crossfit-ceo.html

Livingstone, S. (2005). *Critical Debates in Internet Studies: Reflections on an Emerging Field*. London: LSE Research Online. Retrieved from http://eprints.lse.ac.uk/1011.

Lovink, G. (2012). *Networks without a Cause: A Critique of Social Media*. Cambridge: Polity Press.

Lüders, M. (2008). Conceptualizing personal media. *New Media & Society, 10*(5), 683–702. doi: 10.1177/1461444808094352

Lupton, D. (2013). Understanding the human machine [commentary]. *IEEE Technology and Society Magazine, 32*(4), 25–30. doi: 10.1109/MTS.2013.2286431

Lupton, D. (2016a). The diverse domains of quantified selves: Self-tracking modes and dataveillance. *Economy and Society, 45*(1), 101–122. doi: 10.1080/03085147.2016.1143726

Lupton, D. (2016b). *The Quantified Self: A Sociology of Self-Tracking*. Cambridge: Polity Press.

Lupton, D. (2017). Feeling your data: Touch and making sense of personal digital data. *New Media & Society, 19*(10), 1599–1614. doi: 10.1177/1461444817717515

Lupton, D., Pink, S., Labond, C. H. et al. (2018). Personal data contexts, data sense, and self-tracking cycling. *International Journal of Communication, 12*, 647–666.

Lynch, K., & McLaughlin, E. (1995). Caring labour and love labour. In P. Clancy, S. Drudy, K. Lynch & L. O'Dowd (Eds.), *Irish Society: Sociological Perspectives* (pp. 250–292). Dublin: Institute of Public Administration.

MacMillan, D. and Burrow, P. (2009). Inside the App Economy, *Bloomberg Businessweek*, October 23, 2009. Retrieved from https://www.bloomberg.com/news/articles/2009-10-22/inside-the-app-economy

Madianou, M. (2016). Ambient co-presence: Transnational family practices in polymedia environments. *Global Networks*, *16*(2), 183–201. doi: 10.1111/glob.12105

Madianou, M. (2017). 'Doing family' at a distance: Transnational family practices in poly-media environments. In L. Hjorth, H. A. Horst, A. Galloway & G. Bell (Eds.), *The Routledge Companion to Digital Ethnography* (pp. 102–111). New York: Routledge.

Madianou, M., & Miller, D. (2011). Mobile phone parenting: Reconfiguring relationships between Filipina migrant mothers and their left-behind children. *New Media & Society*, *13*(3), 457–470. doi: 10.1177/1461444810393903

Madianou, M., & Miller, D. (2012). *Migration and New Media: Transnational Families and Polymedia*. London: Routledge.

Mancini, C., Lawson, S., & Juhlin, O. (2017). Animal–computer interaction: The emergence of a discipline. *International Journal of Human-Computer Studies*, *98*, 129–134. doi: 10.1016/j.ijhcs.2016.10.003

Manovich, L. (2011). What is visualization? *Visual Studies*, *26*(1), 36–49. doi: 10.1080/1472586X.2011.548488

Manovich, L. (2012). Trending: The promises and the challenges of big social data. In M. K. Gold (Ed.), *Debates in the Digital Humanities* (pp. 460–475). Minneapolis, MN: University of Minnesota Press.

Marwick, A. (2012). The public domain: Social surveillance in everyday life. *Surveillance & Society*, *9*(4), 378–393. Retrieved from https://search-proquest-com.ezproxy.lib.rmit.edu.au/docview/1314689547?accountid=13552

Marwick, A. & boyd, d. (2018). Understanding privacy at the margins. *International Journal of Communication, 12*. Retrieved from http://ijoc.org/index.php/ijoc/article/view/7053/2293

Matsuda, M. (2009). Mobile media and the transformation of family. In G. Goggin & L. Hjorth (Eds.), *Mobile Technologies: From Telecommunications to Media* (pp. 62–72). New York: Routledge.

McLelland, M., Yu, H., & Goggin, G. (2017). Alternative histories of social media in Japan and China. In J. Burgess, A. Marwick & T. Poell (Eds.), *The Sage Handbook of Social Media* (pp. 53–68). London: Sage.

McCrea, C. (2017). Pokémon's progressive revelation: Notes on 20 years of game design. *Mobile Media & Communication*, *5*(1), 42–46. doi: 10.1177/2050157916678271

McCullough, M. (2013). *Ambient Commons: Attention in the Age of Embodied Information*. Cambridge, MA: MIT Press.

Meese, J., Gibbs, M., Carter, M. et al. (2015). Selfies at funerals: Mourning and presencing on social media platforms. *International Journal of Communication*, *9*(1), 1818–1831.

Meikle, G. (2016). *Social Media: Communication, Sharing and Visibility*. Abingdon: Routledge.

Merel, T. (2018). Ubiquitous AR to dominate focused VR by 2022. *Techcrunch*, 26 January. Retrieved from https://techcrunch.com/2018/01/25/ubiquitous-ar-to-dominate-focused-vr-by-2022/

Mescia, A. (2015, 11 October). Human-sized hamster wheel – booklet. Retrieved from https://issuu.com/adrianomescia/docs/hamster_wheel_booklet

Meyrowitz, J. (2007). Watching us being watched: State, corporate, and citizen surveillance. Paper presented at 'The End of Television? Its Impact on the World (So Far)' symposium, Philadelphia, PA, February.

Mikkonen, I., & Bajde, D. (2013). Happy Festivus! Parody as playful consumer resistance. *Consumption Markets & Culture*, *16*(4), 311–337. doi: 10.1080/10253866.2012.662832

Miller, D. (2016). *Social Media in an English Village: Or How to Keep People at Just the Right Distance*. London: UCL Press.

Miller, D. and Sinanan, J. (2017). *Visualising Facebook*. London: UCL Press.

Miller, D., & Slater, D. (2000). *The Internet: An Ethnographic Approach*. Oxford: Berg.

Milne, E. (2004, January 12). 'Magic Bits of Paste-board'. *M/C: A Journal of Media and Culture, 7*. Retrieved from http://www.media-culture.org.au/0401/02-milne.php

Min, D. A., Kim, Y., Jang, S. A., Kim, K. Y., Jung, S.-E., & Lee, J.-H. (2015). Pretty pelvis: A virtual pet application that breaks sedentary time by promoting gestural interaction. In *Proceedings of the 33rd Annual ACM Conference Extended Abstracts on Human Factors in Computing Systems* (pp. 1259–1264). New York: ACM Press. doi: 10.1145/2702613.2732807

Mol, A. (2008). *The Logic of Care: Health and the Problem of Patient Choice*. London: Routledge.

Mol, A., Moser, I., & Pols, J. (Eds.). (2010). *Care in Practice: On Tinkering in Clinics, Homes and Farms*. Bielefeld: Transcript.

Monahan, T. (2015). The right to hide? Anti-surveillance camouflage and the aestheticization of resistance. *Communication and Critical/Cultural Studies*, *12*(2), 159–178. doi: 10.1080/14791420.2015.1006646

Montfort, N., & Bogost, I. (2009). *Racing the Beam: The Atari Video Computer System*. Cambridge, MA: MIT Press.

Moore, P. and Robinson, A. (2016). The quantified self: What counts in the neoliberal workplace. *New Media and Society*, *18*(11), 2774–2792.

Morgan, D. (1997). *Focus Groups as Qualitative Research* (2nd ed.). Thousand Oaks, CA: Sage.

Morley, D. (2003). What's home got to do with it? Contradictory dynamics in the domestication of technology and the dislocation of domesticity. *European Journal of Cultural Studies*, *6*(4), 435–458. doi: 10.1177/13675494030064001

Morris, M. (1990). Banality in cultural studies. In P. Mellencamp (Ed.), *Logics of Television: Essays in Cultural Criticism* (pp. 119–144). Bloomington, IN: Indiana University Press.

Mowlabocus, S. (2010). *Gaydar Culture: Gay Men, Technology and Embodiment in the Digital Age*. Farnham: Ashgate.

Murray, S., & Anderson, M. (2016). Lez takes time: Designing lesbian contact in geo-social networking apps. *Critical Studies in Media Communication, 33*(1), 53–69. doi: 10.1080/15295036.2015.1133921

Nafus, D., & Sherman, J. (2014). This one does not go up to 11: The Quantified Self movement as an alternative Big Data practice. *International Journal of Communication, 8,* 1784–1794. Retrieved from http://ijoc.org/index.php/ijoc/article/viewFile/2170/1157

Nakamura, L. (2002). *Cybertypes: Race, Ethnicity, and Identity on the Internet.* New York: Routledge.

Nansen, B., Arnold, M., Gibbs, M., & Kohn, T. (2014). The restless dead in the digital cemetery. In C. Moreman & Lewis, A. (Eds.), *Digital Death: Mortality and Beyond in the Online Age* (pp. 111–124). Westport, CT: ABC-CLIO, LLC.

Neff, G. (2012). *Venture Labor: Work and the Burden of Risk in Innovative Industries.* Cambridge, MA: MIT Press.

Neff, G., & Nafus, D. (2016). *Self-Tracking.* Cambridge, MA: MIT Press.

Nelson, J. K., & Shih, P. C. (2017). CompanionViz: Mediated platform for gauging canine health and enhancing human–pet interactions. *International Journal of Human–Computer Studies, 98,* 169–178. doi: 10.1016/j.ijhcs.2016.04.002

Nippert-Eng, C. (2010). *Islands of Privacy.* Chicago: The University of Chicago Press.

Nold, C. (2009). *Emotional Cartography: Technologies of the Self.* Retrieved from http://emotionalcartography.net/

Nye, J. (2004). *Soft Power: The Means to Success in World Politics.* New York: Public Affairs.

Obar, J., & Wildman, S. (2015). Social media definition and the governance challenge: An introduction to the special issue. *Telecommunications Policy, 39*(9), 745–750. doi: 10.2139/ssrn.2647377

Okabe, D., & Ito, M. (2005). Personal, portable, pedestrian images. In M. Ito, D. Okabe & M. Matsuda (Eds.), *Personal, Portable, Pedestrian: Mobile Phones in Japanese Life.* Cambridge, MA: MIT Press.

Okada, T. (2005). The social reception and construction of mobile media in Japan. In M. Ito, D. Okabe & M. Matsuda (Eds.), *Personal, Portable, Pedestrian: Mobile Phones in Japanese Life.* Cambridge, MA: MIT Press.

Oldenburg, R. (1989). *The Great Good Place.* Boston, MA: Da Capo Press.

Olszanowski, M. (2014). Feminist self-imaging and Instagram: Tactics of circumventing sensorship. *Visual Communication Quarterly, 21*(2), 83–95. doi: 10.1080/15551393. 2014.928154

O'Riordan, K. (2005). From usenet to Gaydar: A comment on queer online community. *ACM SIGGROUP Bulletin, 25*(2), 28–32. doi: 10.1145/1067721.1067727

Palmer, D. (2012). iPhone photography: Mediating visions of social space. In L. Hjorth, J. Burgess & I. Richardson (Eds.), *Studying Mobile Media: Cultural Technologies, Mobile Communication, and the iPhone* (pp. 85–97). New York: Routledge.

Palmer, D. (2014). Mobile media photography. In G. Goggin & L. Hjorth (Eds.), *The Routledge Companion of Mobile Media* (pp. 245–255). New York: Routledge.

Papacharissi, Z. (2014). *Affective Publics: Sentiment, Technology, and Politics*. New York: Oxford University Press.

Papacharissi, Z. (2015). We have always been social. *Social Media and Society*, *1*(1), 1–2. doi: 10.1177/2056305115581185

Papailias, P. (2016). Witnessing in the age of the database: Viral memorials, affective publics, and the assemblage of mourning. *Memory Studies*, *9*(4), 437–454. doi: 10.1177/1750698015622058

Parikka, J. (2012). *What is Media Archaeology?* Cambridge: Polity Press.

Parikka, J., & Suominen, J. (2006). Victorian snakes? Towards a cultural history of mobile games and the experience of movement. *Game Studies*, *6*(1), December. Retrieved from http://gamestudies.org/1502/archive

Park, T. W., Kim, S. J., & Lee, G. (2014, June). A study of emoticon use in instant messaging from smartphone. In *International Conference on Human–Computer Interaction* (pp. 155–165). Cham: Springer International.

Pavalanathan, U., & Eisenstein, J. (2016). More emojis, less :) The competition for paralinguistic function in microblog writing. *First Monday*, *21*(11), November. doi: 10.5210/fm.v21i11.6879

Pellegrino, G. (2010). Mediated bodies in saturated environments: Participation as co-construction. In L. Fortunati, J. Vincent, J. Gebhardt, A. Petrovcic & O. Vershinskaya (Eds.), *Interacting with Broadband Society* (pp. 93–105). Frankfurt: Peter Lang.

Perkins, C. (2009). Playing with maps. In M. Dodge, R. Kitchin & C. Perkins (Eds.), *Rethinking Maps* (pp. 167–188). London: Routledge.

Perkins, C. (2012). Playful mapping: The potential of a ludic approach. Paper presented at the International Cartographic Association conference. Retrieved from http://icaci.org/files/documents/ICC_proceedings/ICC2013/_extendedAbstract/121_proceeding.pdf.

Petersen, M. S. (2008). Loser generated content: From participation to exploitation. *First Monday*, *13*(3). doi: 10.5210/fm.v13i3.2141

Pink, S. (2011). Sensory digital photography: Re-thinking 'moving' and the image. *Visual Studies*, *26*(1), 4–13. doi: 10.1080/1472586X.2011.548484

Pink, S., & Hjorth, L. (2012). Emplaced cartographies: Reconceptualising camera phone practices in an age of locative media. *Media International Australia*, *145*, 145–155. doi: 10.1177/1329878X1214500116

Pink, S., Hjorth, L., Horst, H., Nettheim, J., & Bell, G. (2018). Digital work and play: Mobile technologies and new ways of feeling at home. *European Journal of Cultural Studies*, *21*(1), 26–38. doi: 10.1177/1367549417705602

Pink, S., Horst, H., Postill, J., Hjorth, L., Lewis, T., & Tacchi, J. (2016). *Digital Ethnography: Principles and Practices*. London: Sage.

Pink, S., Sinanan, J., Hjorth L., & Horst, H. (2016). Tactile digital ethnography: Researching mobile media through the hand. *Mobile Media and Communication, 4*(2), 237–251. doi: 10.1177/2050157915619958

Prøitz, L. (2007). The mobile phone turn: A study of gender, sexuality and subjectivity in young people's mobile phone practices. Doctoral thesis, University of Oslo, Oslo, Norway. Retrieved from www.duo.uio.no/bitstream/handle/10852/27243/NY_314_Proitz_hele.pdf?sequence=2

Quan-Haase, A., & Martin, K. (2013). Digital curation and the networked audience of urban events. *International Communication Gazette, 75*(5–6), 521–537. doi: 10.1177/17 48048513491910

Raessen, J. (2006). Playful identities, or the ludification of culture. *Games and Culture, 1*(1), 52–57.

Reading, A. (2009a). Memobilia: Mobile phones making new memory forms. In J. Garde-Hansen, A. Hoskins & A. Reading (Eds.), *Save As… Digital Memories* (pp. 81–95). Basingstoke: Palgrave Macmillan.

Reading, A. (2009b). Mobile witnessing: Ethics and the camera phone in the war on terror. *Globalizations, 6*(1), 61–76. doi: 10.1080/14747730802692435

Refslund Christensen, D., & Gotved, S. (2014). Online memorial culture: An introduction. *New Review of Hypermedia and Multimedia, 21*(1–2), 1–9. doi: 10.1080/1361 4568.2015.988455

Reuters/ABC. (2018, 30 January). Pentagon reviewing security after *Strava* fitness app broadcast military personnel locations. Retrieved from www.abc.net.au/news/2018-01-30/pentagon-reviewing-security-after-strava-app-reveals-locations/9373054

Richardson, K., & Hessey, S. (2009). Archiving the self? Facebook as biography of social and relational memory. *Journal of Information, Communication and Ethics in Society, 7*(1), 25–38. doi: 10.1108/14779960910938070

Rieck, J. (2016). Attacks on Fitness Trackers Revisited: A Case-Study of Unfit Firmware Security. *arXiv.* arXiv:1604.03313.

Rieser, M. (2011). *The Mobile Audiences: Media Art and Mobile Technologies.* London: ICI Global.

Rogers, R. (2018). Digital methods for cross-platform analysis. In J. Burgess, A. Marwick & T. Poell (Eds.), *The SAGE Handbook of Social Media* (pp. 158–186). E-book version. London: Sage.

Roquet, P. (2016). *Ambient Media: Japanese Atmospheres of Self.* Minnesota, MN: Minnesota University Press.

Rose, G. (2014). On the Relation between 'visual research methods' and contemporary visual culture. *The Sociological Review, 62*(1), 24–46.

Rosenberg M., N. Confessore, & C. Cadwalladr (2018). How Trump consultants exploited the Facebook data of millions. *The New York Times*, 17 March. Retrieved from https://www.nytimes.com/2018/03/17/us/politics/cambridge-analytica-trump-campaign.html.

Rosenblatt, P. (1996). Grief does not end. In D. Klass, P. R. Silverman & S. L. Nickman (Eds.), *Continuing Bonds*. Washington, DC: Taylor & Francis.

Rubinstein, D., & Sluis, K. (2008). A life more photographic: Mapping the networked image. *Photographies*, *1*(1), 9–28. doi: 10.1080/17540760701785842

Rushkoff, D. (1994). *Cyberia: Life in the Trenches of Cyberspace*. New York: Clinamen Press.

Russo, A., Watkins, J., Kelly, L., & Chan, S. (2008). Participatory communication with social media. *Curator: The Museum Journal*, *51*(1), 21–31. doi: 10.1111/j.2151-6952.2008.tb00292.x

Salen, K. (2017). Afraid to roam: The unlevel playing field of Pokémon GO. *Mobile Media & Communication*, *5*(1), 34–37. doi: 10.1177/2050157916677865

Salen, K., & Zimmerman, E. (2003). *Rules of Play: Game Design Fundamentals*. Cambridge, MA: MIT Press.

Schloss, J., & Boyer, B. (2014). Urban echoes: The boombox and sonic mobility in the 1980s. In S. Gopinath & J. Stanyek (Eds.), *The Oxford Handbook of Mobile Music Studies* (*Vol. 1*, pp. 399–412). Oxford: Oxford University Press.

Scholz, T. (Ed.). (2012). *Digital Labour: The Internet as Playground and Factory*. New York: Routledge.

Schüll, N. D. (2016). Data for life: Wearable technology and the design of self-care. *BioSocieties*, *11*(3), 317–333. doi: 10.1057/biosoc.2015.47

Schwartz, R., & Halegoua, G. R. (2014). The spatial self: Location-based identity performance on social media. *New Media & Society*, *7*(10), 1643–1660. doi: 10.1177/1461444814531364

Senft, T., & Baym, N. (2015). What does the selfie say? Investigating a global phenomenon. *International Journal of Communication*, *9*(1), 1588–1606. Retrieved from http://ijoc.org

Sengupta, S. (2012). 'Big Brother'? No, it's parents. *The New York Times*, 26 June. Retrieved from www.nytimes.com/2012/06/26/technology/software-helps-parents-monitor-their-children-online.html?pagewanted=all

Serrano-Telleria, A. (2017). *Between the Public and Private in Mobile Communication*. London: Routledge.

Shade, L. R., & Singh, R. (2016). 'Honestly, we're not spying on kids': School surveillance of young people's social media. *Social Media & Society*, *2*(4). doi:10.1177/2056305116680005

Sheller, M. (2014). Mobile art: Out of your pocket. In G. Goggin & L. Hjorth (Eds.), *The Routledge Companion to Mobile Media* (pp. 197–205). New York: Routledge.

Sheller, M., Aceti, L., & Iverson, H. (Eds.). (2016). L.A. Re.Play: Mobile Network Culture in Placemaking. *Leonardo Electronic Almanac*, *21*(1). Retrieved from: www.leoalmanac.org/l-a-re-play-volume-21-no-1/

Shirky, C. (2008a). Here comes everybody. Presentation at The Aspen Ideas Festival, Aspen, CO, 30 June–8 July. Retrieved from www.channels.com/episodes/show/12772338/Clay-Shirky-Here-Comes-Everybody?page=5

Shirky, C. (2008b). It's not information overload. It's filter failure. Keynote address presented at Web 2.0 Expo, New York, 16–19 September. Retrieved from https://conferences.oreilly.com/web2expo/webexny2008/public/schedule/detail/4817

Shirky, C. (2009). *Here Comes Everybody: The Power of Organizing without Organizations*. New York: Penguin.

Sicart, M. (2014). *Play Matters*. Cambridge, MA: MIT Press.

Sicart, M. (2017). Reality has always been augmented: Play and the promises of Pokémon GO. *Mobile Media & Communication*, *5*(1), 30–33. doi: 10.1177/2050157916677863

Simon, N. (2010). *The Participatory Museum*. Santa Cruz, CA: Museum 2.0.

Singer, R. W., & Perry, A. J. (2015). Wearables: The well-dressed privacy policy. *Intellectual Property & Technology Law Journal*, *27*(7), 24–27.

Soukup, C. (2006). Computer-mediated communication as a virtual third place: Building Oldenburg's great good places on the world wide web. *New Media & Society*, *8*(3), 421–440.

Standage, T. (1998). *The Victorian Internet: The Remarkable Story of the Telegraph and the Nineteenth Century's on-Line Pioneers*. London: Weidenfeld & Nicolson.

Stanyek, J., & Piekut, B. (2010). Deadness technologies of the intermundane. *TDR/The Drama Review*, *54*(1), 14–38. doi: 10.1162/dram.2010.54.1.14

Stark, L., & Crawford, K. (2015). The conservatism of emoji: Work, affect, and communication. *Social Media & Society*, *1*(2), 1–11. doi: 10.1177/2056305115604853

Stewart, Phil (2018) "Pentagon reviewing security after fitness apps show locations". *Reuters*. Jan 30, 2018. Retrieved form https://www.reuters.com/article/us-usa-military-devices/pentagon-reviewing-security-after-fitness-apps-show-locations-idUSKBN1FI2EH

Stephenson, N. (1992) *Snow Crash*. New York: Bantam Books.

Stevenson, M. (2018). From hypertext to hype and back again: Exploring the roots of social media in early web culture. In J. Burgess, A. Marwick & T. Poel (Eds.), *The Sage Handbook of Social Media* (pp. 69–88). London: Sage.

Stinson, E. (2013). Stereopublic: A crowd sourced app for finding the best places for peace and quiet. *Wired*, 22 November. Retrieved from www.wired.com/2013/11/stereopublic-an-app-to-help-you-find-peace-and-quiet/

Stopher, B. (Ed.). (2015). *Tangible Evidence 02: Systems, Platforms and Prototypes*. London: University of the Arts London. Retrieved from http://ualresearchonline.arts.ac.uk/9435/1/TE02_web.pdf

Sturken, M. and Cartwright, L. (2009). *Practices of Looking: An Introduction to Visual Culture* (2nd ed.), Oxford: Oxford University Press.

Subramonyam, H. (2015). SIGCHI: Magic mirror – embodied interactions for the Quantified Self. In *Proceedings of the 33rd Annual ACM Conference Extended Abstracts on Human Factors in Computing Systems* (pp. 1699–1704). New York: ACM Press. doi: 10.1145/2702613.2732884

Suess, A. (2017). *Art Gallery Visitors and Instagram*. PhD thesis, Queensland University of Technology, Brisbane. Retrieved from www.academia.edu/12086365/Art_Gallery_Visitors_and_Instagram

Surman, D. (2009). Pokémon 151: Complicating *kawaii*. In L. Hjorth & D. Chan (Eds.), *Gaming Cultures and Place in Asia-Pacific* (pp. 158–178). London: Routledge.

Sutton-Smith, B. (1997). *The Ambiguity of Play*. London: Routledge.

Swan, M. (2013). The Quantified Self: Fundamental disruption in Big Data science and biological discovery. *Big Data*, *1*(2), 85–99. doi: 10.1089/big.2012.0002

Swan, M. (2015). Connected car: Quantified Self becomes quantified car. *Journal of Sensor and Actuator Networks*, *1*(1), 2–29. doi: 10.0.13.62/jsan4010002

Szcześniak, M. (2014). Blending in and standing out: Camouflage and masking as queer tactics of negotiating visibility. *Widok. Teorie I Praktyki Kultury Wizualnej*, *0*(5), 1–28.

Tang, D. T. S. (2015). Essential labels? Gender identity politics on Hong Kong lesbian mobile phone application Butterfly. In L. Hjorth & O. Khoo (Eds.), *Routledge Handbook of New Media in Asia* (pp. 348–362). New York: Routledge.

Taylor, T. L. (2012). *Raising the Stakes*. Cambridge, MA: MIT Press.

Tencent (2014). *Internet Social User Experience Center: China Emoji Usage*. Report. Retrieved from http://isux.tencent.com/china-emoji-usage-report.html (in Chinese).

Tencent (2016). *Annual Report*. Retrieved from www.tencent.com/zh-cn/content/ir/rp/2016/attachments/201601.pdf (in Chinese).

Teranova, T. (2000). Free labor: Producing culture for the digital economy. *Social Text*, *18*(2), 33–58.

Thumim, N. (2017). Self-(re)presentation now. *Popular Communication*, *15*(2), 55–61. doi: 10.1080/15405702.2017.1307020

Tiidenberg, K. (2014). Bringing sexy back: Reclaiming the body aesthetic via self-shooting. *Cyberpsychology*, *8*(1). doi: 10.5817/CP2014-1-3

Tiidenberg, K. (2015a). Great faith in surfaces: A visual narrative analysis of selfies. In A.-A. Allaste & K. Tiidenberg (Eds.), *In Search of... New Methodological Approaches to Youth Research*. Cambridge: Cambridge Scholars Publishing.

Tiidenberg, K. (2015b). Odes to heteronormativity: Presentations of femininity in Russian-speaking pregnant women's instagram accounts. *International Journal of Communication*, *9*(1), 1746–1758. Retrieved from http://ijoc.org/index.php/ijoc

Tiidenberg, K. (2018). Visibly ageing femininities: Women's visual discourses of being over-40 and over-50 on Instagram. *Feminist Media Studies*, *18*(1), 61–76. doi: 10.1080/14680777.2018.1409988

Tokunaga, R. (2011). Social networking site or social surveillance site? Understanding the use of interpersonal electronic surveillance in romantic relationships. *Computers in Human Behavior*, *27*(2), 705–713. doi: 10.1016/j.chb.2010.08.014

Treem, J., & Leonardi, P. (2013). Social media use in organizations: Exploring the affordances of visibility, editability, persistence, and association. *Annals of the International Communication Association, 36*(1), 143–189.

Troyer, J. (2014). Death isn't taboo, we're just not encouraged to talk about it. *The Conversation*. Retrieved from https://theconversation.com/death-isnt-taboo-were-just-not-encouraged-to-talk-about-it-25001

Troyer, J. (2017, 30 August). Annual Public Lecture: The Future of Human Mortality: Death, Technology and the Law. *Law and Justice* (La Trobe Law School Blog). Melbourne, Australia: State Library of Victoria. Retrieved from https://law.blogs.latrobe.edu.au/2017/09/08/annual-public-lecture-future-human-mortality-dr-john-troyer/

Turkle, S. (1984). *The Second Self: Computers and the Human Spirit*. Cambridge, MA: MIT Press.

Turkle, S. (1995). *Life on the Screen: Identity in the Age of the Internet*. New York: Simon & Schuster.

Turkle, S. (2011). *Alone Together: Why We Expect More from Technology and Less from Each Other*. New York: Basic Books.

Tuters, M., & Varnelis, K. (2006). Beyond locative media: Giving shape to the internet of things. *Leonardo, 39*(4), 357–363.

Uricchio, W. (2011). The algorithmic turn: Photosynth, augmented reality and the changing implications of the image. *Visual Studies, 26*(1), 25–35. doi: 10.1080/1472586X.2011.548486

Vaidhyanathan, S. (2011). *The Googlization of Everything*. Berkeley, CA: University of California Press.

van Djick, J. (2007). *Mediated Memories in the Digital Age*. Stanford, CA: Stanford University Press.

van Dijck, J. (2008). Digital photography: Communication, identity, memory. *Visual Communication, 7*(1), 57–76. doi: 10.1177/1470357207084865

van Djick, J. (2013). *The Culture of Connectivity: A Critical History of Social Media*. Oxford: Oxford University Press.

van Dijck, J. (2014). Datafiction, dataism and dataveillance: Big Data between scientific paradigm and secular belief. *Surveillance & Society, 12*(2), 197–208. Retrieved from http://hdl.handle.net/11245/1.435997

van Djick, J. (2016). Big Data, grand challenges: On digitization and humanities research. *KWALON, 21*(1), 8–18.

van Dijck, J. (2017). *The Platform Society*. Digital Media Symposium. Retrieved from www.youtube.com/watch?v=BE8Tw9Hc6kE

van Dijck, J., & Poell, T. (2013). Understanding social media logic. *Media and Communication, 1*(1), 2–14. Retrieved from http://hdl.handle.net/11245/ 1.396993

Van House, N. (2011). Personal photography, digital technologies and the uses of the visual. *Visual Studies, 26*(2), 125–134. doi: 10.1080/1472586X.2011.571888

Van House, N., Davis, M., Ames, M., Finn, M., & Viswanathan, V. (2005). The uses of personal networked digital imaging: An empirical study of cameraphone photos and sharing. In *CHI 2005*, Portland, OR, 2–7 April. New York: ACM Press.

Varnelis, K. (2008). *Networked Publics*. Cambridge, MA: MIT Press.

Varol, O., Ferrara, E., Davis, C., Menczer, F., & Flammini, A. (2017). Online human–bot interactions: Detection, estimation, and characterization. Retrieved from https://arxiv.org/pdf/1703.03107.pdf

Veale, K. (2003). A virtual adaptation of a physical cemetery for diverse researchers using information science methods. *Computers in Genealogy*, *8*(4), 16–38.

Vella, K., Johnson, D., Wan Sze Cheng, V., Davenport, T., Mitchell, J., Klarkowski, M., & Phillips, C. (2017). A sense of belonging: Pokémon GO and social connectedness. *Games and Culture*, 20 July (Online First), 1–21. doi: 10.1177/1555412017719973

Verhoeff, N. (2012). *Mobile Screens: The Visual Regime of Navigation*. Amsterdam: Amsterdam University Press.

Verhoeff, N. (2013). The medium is the method: Locative media for digital archives. In J. Eckel, B. Leiendecker, D. Olek & C. Piepiorka (Eds.), *(Dis)Orienting Media and Narrative Mazes* (pp. 17–30). Bielefeld: Transcript.

Villi, M., & Stocchetti, M. (2011). Visual mobile communication, mediated presence and the politics of space. *Visual Studies*, *26*(2), 102–112. doi: 10.1080/1472586X.2011.571885

Vincent, J. (2017). Former Facebook exec says social media is ripping apart society. *The Verge*, 11 December. Retrieved from www.theverge.com/2017/12/11/16761016/former-facebook-exec-ripping-apart-society

Vivienne, S., & Burgess, J. (2012). The digital storyteller's stage: Queer everyday activists negotiating privacy and publicness. *Journal of Broadcasting & Electronic Media*, *56*, 362–377. doi:10.1080/08838151.2012.705194

Volkmer, Ingrid (Ed.). (2006). *News in Public Memory: An International Study of Media Memories across Generations*. New York: Peter Lang.

Wajcman, J. (1991). Patriarchy, technology, and conceptions of skill. *Work and Occupations*, *18*(1), 29–45. doi: 10.1177/0730888491018001002

Wajcman, J. (2017). Automation: Is it really different this time? *The British Journal of Sociology*, *68*, 119–127. doi: 10.1111/1468-4446.12239

Wajcman, J., Bittman, M., & Brown, J. (2008). Families without borders: Mobile phones, connectedness and work–home divisions. *Sociology*, *42*(4), 635–652. doi: 10.1177/0038038508091620

Walker Rettberg, J. (2014). *Seeing Ourselves through Technology: How We Use Selfies, Blogs and Wearable Devices to See and Shape Ourselves*. London: Palgrave Macmillan.

Walter, T., Hourizi, R., Moncur, W., & Pitsillides, S. (2011). Does the internet change how we die and mourn? Overview and analysis. *Omega: Journal of Death and Dying*, *64*(4), 275–302. doi: 10.2190/OM.64.4.a

Warner, M. (2002). *Publics and Counterpublics*. New York; Cambridge, MA: Zone Books; distributed by MIT Press.

Watts, L., & Nafus, D. (2013). *Data Stories*. Kirkwall: Brae Editions.

Wawro, A. (2016). How did Pokémon GO conquer the planet in less than a week? *Gamasutra*, 13 July. Retrieved from www.gamasutra.com/view/news/276955/How_did_Pokemon_Go_conquer_the_planet_in_less_than_a_week.php

Weiss, G. M., Nathan, A., Kropp, J. B., & Lockhart, J. W. (2013). WagTag: A dog collar accessory for monitoring canine activity levels. In *Proceedings of the 2013 ACM Conference on Pervasive and Ubiquitous Computing Adjunct Publication* (pp. 405–414). New York: ACM Press. doi: 10.1145/2494091.2495972

Wellman, B., & Gulia, M. (1999). Virtual communities as communities: Net surfers don't ride alone. In M. A. Smith & P. Kollock (Eds.), *Communities in Cyberspace* (pp. 167–194). London: Routledge.

Wellman, B., & Haythornthwaite, C. A. (2002). *The Internet in Everyday Life*. Malden, MA: Blackwell.

Wellman, B., et al. (2003). The social affordances of the internet for networked individualism. *Journal of Computer-Mediated Communication*, *8*(3). Retrieved from http:// jcmc.indiana.edu/vol8/issue3/wellman.html.

Wen, D., Zhang, X., & Lei, J. (2017). Consumers' perceived attitudes to wearable devices in health monitoring in China: A survey study. *Computer Methods and Programs in Biomedicine*, *140*, 131–137. doi: 10.1016/j.cmpb.2016.12.009

Wendt, B. (2014). *The Allure of the Selfie: Instagram and the New Self-Portrait*. Amsterdam: Institute of Network Cultures, Hogeschool van Amsterdam.

West, P., Giordano, R., Van Kleek, M., & Shadbolt, N. (2016). The quantified patient in the doctor's office: Challenges & opportunities. In *Proceedings of the 2016 CHI Conference on Human Factors in Computing Systems* (pp. 3066–3078). New York: ACM Press. doi: 10.1145/2858036.2858445

Whitaker, R. (1999). *The End of Privacy: How Total Surveillance is Becoming a Reality*. New York: New Press.

Whitson, J. R. (2013). Gaming the Quantified Self. *Surveillance & Society, 11*(1/2), 163–176.

Whittaker, S., Bergman, O., & Clough, P. (2010). Easy on the trigger dad: A study of long-term family photo retrieval. *Personal and Ubiquitous Computing*, *14*(1), 31–43. doi: 10.1007/s00779-009-0218-7

Wilding, R. (2006). 'Virtual' intimacies? Families communicating across transnational contexts. *Global Networks*, *6*(2), 125–142. doi:10.1111/j.1471-0374.2006.00137.x

Williams, R. (1975). *Television: Technology and Cultural Form*. New York: Schocken Books.

Williams, R. (1977). *Marxism and Literature*. New York: Oxford University Press.

Williams, R. (2002 [1958]). Culture is ordinary. In B. Highmore (Ed.), *The Everyday Life Reader* (pp. 91–100). London: Routledge.

Wilmott, C., Fraser, E., & Lammes, S. (2017). 'I am he. I am he. Siri rules': Work and play with the Apple Watch. *European Journal of Cultural Studies*, *21*(1), 78–95. doi: 10.1177/1367549417705605.

Wolf, G. (2010). Gary Wolf: The quantified self. Ted Talk. Retrieved from www.ted.com/talks/gary_wolf_the_quantified_self

Yeates, N. (2004). Global care chains. *International Feminist Journal of Politics*, *6*(3), 369–391. doi: 10.1080/1461674042000235573

Yu, H., & Xu, J. (2017). E'gao as a networked digital leisure practice. In S. Carnicelli, D. McGillivray & G. McPherson (Eds.), *Digital Leisure Cultures: Critical Perspectives* (pp. 152–156). Abingdon: Routledge.

Zylinska, J. (Ed.). (2015). *Photomediations*. Open Press. Retrieved from http://photomediationsopenbook.net

Index